# THE UNITED NATIONS
## A Place of Promise and of Mischief

**RICHARD S. WILLIAMSON**

University Press of America
Lanham, New York, London

Hudson Institute

**Hudson Institute** was founded by the late Herman Kahn in 1961 to examine important issues of public policy. It is a nonprofit, nonpartisan organization; there are no "official" Hudson positions. Its independent and objective analyses address educational, economic, political and national security issues. For additional information: Hudson Institute, Herman Kahn Center, 5395 Emerson Way, P.O. Box 26-919, Indianapolis, IN 46226.

**Library of Congress Cataloging-in-Publication Data**

Williamson, Richard S.
The United Nations : a place of promise and of mischief
/ Richard S. Williamson.
p.   cm.
Includes bibliographical references.
1. United Nations.   2. United Nations—United States.
3. Diplomatic negotiations in international disputes.
4. Human rights.   I. Title.
JX1977.W54   1989   341.23—dc20   90-12792 CIP

ISBN 0–8191–7950–7 (cloth : alk. paper)
ISBN 0–8191–7951–5 (paper : alk. paper)

The paper used in this publication meets the minimum requirements of American National Standard for Information Sciences—Permanence of Paper for Printed Library Materials, ANSI Z39.48–1984.

# DEDICATION

To Marion and Donald Williamson

**The acorn does not fall
far from the tree.**

**And to Jane, and to Elisabeth, Craig and Richard**

# ACKNOWLEDGEMENTS

The speeches and articles collected in this volume represent my analysis and views on the United Nations and United States diplomacy in that arena during recent years. I am indebted to the people who asked me to serve as U.S. Permanent Representative to the United Nations offices in Vienna, Austria, on U.S. delegations to the U.N. Human Rights Commission, and later as Assistant Secretary of State for International Organization Affairs; to my colleagues in Vienna and at the International Organizations Bureau at the Department of State; and to mentors, colleagues and outside experts who helped give me greater insights into the promise and mischief of the U.N. I want to thank President Ronald Reagan, Secretary of State George Shultz, Ambassador Jeane Kirkpatrick and Ambassador Vernon Walters. I wish to thank the following friends, and former and current colleagues whose support, help and insights have guided me in this area: Ken Quinn and Penny Eastman; Kristina Arriaga, Bruce Chapman, Marion Creekmore, Barry Gidley, Steve Grummon, John Herzberg, Senator Robert Kasten, Alan Keyes, Lester Korn, Charles Lichenstein, Joseph Petrone, Charlie Ponticelli, Jose Sorzano, Richard Stanley, Tom Turqman, Brian Urquhart, Armando Valladares, Fran Westner and John Whitehead.

A special thanks to Sandy Kwiecien and Jan Hester for their infinite patience and help.

Finally, I want to thank the Hudson Institute, and especially its President, Mitch Daniels, for their support in this project.

# TABLE OF CONTENTS

# INTRODUCTION

The United Nations matters. It should be taken seriously; and the United States should energetically engage the U.N. at all levels.

The United Nations is playing a larger role on the world stage. It is incumbent on the U.S. to work vigorously with other member states and the U.N. Secretariat for the U.N. to achieve the promise of its founders and of its charter while, at the same time, recognizing its limits and its mischief.

## The Promise

The hopes of people all over the world rest upon the wings of the U.N. In some areas the U.N. can help realize those hopes. At the same time we do a disservice to those hopes and to the U.N. itself if we overload it. The U.N. can make many contributions to a better world, especially through its specialized agencies. But the U.N. is not the solution alone to any of our ills. A major reason for the frustrations with the U.N. that, in turn, have contributed to its mischief has been vastly unrealistic expectations for the U.N. that exceed its capacity to deliver.

The promise of the United Nations was forged by the horrors of World War II. During the war, President Roosevelt initiated consultations amongst the allies that nurtured its creation. After turning its back on the League of Nations and fighting another world war, American idealism embraced the work in San Francisco in 1945 to create a world assembly.

We are an idealistic and hopeful people. The moral imperative of the U.N. Charter embraces our own aspirations. That Charter states two overriding goals: "to save succeeding generations from the scourge of war which twice in our lifetime has brought untold sorrow to mankind," and "to reaffirm faith in fundamental human rights in the dignity and worth of the human person, in the equal rights of men and women and of nations large and small."

In speaking of the Charter, in 1983, President Reagan reflected the desires of the American people when he told the U.N. General Assembly that "the Government of the United States will continue to view the U.N. Charter's concern for human rights as the moral center of our foreign policy."

In addition to working to avert war, the U.N. held out the prospect of making the world a better place. There are global problems that do not respect nations' borders: nuclear non-proliferation, acid rain, global warming, the spread of AIDS, illicit drugs and the tragic flows of refugees. These and many other problems require multilateral solutions. The U.N. was designed to help mankind cope with these sorts of global issues.

In contrast to the General Assembly, the U.N. agencies were established for non-political purposes. Some act as international clearing houses; others advance international standards or provide technical assistance. In the United States, so much attention focuses upon the United Nations in New York, its political and rhetorical excesses, and the need for administrative reform, that the solid work of the important technical agencies in the U.N. system are often overlooked.

From 1983-1985 I served as U.S. ambassador to the United Nations in Vienna, Austria. Based in Vienna are nine international organizations in the U.N. system dealing with such varied subjects as nuclear non-proliferation, work to curb illicit drugs, the welfare and education of Palestinian refugees in the Middle East, international trade law, and global industrial development. Later as Assistant Secretary of State for International Organizations, I had oversight responsibility for all technical and specialized agencies in the U.N. system, in addition to the U.N. General Assembly.

Some of these organizations are not serious. They ignore their charters and are primarily forums for political posturing and recycling tired, sterile North-South debates. But many others are serious and important to U.S. interests.

For example, the World Health Organization (WHO), which is headquartered in Geneva, led the fight that eradicated smallpox. Today WHO is leading the international effort to coordinate the attack on the pandemic of AIDS. The successful completion of work on a new vaccine against malaria, carried out by WHO in cooperation with U.S. government agencies and others, is having revolutionary social and economic impact throughout the world. WHO has played a major role in developing oral rehydration salts, which are used to combat diarrheal diseases. I have been inspired by visits to U.N. facilities in villages in Latin America, Africa and Asia where I have seen committed WHO technicians work with desperately poor and illiterate mothers on the use of oral rehydration to help save the lives of their babies. They receive no attention on the world stage, but they are making it a better place.

The International Atomic Energy Agency (IAEA) is a U.N. specialized agency headquartered in Vienna. An outgrowth of President Eisenhower's "Atoms for Peace Program," the IAEA is the cornerstone of international efforts to prevent the spread of nuclear weapons. IAEA serves as the focal point for efforts to improve nuclear safety practices around the world. Its safeguards constitute a unique international system of verification, providing essential assurance that nuclear material in peaceful nuclear programs is used exclusively for peaceful purposes. IAEA's system of on-site verification provided a critical model for the on-site verification provisions of the 1988 U.S.-Soviet Intermediate Nuclear Forces Treaty (INF) that eliminated intermediate-ranged nuclear weapons from Europe. The IAEA is the primary forum for keeping the nuclear non-proliferation norm. It is the body that carries out vital articles of the Nuclear Non-Proliferation Treaty, the world's most widely observed arms control treaty. Throughout my tenure in Vienna, I was impressed by the non-polemic behavior of the member nations of the IAEA, and the professionalism of its secretariat. Because of this U.N. agency the world is a safer place.

The International Civil Aviation Organization (ICAO), a U.N. organization headquartered in Montreal, promotes safety in air navigation by setting up commonly accepted standards for radio transmission, landing systems, and communication. Its pioneer work in combating international terrorism has led to creation of new procedures for dealing with airplane hijackings, bombings, and attacks on airports. ICAO served the international community by facilitating discussion of the bombing by North Korea of Korean Air Flight 858. As head of the U.S. delegation to ICAO in July 1988, for talks on the U.S. accidental shooting of Iranian Airline flight 665, I was impressed by the businesslike approach, professional investigation, and non-polemical discussions in ICAO of this tragic incident.

Similarly, the International Maritime Organization is promoting, through a new convention, safeguards against terrorism at sea, such as the vicious attack on the passengers of the Achille Lauro. The World Meterological Organization has pioneered new efforts to forecast the weather and bring these benefits to farmers around the world. The International Labor Organization helps set minimum standards of employment for workers all over the world, and effectively promotes human and workers' rights. The U.N. Commission on International Trade Law developed model codes of arbitration used by the United States in negotiating the release of the hostages in Iran. Three U.N. organizations in Vienna; the International Narcotics Control Board, the Division of Narcotic Drugs, and the U.N. Fund for Drug Abuse Control, make important contributions to fight illicit drugs, including the recent convention on Drug Trafficking. These and most other U.N. technical and specialized agencies are helping to make the world a better place.

In 1988, the U.N. Peacekeeping Forces received the Nobel Prize for Peace, further recognition of areas in which the U.N. was keeping faith with its promise. That year, in addition to existing peacekeeping forces in the Middle East and elsewhere, the U.N. played a major role in advancing peace in Afghanistan, the Iran-Iraq war and Namibia.

The small nation of Afghanistan, with a population of 15 million, was invaded by the Soviet Union in 1979. Over the next nine years of conflict and violence, over one million Afghans died and 5-1/2 million Afghans fled as refugees to Pakistan and Iran. The United Nations played an important role in ending that occupation. First, the U.N. provided the forum through which world attention focused on Afghanistan. Following the brutal Soviet invasion, each year the U.N. General Assembly passed resolutions on Afghanistan, calling for the withdrawal of foreign forces, the establishment of a broad-based government through self-determination, the safe and honorable return of the refugees and a non-aligned Afghanistan. Secondly, using the authority of his office, Secretary General de Cuellar appointed special negotiator, Diego Cordovez, to explore with the parties involved ideas and ways of resolving the crisis. These U.N. proximity talks contributed to the Geneva Accords of April 1988. The Accords established a new peacekeeping operation: the United Nations Good Offices in Afghanistan and Pakistan (UNGOMAP). This U.N. force monitored the implementation of the Accords, especially the Soviet troop withdrawal. While the Soviet withdrawal resulted from the brave fighting of Afghan freedom fighters, the mujaheddin, the U.N. did make a solid contribution. And once fighting stops, the Afghanistan Coordinator for U.N. Refugee Relief, Prince Sadruddin Aga Khan, will play a major role in the safe repatriation of the millions of Afghans that have been driven from their homeland by eleven years of brutal Soviet occupation and civil war.

The bloody eight-year war between Iran and Iraq is another example of a regional conflict in which the U.N. helped facilitate a settlement. While a breakthrough required the parties themselves, fighting to exhaustion, to finally conclude that it was in their respective interests to negotiate, the U.N. played an important role in 1988 by helping to put into effect a cease-fire and initiate direct talks between the parties.

Also, 1988 witnessed the U.N. make a real contribution to settle the conflict over Namibia involving South Africa, Angola, and the Southwest African Peoples Organization (SWAPO), and the related threats from Cuban military forces in Angola and the need for internal reconciliation in that country. In 1978, the U.N. Security Council passed Resolution 435 establishing the United Nations Namibia Transition Assistance Group (UNTAG). For the next ten years intense U.S. and U.N. diplomatic efforts sought peace in this troubled region. Now, the fruits of these efforts are being borne out. Today Namibia is the world's newest independent nation. Again, the key for peace was the recognition by Angola and South Africa of the futility of their conflict and the vigorous pressure of their allies on them to seek a settlement. However, once the combatants reached this stage, the U.N. has played a major role to facilitate the resolution.

In Afghanistan, Iran-Iraq, and Namibia, the U.N. has contributed to the pursuit of peace. In none of these conflicts was the U.N. the decisive factor in advancing peace. In each the combatants themselves and their sponsors had reached a point where they wanted to stop the fighting. But also, in each case, at that point the United Nations played a major role in advancing the peace process and thereby realized its promise.

The United Nations also has realized its prospects recently through helping to insure fair elections in Nicaragua, in a WHO Emergency Team rushing to Romania to assess AIDS cases, and an international treaty to protect the global ozone layer. The U.N. Committee on Disarmament has become the preferred forum to work for a Chemical Weapons treaty. The U.N. Human Rights Commission, after years of hesitation and avoidance, in recent years has put pressure on the regimes in Cuba and Iran to improve their dastardly human rights record. And, if progress is to be made to achieve peace in war-torn Cambodia, the U.N. will play a major role. At the same time, the U.N. has been and remains a seriously flawed institution, an incubator for mischief, and sometimes, harm to world peace.

## The Mischief

To keep peace, to promote political self-determination, to foster global prosperity, to strengthen the bonds of civility among nations, to make the world a better place: this is the promise of the United Nations. Thereby, the U.N. was to speak with the voice of moral authority, its greatest power. But over the years the voice of the United Nations became louder and its moral authority deteriorated. The collective aspirations for a great, global town meeting too often became lost under the sound and fury, the clamor and rigid rhetoric of petty politicalization.

The United Nations was founded by 51 member states. The overwhelming majority were like minded democracies with a commitment to liberal principles.  During the United Nations' first twenty years, the Soviet Union led a hostile minority that sought to frustrate the majority. However, generally debates avoided name calling, general consensus was possible, and rational problem solving prevailed.  Beginning in the 1960's, the composition of the United Nations changed dramatically and the character of the U.N. fundamentally changed as a consequence.  Today there are 159 members of the United Nations.  Of those, 32 have fewer than one million citizens each.  Two-thirds of the vote in the General Assembly speak for less than ten percent of the world's people and thirty practicing democracies pay over two-thirds of the bills.

In the 1960's and 1970's rhetorical excess grew in the U.N. General Assembly.  Many newly independent nations, lacking military power, economic wealth and a history of conducting their own diplomacy, found in the United Nations one of the few arenas in which to give voice to their new sovereignty.  In the U.N. General Assembly they had a global platform denied them in the real world.  Exuberance with their new freedom and long simmering frustrations and resentments toward former colonial powers gave voice to harsh rhetoric, often disconnected to the reality beyond the U.N.  As the clamor grew louder and the rhetoric more harsh, the opportunity for dialogue was drowned out.  And the United States, more than any other nation, became the target of name calling in the U.N. while brutal totalitarian regimes in Moscow, Havana and elsewhere avoided the U.N.'s rhetorical sting.

The structure of the U.N. as devised by its members is based on sovereign equality (one nation, one vote) and on the General Assembly, a quasi-legislative body, which makes decisions by votes.  Therefore, it is not surprising that the many new member states in the 1960's, which were mostly poor and weak, sought to bind together into voting blocs.  This provided the new members fellowship, security, and maximized their influence.  The blocs are geographic, political, and ethnic in character.

The largest blocs are dominated by the new members: the group of 77 (G-77) consists of over 120 less-developed countries and the Non-Aligned Movement (NAM) includes close to 100 of the 159 U.N. member states. The G-77 or NAM constitute an automatic majority.  The blocs have become the multilateral equivalent of political parties.  The dynamics of the U.N. voting blocs are familiar to U.S. politicians.  It is almost identical to legislative parties and caucuses in city councils, state legislatures, and the U.S. Congress.  But the "party discipline" of the U.N. blocs is much stronger than it is in most American legislative bodies.  Rarely do member states break ranks from the "party position" agreed to within their bloc. The forces to conform within the bloc override other considerations.

The U.N. deliberations reflect the internal U.N. dynamics more than the real world out beyond Turtle Bay. They are distorted by a U.N. prism dominated by the North-South debate, the Arab-Israeli clash and South Africa apartheid. This dislocation between what goes on within the U.N. and what goes on outside the U.N. has helped erode its legitimacy on the world stage, given license for member state irresponsibility, encouraged mischief, and often led to U.N. irrelevancy.

Since U.N. resolutions have no binding authority on member states, no independent sanctions on the real world beyond the U.N., increasingly they became a vehicle to make a political point or to posture rather than to impact real events. Since there were no real consequences to actual events from U.N. debates or U.N. resolutions there was no discipline compelling deliberations toward reasonable dialogue and constructive compromise. Often resolutions were crafted to blame others, usually developed nations for other countries failed policies at home, such as the deteriorating standard of living of Third World countries caused by central economic planning. The result has been extreme rhetoric, irresponsible posturing, and growing irrelevancy.

For example, on fundamental issues of economic development, for years countries within the United Nations engaged in heated confrontation on political documents. For example, the U.N.'s Lima and New Delhi Declarations called for massive shifts of industrial capacity and production from developed to developing countries by dates certain. They called for redistribution not economic growth. There were no incentives provided, no practical proscription to realize the stated goals, no appreciation for market forces in the real world, no recognition of the benefits of overall global economic growth. They were simple declarative policies. Overtures within the U.N. by developed nations to forge practical partnerships on specific programs for technical assistance were discounted or even rebuffed as continued economic imperialism. These documents may have been good politics back home for governments in developing countries, but they did not create new jobs. They did not harmonize nations on a challenge in which all countries have a vital interest but polarized them. The U.N. proved a damaging and even noxious forum to address economic development.

On issues regarding the Middle East, the U.N. has a particularly pernicious record. Tragically, the United Nations has exacerbated the problems of that region more than helped resolve them. The Palestine Liberation Organization and radical Arab states have turned the U.N. into a forum for waging war against Israel by other means. It is a platform upon which the PLO seeks to unilaterally enhance its position at the expense of Israel.

In 1975, the U.N. membership passed a corrosive resolution asserting that "Zionism is a form of racism." This gave great political and intellectual credibility to attacks on Zionism. It endowed that attack with moral value and legitimizing force. There have been more than 150 anti-Israel resolutions passed in the U.N. Security Council, General Assembly and the Commission on Human Rights. Israel has been the most frequent target of U.N. resolutions condemning or deploring its actions by a ratio of more than ten to one. The U.N. is a battlefield wherein the PLO and radical Arab states seek to delegitimize Israel. And not a single General Assembly resolution on the Arab-Israeli conflict calls for negotiations between the parties.

The U.N. has not been an arena for conflict resolution in the Middle East. It has been used for political posturing, name-calling and polarizing the parties.

In 1948, the member states of the United Nations adopted the Universal Declaration of Human Rights. This glorious document set forth principles of fundamental human rights and fundamental freedoms, values embraced in our own Declaration of Independence and Constitution. This document was intended to protect the weak against the strong. It set minimum standards of decency for every government to meet in dealing with their own citizens.

The U.N. Human Rights Commission provided a process by which callous governments that violate the human rights of their own people could be brought before the court of world opinion. Unfortunately, over the years the U.N. Human Rights Commission sunk from being an objective court intended to judge human rights records to a smoke-filled room of petty politics. In the process, the member states debased the Universal Declaration on Human Rights and, worst of all, turned their back on the oppressed.

Tragically, notwithstanding the hopes and noble intent of the drafters of the Declaration, abuses of human rights have continued to be a constant reality in many corners of the globe. Nonetheless, often the U.N. Human Rights Commission has turned a blind eye to abuses by the strong or those countries protected by bloc support. In 1968, Soviet tanks rumbling into Prague went unnoticed. Throughout the 70's, Fidel Castro's repressive regime escaped U.N. attention. At the same time, some nations that are medium or small powers isolated and not members of blocs, such as Israel, are repeatedly challenged by the commission, even when the facts do not sustain the allegations.

The U.N. is a sprawling institution with rampant waste and mismanagement. The United Nations disaster-relief organization, UNDRO, in the mid-1980's spent more money on its own air conditioning than on sending staff to disaster zones. While millions are starving in Ethiopia, the U.N. Economic Commission for Africa, based in Addis Ababa, proposed to spend $73.5 million building a conference center for itself there.

Many member states treat U.N. agencies as convenient dumping grounds for people they would rather not have at home, because they are incompetent or a political threat. Member governments' intrusive backing of their own nationals has created a system in which merit plays little role. Too many U.N. staff are there not because of what they achieved but because of where they came from, who they knew or who owed them a favor. And the financial benefits for holders of top U.N. posts can be considerable. One under secretary-general received a $500,000 handshake when he retired, a pension of $50,000 a year, and a $125,000-a-year consultant contract

In voluntary and assessed contributions, the United States taxpayers pay almost $1 billion a year to the United Nations and its affiliated agencies. Our assessed contribution is 25 percent of the U.N. budget and our voluntary contributions exceed that, yet we have but a single vote in the U.N. General Assembly. While we pay the piper, we rarely call the tune.

The United Nations is a flawed institution. The majority of member states too often have failed themselves and others by failing to keep faith with the promise of the United Nations founders and their Charter. The secretariat's waste and mismanagement is a travesty given the enormity of the challenge and opportunity for good for the U.N. But the promise of the U.N. remains and in the past decade progress has been made to meet it.

## A Decade of Change

The 1980's were turbulent years at the United Nations. There was confrontation, occasional crisis, and change. In the early 1980's, the United Nations was braced by a cold shower that helped jolt member states into recognizing how the U.N. had declined and led to constructive reassessments. The result is a U.N. with brighter prospects than a decade ago.

Many of President Reagan's predecessors did not take the institution seriously. President Eisenhower had appointed Senator John Cabot Lodge to be the U.S. Permanent Representative to the U.N. and President Kennedy had appointed Governor Adlai Stevenson. Both men were leading public figures in their day. Both men brought energy, eloquence and stature to their U.N. job. But they have been the exception. President Nixon appointed the able career foreign service officer Charles Yost to the post precisely because he wanted to down-play the U.N. Yost was bright and experienced, unlikely to make a mistake, and being a career bureaucrat he lacked a political base from which to yield independent influence or garner attention. Of course from time to time there have been U.N. Ambassadors with great skill and stature such as George Bush and Pat Moynihan, but they remained the exception. In contrast to many of his predecessors, Ronald Reagan believed in the importance of the U.N. He was willing to engage the institution in a determined, consistent, forceful manner and to work for change.

Reagan's first U.N. Ambassador, Jeane Kirkpatrick, took the "kick me" sign off the United States. We no longer passively accepted outrageous charges and name-calling. Those who had challenged the United States with impunity in the past began to realize that such reckless accusations would be met by an equally forceful challenge and the truth. The U.S., by taking the words seriously of other delegations, led them to take their own words seriously. The United Nations was not just an expensive Turkish bath for countries to let off steam. Ideas matter and words are the currency of ideas. Within the U.N. nations would be expected to talk and act responsibly.

With his appointment of Ambassador Kirkpatrick and later Ambassador Vernon Walters, President Reagan signaled a renewed determination with respect to the United Nations. Political, diplomatic and financial leverage were engaged to advance U.S. interests in the U.N. Ronald Reagan himself made seven visits to the General Assembly, a record number of appearances by any President of the United States. In the area of human rights, the United States attacked the prevailing double standards, aggressively pursuing uniform application of the Universal Declaration of Human Rights. And in the area of management and administration, the United States engaged in a multi-year campaign to bring some sanity to the reckless, spendthrift practices of the United Nations. This aggressive U.S. diplomacy at the U.N. jarred the status quo. Some startled members of the U.N. community were offended at first. But gradually the rhetoric changed. From name calling and posturing the U.N. debate moved toward real dialogue.

Just as important as the Reagan Administration's efforts to reform the U.N., was the changing role of Third World countries within the U.N. during the 1980's. Over a period of time developing nations had learned that excessive rhetoric in the United Nations did have a cost. They were taken less seriously. Their sweeping resolutions mandating great changes had little impact on their very urgent and real needs. They began to understand that passing a broad resolution calling for a new international economic order did not put more food on the table, did not create new jobs, did not create further markets for their products.

The result of these developments has been a gradual movement of the G-77 nations toward more constructive behavior. There has been a recognition that the spendthrift ways of the United Nations hurt their interests, which they feel are so dependent on a viable and vital United Nations, more than any other group of countries. Leading developing countries have embraced the U.N. reform process and helped advance it. To strengthen the United Nations is to strengthen their own capacities. In U.N. economic fora, sweeping condemnations of industrialized countries have diminished and been replaced by work programs for specific projects, technical assistance and joint ventures.

This reformed behavior by the developing nations majority has had profound consequences for the United Nations. These changes have contributed significantly to improvements within the U.N. This is not to say that posturing and confrontation have disappeared. It is not to say that we don't continue to have major differences on fundamental issues with developing countries. But the range of issues in the U.N. on which we can constructively work with the G-77 has grown enormously. This trend is very positive for the United States, for developing countries, and for the United Nations.

A third major factor in recent years that improved the climate and constructiveness in the U.N. has been the adjusting U.S.-Soviet relationship. While the Soviet Union remains our primary adversary and the East-West confrontation the primary threat, the revolutionary events going on in the Soviet Union have profoundly changed the U.S.-Soviet relationship. The foreign adventurism of General Secretary Breznev has been replaced by President Gorbachev's more modest aspirations. The softened rhetoric and efforts to avoid direct confrontation by both superpowers have created a new environment and opportunity for the United Nations.

In recent years, the superpowers have used their influence to help work toward resolutions of regional wars in Afghanistan, Namibia and Iran-Iraq. They are working to end the tragic war in Cambodia. And in each one of these conflicts, the United Nations has been a constructive instrument to help the peace process. The U.S. has served as a convenient facilitator to help bridge the final gaps toward peace, to provide a buffer for graceful exits of combatents, and to provide a framework for reconstruction.

The shifting U.S.-Soviet relationship also has helped lower the rhetorical cacophony within the United Nations. Instead of seeking out clash and confrontation with the West, generally the Soviet delegation has quieted its rhetoric. Client states of the Soviet Union have followed their lead. And developing countries have learned that trying to force all issues through an East-West prism is no longer fertile ground for mischief. While the language of U.S. debate still often falls far short of reasoned discourse and considered deliberations, it is better.

A final major element that has helped the U.S. improve in recent years has been the performance of Secretary General Perez de Cuellar. An able and experienced diplomat, the Secretary General is often criticized as too passive. He is not an activist by nature. But by nature, he is a man of prudence, fairness and decency. By training he is a man of skill. Secretary General de Cuellar has enhanced the office he holds, and he has been willing to draw on his capital of good will constructively on issues such as gaining a cease-fire in the Iran-Iraq war.

## The Opportunity

The 1980's were an exciting time at the United Nations. To keep faith with the promise of the U.N. Charter, the 1990's need to build on the progress of recent years. All member states should recognize the limits of the organization. We should not over-burden it. We should not expect it to be the solution to our ills. It can help in making the world a better place, but only if member states are realistic about the U.N.'s capacity and they act responsibly and constructively within the U.N. The tendency toward mischief is considerable. To succumb to that temptation is to go backward.

The United States should be vigilant in advancing the U.N. reform process. Unacceptable waste and mismanagement remains. The United States should not accept name calling nor should it stand idle when U.N. debate moves to rhetorical excess. Sweeping U.N. resolutions that are counter productive must be vigorously opposed and constructive concrete work plans advanced. The United States should lead the fight to repeal the U.N.'s resolution that equates Zionism with racism. We must fight U.N. double standards, especially on human rights. At the same time, a successful United Nations is in our interests. The opportunity of the 1990's is to help the U.N. realize its promise.

PART ONE

U.S. DIPLOMACY AND THE U.N.

## OUR UNESCO DEPARTURE:
### A Wise Decision, But the U.N. Remains Vital to the U.S.

There has been a great deal of public debate leading up to and since President Reagan's decision to withdraw the United States from UNESCO. Unfortunately, most of this debate has been above the battle and beside the point: it has blurred rather than clarified the issue.

President Reagan made a courageous and correct decision, but not for the reasons we read so much about.

Those who point to the waste, inefficiency, and wrong-headed policies of UNESCO and say the entire United Nations system is worthless, or worse, that the entire U.N. is harmful to U.S. interests, are wrong. In many ways and many areas, the U.N. benefits America.

But those who point to the high ideals of the U.N. founders and suggest that we must have limitless patience with U.N. failings and stay within every one of its various houses to reform it from within, no matter how corrupt and rotten its foundation, are equally wrong. If the U.N. matters, if we are going to take it seriously, at some point we must be willing to say enough is enough, we will accept no more.

It is precisely because of the high ideals of the U.N charter, because of the vital importance to U.S. interests of certain organizations within the U.N. system, because of its potential to benefit the world that President Reagan was correct to withdraw the United States from UNESCO.

The U.N. system is important to the world community and to U.S. interests. Debates in the U.N. set the international agenda for much of the world. These debates legitimize and delegitimize issues on the world stage and focus world attention, often establishing the framework for progress.

---

Appeared in The Washington Times, January 18, 1985.

While American coverage of the U.N activities usually is buried deep inside our newspapers and seldom commands notice on the network news, in New Delhi and Lagos and elsewhere throughout the world the U.N. is front-page news daily.   To the extent the United States seriously wants to wage battle in the worldwide war of ideas - and we must - the U.N. cannot be ignored.

Also, the U.N. serves the valuable role of bringing scores of nations together to meet, to discuss, to seek answers.   While we can be discouraged, often dismayed, with the low level of debate and violently oppose certain proposed conclusions, that does not eliminate the valuable diplomatic benefits of the U.N. as a gathering place for the world.

Further, and most important, many of the U.N.'s specialized agencies carry out vital work important to U.S. interests. Indeed, from my vantage point, it is precisely because of the importance of work in certain of these other U.N. agencies that the United States was compelled to withdraw from UNESCO.

For the past 20 months I have been serving as U.S. ambassador to the United Nations in Vienna, Austria.   Based in Vienna are nine international organizations in the U.N. system dealing with such varied subjects as nuclear nonproliferation, controlling illicit drugs, the welfare and education of Palestinian refugees in the Middle East, international trade law, and global industrial development.

Some of these organizations are not serious.   They ignore their charters and are primarily forums for political posturing and recycling tired sterile North-South and East-West debates.   But others are serious and important to U.S. interests.

The International Atomic Energy Agency, like UNESCO, is a U.N. specialized agency.   An outgrowth of President Eisenhower's "Atoms for Peace Program," the IAEA is a linch pin of the worldwide nuclear nonproliferation regime.

With its newest member, the Peoples Republic of China, bringing its membership to 112 nations, the IAEA is the focal point for multilateral discussions on the peaceful uses of nuclear energy and assurances of nuclear supplies.   It is the multilateral vehicle for the safe transfer of peaceful nuclear technology.   And it has the critical responsibility of providing international inspections and safeguards on peaceful nuclear material to military purposes.

It is the primary forum for keeping the nuclear nonproliferation norm. And it is the body which carries out vital articles of the Nuclear Non-proliferation Treaty, the most widely adhered-to arms control treaty in the world.

The work of the IAEA is important to the United States and to the peace of the world. Without this U.N. organization it is hard to envision an effective nuclear nonproliferation regime. All of us would be less secure.

Less dramatic perhaps, but no less vital to America, is the need to fight drug abuse; a curse that kills thousands and harms millions every year in the United States. For those plagued by drug abuse, future progress is little consolation. But if there is to be progress, part of the answer lies with three U.N. organizations in Vienna - the International Narcotics Control Board, the Division of Narcotic Drugs, and the U.N. Fund for Drug Abuse Control.

In Vienna, similar serious nonpolemic work is done by the U.N. Commission on International Trade Law which, for example, developed model codes of arbitration used by the United States in negotiating the release of hostages in Iran, and by the U.N. Scientific Committee on the Effects of Atomic Radiation, which compiles information from research worldwide on the health impacts resulting from radiation exposure.

These are serious enterprises. Through them the U.N. system benefits all of us. But these activities are under constant threat.

All large bureaucracies, especially those in the public sector that lack the bottom-line discipline of the profit motive, tend toward inefficiencies and waste. Within the U.N. system, this organizational weakness is aggravated by political necessities that result often in personnel hiring more dictated by geographic distribution than by experience or competence. Common sense and good management practices are too often absent.

Even more disturbing, however, is the temptation for wholesale politicalization. Some member-states, seeing no cost to themselves, are willing to distort grossly any and all of the international organizations within the U.N. for political purposes unrelated to the charter and purposes of those agencies.

To these countries, each U.N. agency is a target of opportunity, another platform from which to shout their sound and fury, another vehicle to carry out their ideological warfare. The results are most disturbing, even shameful at times.

In Vienna, I have seen the annual IAEA general conference, once a business-like gathering of nuclear experts from throughout the world, distorted to a political battleground where thwarting the attacks on the rights of Israel has become our primary focus of attention. I have sat in meetings of the U.N. Industrial Development Organization in which the Soviets and their clients, one after repetitious other, gave long speeches on missile deployment in Europe and barely mentioned industrial development at all.

President Reagan's decision to withdraw the United States from UNESCO is having a profound, immediate, beneficial impact within the U.N. system.

Weekly I deal with ambassadors from every region of the globe. Not one has defended the practices of UNESCO to me. True, a few have expressed the hope the United States would work within UNESCO for reform rather than leave. But none have questioned the merits of the U.S. case against UNESCO.

More important, many - even from Africa, Asia, and Latin America - have expressed their personal support for the U.S. decision. Invariably they explain to me that they are pleased by our decision not because they hold any personal brief against UNESCO but because they believe the U.N. system is vital to their own countries' interests. They recognize the waste in the U.N. system. They realize that extraneous political issues are intruding on the serious work of many U.N. organizations. And they look to the United States for leadership.

By giving notice to UNESCO one year ago that inefficiency, waste, and politicalization would no longer be tolerated there, the United States was providing leadership.

By withdrawing, the United States demonstrated the courage of its convictions regarding UNESCO; but more important, we said the U.N. is important, it matters to us, we will not sit by and let U.N. agencies degenerate.

This is having a sobering and highly beneficial impact throughout the U.N. system.

# U.S. MULTILATERAL DIPLOMACY AT THE UNITED NATIONS

While we have had some stunningly successful performances by our ambassadors at the United Nations (witness Jeane Kirkpatrick and Daniel Patrick Moynihan), overall the United States quite simply is not very good at multilateral diplomacy within the U.N. The result is that U.S. interests are ill served. Too often within the United Nations we are on the defensive, engaged in damage control, and on occasion little more than mere spectators witnessing setback after setback.

Admittedly, some United Nations forums are above the battle and beside the point. But others that deal with crucial issues of nuclear nonproliferation or world health, refugees, or control of illicit drugs do indeed matter, and some are even vital to U.S. interests.

A large part of U.S. ineffectiveness in certain multilateral organizations such as the U.N. is because of the distribution of voting strength. But that alone cannot account for U.S. impotence in so many multilateral forums. As Senator Daniel Patrick Moynihan wrote in his book, A Dangerous Place, in 1974 the United States was frequently reduced to voting alone or only alongside Chile and the Dominican Republic.1/ Ambassador Jeane Kirkpatrick has written that during the following years it got even worse; we lost Chile and the Dominican Republic.2/ Even our closest bilateral allies frequently abandon us in the U.N. Why?

A large part of our current relative weakness within the institution stems from the United States' failure to recognize international organizations for what they are - highly political arenas. They are political bodies in the same sense as city councils, state assemblies, or the U.S. Congress. Failing to appreciate this fact, we neither recruit nor train foreign service officers (FSOs) for the politics of multilateral diplomacy. Generally, foreign service officers see a tour with international organizations posts as something to be avoided, something that will not enhance their careers and, at best, a necessary evil that sidetracks them briefly and then they get back to their real career as bilateral diplomats.

But, as noted above, multilateral diplomacy is fundamentally different from bilateral diplomacy. There are very real political skills needed in legislative bodies. Generally, foreign service officers are trained in the craft of bilateral diplomacy, spend most of their careers in bilateral posts, and are rewarded within the system for their proficiency in bilateral diplomacy. There should be no surprise, therefore, that generally foreign service officers, while bright and dedicated public servants, are not very good multilateral diplomats. And this lack of political skill in multilateral diplomacy by U.S. career diplomats fundamentally weakens U.S. effectiveness in the U.N. system. Senator Claiborne Pell has written,

> As a former career diplomat, I would like to see the Foreign Service give greater attention to developing and rewarding skills in multilateral diplomacy. It ought to be regarded as a national disgrace when others outperform us in the multilateral arena.3/

### The U.N. Matters

The United Nations system is important to the world community and to U.S. interests. Debates in the U.N. set the international agenda for much of the world. These debates legitimize issues on the world stage and focus world attention, often establishing the framework for progress.

While U.S. coverage of U.N. activities usually is buried deep inside our newspapers and seldom commands notice on the network news, in New Delhi and Lagos and elsewhere throughout the world the U.N. is frontpage news daily. To the extent that the United States seriously wants to wage battle in the worldwide wars of ideas - and we must - the U.N. cannot be ignored.

Also, the U.N. serves the valuable role of bringing scores of nations together to meet, to discuss, and to seek answers.4/ While we can be discouraged, often dismayed, with the low level of debate and violently oppose certain proposed conclusions, that does not eliminate the valuable diplomatic benefits of the U.N. as a gathering place for the world.

Further, and most important, many of the United Nations' specialized agencies carry out vital work important to U.S. interests. From 1983-1985 I served as U.S. ambassador to the United Nations in Vienna, Austria. Based in Vienna are nine international organizations in the U.N. system dealing with such varied subjects as nuclear nonproliferation, controlling illicit drugs, the welfare and education of Palestinian refugees in the Middle East, international trade law, and global industrial development.

Some of these organizations are not serious. They ignore their charters and are primarily forums for political posturing and recycling tired, sterile North-South and East-West debates. But others are serious and important to U.S. interests.

The International Atomic Energy Agency (IAEA) is a U.N. specialized agency.5/ An outgrowth of President Eisenhower's "Atoms for Peace Program," the IAEA is a linchpin of the worldwide nuclear nonproliferation regime.6/ With its newest member, the People's Republic of China, the IAEA is the focal point for multilateral discussions among its 112 members on the peaceful uses of nuclear energy and assurances of nuclear supplies. It is the multilateral vehicle for the safe transfer of peaceful nuclear technology. And it has the critical responsibility of providing international inspections and safeguards on peaceful nuclear facilities to ensure there is no diversion of sensitive nuclear material to military purposes.

The IAEA is the primary forum for keeping the nuclear nonproliferation norm. It is the body that carries out vital articles of the Nuclear Non-Proliferation Treaty, the world's most widely observed arms control treaty. The work of the IAEA is important to the United States and to the peace of the world. Without this U.N. organization it is hard to envision an effective nuclear nonproliferation regime. All of us would be less secure.

Less dramatic perhaps, but no less vital, is the need to fight drug abuse, a curse that kills thousands and harms millions every year in the United States. For those plagued by drug abuse, future progress is little consolation; but if there is to be progress, part of the answer lies with three U.N. organizations in Vienna - the International Narcotics Control Board, the Division of Narcotic Drugs, and the U.N. Fund for Drug Abuse Control.

In Vienna, similar serious nonpolemic work is done by the U.N. Commission on International Trade Law which, for example, developed model codes of arbitration used by the United States in negotiating the release of hostages in Iran. Also in Vienna, the U.N. Scientific Committee on the Effects of Atomic Radiation compiles information from research worldwide on the effects on health resulting from radiation exposure.

For all of these reasons, it is easy to conclude that the United Nations system does matter to us and to the world.

## Poor Performance in the U.N.

The record of the United States' disappointing performance in the U.N. system is overwhelming. We have become isolated inside its bodies and have been outvoted repeatedly. Generally it is not because other nations want to avoid us. Other countries seek our support and are pleased when we join them. Our isolation is self-inflicted. Having taken a position, we fail to gain support from other nations, fail to build coalitions, and often fail to get even our closest bilateral allies to join us.

The annual State Department reports to Congress on voting practices in the United Nations General Assembly (UNGA) eloquently and forcibly demonstrate this fact. During the 38th UNGA, our Western European allies cast votes coincident with the United States only 53.8 percent of the time; the Americas 26.8 percent; Asia and the Pacific 21.5 percent; Africa 18.6 percent; and Eastern Europe 14.2 percent. Nations of the Non-Aligned Movement and Western nations agreed on about 20 percent of contested votes, whereas the Non-Aligned and the Soviet bloc were in agreement 80 percent of the time.7/ It is true that votes are not the only means by which member states can be supportive of the United States. Speeches, lobbying inside their own meetings, and behind the scenes efforts to moderate offensive resolutions all can aid the United States. However, the pattern of these cumulative voting records clearly shows our relegation.

Beyond voting, the tone of debate within the U.N. and the wording of resolutions tend too easily to abuse the United States. During the 38th UNGA, the United States was the only major nation singled out for criticism by name. One resolution falsely attacked the United States for violating the South African arms embargo; one unfairly attacked the United States for nuclear cooperation with South Africa; and another attacked the United States for its assistance to Israel. It is noteworthy and perhaps instructional that such attacks seldom, if ever, are aimed at the Soviet Union. Notwithstanding the Soviet Union's maintenance of more than 100,000 occupation troops within Afghanistan, the Soviets have not been the object of specific disapproval in a UNGA resolution.8/

During the summer of 1983, the major U.N. forum for the North-South economic debate was in Belgrade, Yugoslavia, at UNCTAD VI. The U.N. Conference on Trade and Development was founded in 1964 to consider the relationship between international trade policies and economic development in the Third World. Over time UNCTAD's rhetoric, resolutions, and actions have become increasingly hostile to the West, free enterprise, multinational corporations, and the private sector. Whereas the original logic underlying UNCTAD was that developing counties should obtain the external resources they need for development programs through increased trade instead of aid, by the sixth plenary meeting in 1983 UNCTAD primarily focused on organizing cartels, intervening in markets, and extracting funds from developed countries.9/ Perhaps most offensive and far reaching is UNCTAD's proposal for an Integrated Program for Commodities (IPC). This proposal is a centerpiece of certain nations' efforts to utilize U.N. bodies to create a New International Economic Order (NIEO). The IPC proposes manipulations of the essential commodity market in ways offensive to the free market and free trade, and methods to extract artificially high prices from developed countries through price fixing and cartels.

At UNCTAD VI the United States did not break consensus on the resolutions adopted, but did lead a small number of Western developed countries in expressing reservations about the most offensive portions of the consensus resolution after its adoption. The United States' ineffectiveness is documented not only by its inability to negotiate acceptable resolutions and by the small minority of countries which followed our lead in expressing reservations, but more fundamentally and more troubling by the U.S. delegation's unwillingness to stand on principle and vote "no."

As Ambassador Kirkpatrick has said,

It is not pleasant to lose . . . it is also not pleasant to provoke the disapproval of almost everyone. It is not agreeable to decline the good offices of colleagues eager to work out compromises on any issue, and principle.10/

But the UNCTAD VI resolutions offended basic principles of free-market economies and clear U.S. positions. Nonetheless, the U.S. delegation to UNCTAD VI apparently felt so isolated, so unwilling to lead, so powerless, that it did not break consensus, did not so offend the other delegates, but merely expressed more genteel reservations.

As noted above, the IAEA is critical to the nuclear nonproliferation regime and therefore does have vital importance to us. Nonetheless, for a number of months in 1982-1983 we were forced to suspend our participation in the agency due to a political defeat during the September 1982 IAEA General Conference. This withdrawal, if it had become permanent, would have seriously weakened the worldwide nuclear nonproliferation regime and weakened our own security.

The cause of our withdrawal was the denial of Israeli credentials by the IAEA General Conference. We lost this key issue by a single vote. It is not constructive to point fingers or reflect on how things might have been different in 1982. But it is instructive to wonder how the United States, as a country that played a leading role in the creation both of the United Nations and the International Atomic Energy Agency, and remains by far the largest financial contributor to these organizations and the largest provider of direct peaceful nuclear cooperation to Third World countries worldwide, could lose by a single vote on a matter of pivotal political importance to us.

The recent U.S. withdrawal from the United Nations Educational, Scientific, and Cultural Organization (UNESCO) is a further demonstration of our ineffectiveness in U.N. specialized agencies. The United States was a founding member of UNESCO and its largest contributor. UNESCO, at its best, was viewed as a valuable instrument for cooperation in education, science, culture, and communication. But it had increasingly diverted its energies to costly and politicized activities, harmed U.S. interests, criticized Western values, attacked free-market economic principles, the free flow of information, and further mismanaged itself.

From 1981 through 1984, the United States engaged in a concerted campaign to encourage UNESCO to eliminate its anti-Western tone, its unwillingness to defend the ideals of free thought and free expression upon which it was founded, and to reform its expensive and inefficient management practices.

UNESCO failed to respond meaningfully to U.S. efforts for reform. This distorted wasteful spending of the agency's Director General Amadou-Mahtar M'Bow continues unchecked. Alone among U.N. agencies, UNESCO passed a budget for 1984-1985 that included substantial program growth. While UNESCO is supposed to promote scientific and cultural programs in the developing world, it continues to spend 78 percent of its inflated budget on headquarters in Paris. UNESCO continues to promote the "New World Information and Communications Order" which directly threatens the principle of free press. It promotes collective rights rather than individual human rights and continues to allow Soviet manipulation of peace and disarmament themes in its technical areas. UNESCO continued to show itself to be ideologically hostile to Western values in general and the United States in particular. Having been ineffective in reforming UNESCO, the United States withdrew in December 1984.11/

While the foregoing is only a partial list of U.S. setbacks in the United Nations, it clearly demonstrates our too consistently poor performance in the U.N..

### The U.N. is a Political-Legislative Arena

After turning its back on the League of Nations and fighting another world war, traditional American idealism heartily embraced the work in San Francisco in 1945 to create a world assembly. The United Nations was oversold to the American people. As Dean Acheson observed, the United Nations' "presentation to the American people as almost Holy Writ and with the evangelical enthusiasm of a major advertising campaign seemed to me to raise popular hopes which could only lead to bitter disappointment."12/ Perhaps it is because of our idealism, coupled with our initial unrealistic expectations, that the United States has been so slow to fully recognize the fact that the U.N. is a highly political body, and so inept at acting upon that fact.

Americans are an idealistic and hopeful people. The moral imperative of the U.N. Charter embraces our own aspirations. That Charter states two overriding goals: "to save succeeding generations from the scourge of war which twice in our lifetime has brought untold sorrow to mankind," and "to reaffirm faith in fundamental human rights, in the dignity and worth of the human person, in the equal rights of men and women and of nations large and small."13/

In speaking of the Charter, in 1983 President Reagan reflected the desires of the American people when he told the U.N. General Assembly that "the Government of the United States will continue to view the U.N. Charter's concern for human rights as the moral center of our foreign policy."14/

The United Nations was founded to keep peace, to promote political self-determination, to foster global prosperity, and to strengthen the bonds of civility among nations. Thereby, the United Nations was to speak with the voice of moral authority, its greatest power. Over the past 40 years, however, as the voice of the United Nations has become louder, its moral authority has enervated. The collective aspirations for a great, global town meeting have been lost under the clamor and rigid rhetoric of petty politicalization.15/

The tremendous proliferation of member states began this transformation. The United Nations was founded by 51 member nations. Most were democracies with a commitment to liberal principles. During the United Nations' first two decades, the Soviet Union led a hostile minority in the organization that sought to frustrate the majority.16/ General consensus was possible, however, and rational problem solving prevailed.

Beginning in the 1960s, the composition of the United Nations changed drastically and, consequently, fundamentally changed the character of the U.N. Today there are 158 members of the United Nations. Of those, 32 have fewer than one million citizens each. Two-thirds of the vote in the General Assembly speak for less than 10 percent of the world's people and 30 practicing democracies pay two-thirds of the bills.

More important, the world view of most of the new members is significantly different that that of the majority of the founding nations.17/ Most of these former colonies are not democracies, do not embrace liberal principles, and lack experience in foreign affairs. Most are economically undeveloped and politically weak. According to one analysis, the proportion of prodemocratic countries in the United Nations has dropped from 60 percent to 40 percent.18/

The structure of the United Nations as devised by its founding members is based on sovereign equality (one nation, one vote) and on the General Assembly, a quasi-legislative body, which makes decisions by votes. Therefore, it is not surprising that the many new member states in the 1960s, which were mostly poor and weak, sought to bind together into voting blocs. This provided the new members fellowship, security, an issue resource bank, and maximized their influence.19/ The blocs are geographic, political, and ethnic in character.

The largest blocs are dominated by the new members: the group of 77 (G-77) consists of over 120 less-developed countries and the Non-Aligned Movement (NAM) included 95 of the 158 U.N. member states. The G-77 or NAM constitute an automatic majority. The blocs have become the multilateral equivalent of political parties.20/

Both our friends and allies and the Soviet Union have come to terms with the political importance of United Nations blocs.21/ There is the European Community, or "the 10" bloc with very strict rules of cohesion. Furthermore, France works closely with the network of its former colonies and other regional and political blocs. Similarly, Britain works with members of the Commonwealth.22/

There is the Soviet bloc with nations of Eastern Europe and Soviet satellites. A number of Soviet satellites also have membership in other regional and political blocs. For example, Cuba is a member of the Latin American Group and the NAM.23/ By infiltrating these majority blocs, the Soviets both are fully informed about their deliberations and, through their proxies, they are in a position to influence significantly positions taken by the NAM or G-77, both of which seek to adopt positions by consensus.

The dynamics of the U.N. voting blocs are familiar to U.S. politicians. It is almost identical to legislative parties and caucuses in city councils, state legislatures, and the U.S. Congress. Nonetheless, the United States in the United Nations belongs to no voting bloc 24/ and is notoriously poor at the type of legislative give-and-take in the U.N. that our successful legislators have perfected domestically.

Ambassador Kirkpatrick has noted perhaps the most important dimension of bloc politicalization within the United Nations:

> The pattern of blocs conflict encourage solidarity with entities that have reality only in the U.N. Most serious, they breed a process in which the concrete national interests of real nations may be subordinated to the interests of a group that has no relevance to the welfare of its member states.25/

The political influence of blocs and the politicalization of the United Nations are increased by the incredibly large number of annual meetings and conferences. According to one source, in 1982 there were more than 11,600 United Nations meetings in just New York and Geneva. The 1982 General Assembly alone produced 236 million pages of documents.26/ Relatively few nations have the manpower or organizational resources to analyze the documents, produce instructions for its delegations, or to staff all the meetings.

Frequently, technical meetings will be covered by locally stationed delegates with little or no technical backup. Understandably, they feel more comfortable in the recycled political rhetoric and political resolutions common in U.N. forums than in technical discourse they do not fully understand. The result is the spectrums of U.N. politics engulfing many technical meetings.

A delegation lacking its own independent technical expertise will rely on guidance from its voting bloc. Since many technical issues do not lend themselves to only one analysis or a single solution, many delegations will turn to their bloc for answers. The ill-informed delegation that votes with its bloc has political coverage back home. And it is the political decision by majority vote in these meetings that determines the United Nations' position.27/

A further consequence of this proliferation of meetings is that it has tended to eliminate the Untied Nations division of labor. Originally, the United Nations was an integrated system comprised of separate but interrelated bodies discharging different functions. Today, once-technical U.N. bodies squander enormous time and energy dealing with a handful of political issues. Each United Nations specialized agency has become a target of opportunity to be transformed by the Soviet bloc or radical Third World nations to their own congretio de propaganda fide.

Today the focal point of the International Atomic Energy Agency General Conference, once an elite gathering place of the world's nuclear physicists devoid of political issues, is Israeli credentials. Enormous resources were spent at the U.N. International Decade for Women on the issue of the Palestinians and the West Bank. The United Nations Industrial Development Organization Permanent Committee must suffer through lengthy dissertations and resolutions by the Soviet Union and its client states on its peace and disarmament propaganda. Such politicalization of the United Nations system distorts the purpose and effectiveness of its bodies. Nonetheless, it is a reality which must be addressed by the United States thoughtfully, professionally, and effectively. Withdrawal in every case is not the answer. The United States must develop and exercise the political skills to depoliticize the technical agencies.

Rather than working constructively to depoliticize the technical agencies, too often the United States has been an unwitting accomplice. The Soviet bloc and radical Third World nations have policies to introduce deliberately political items onto the agendas of almost all parts of the United Nations, including technical agencies. Their goal is not necessarily to gain adoption for their proposal but to gain legitimacy for their propaganda and engage in the politics of embarrassment. As some analysts have observed,28/ many disputes are brought to the United Nations without any intention of settlement. The intent is to embarrass and hurt an opponent. Other disputes are brought to legitimize issues or provide global status. Whichever the goal, this politicalization occurs, and the United States contributes to the success of this harmful process by its customary policy of not opposing the inscription of each and every such item in the agenda of U.N. specialized agencies. Motivated by a sense of fair play and historical morals that all issues deserve a fair hearing, the United States is politically naive and ineffectual.29/ Most issues do deserve deliberation, but each in its proper forum and only there, not in each and every forum, whether germane or not.

As former Congressman Otis Pike said at the U.N.'s 40th anniversary,

> the United Nations was to be a gathering, not of politicians, but of nations, and the nations would put forth every effort to act as citizens of the world, not as ward-heeling representatives of some local constituency back home. That was the hope. The reality is that the nations are acting exactly like politicians. Anyone who has ever served in any legislative body would recognize the cast of characters.30/

### FSOs Poorly Equipped

My experience, both while serving in the Reagan White House and in Vienna, has been that foreign service officers are among the brightest employees of the U.S. government. By the nature of their training and experience they have broad familiarity with world affairs. However, they are not given the particular tools to become good multilateral diplomats. That is not to say that there are no FSOs good at multilateral diplomacy; some are excellent. But they are the exception, not the rule.

Bilateral diplomacy, where most FSOs spend most of their careers, is different in nature from multilateral diplomacy. Intimate substantive knowledge of the host country is required. A discerning eye to pick up information and relay data back to the State Department is required. An ability to forge professional and social bonds with interlocutors from the host government is needed. Skill at delivering demarches so as to make the views of Washington clearly known, while at the same time not hemorrhaging personal relationships, is important.  A host of other skills are also helpful, but legislative skills are not required.

Within the United Nations system it is necessary for a diplomat to be fully familiar with rules of procedure and the varied parliamentary tactics.  Knowledge of the interplay between the UNGA and the specialized agencies and among the agencies themselves is crucial.  Awareness of thematic-issue evolution within the various U.N. organs is important.  Since such a wide range of issues are debated in each U.N. forum, a wider range of substantive knowledge often is required by multilateral diplomats, and an ability to extemporaneously make cogent arguments.

Most important, rather than a targeted focus on the concerns, needs, and limits of a single host country, the multilateral diplomat must be politically sensitive simultaneously to the national interests of scores of countries covering the entire spectrum of geographic, ethnic, economic, and political orientations.  He must be ever conscious of the subtle interplay among these many players.  He should be capable of reading minute differences among states and within voting blocs even as positions are constantly changing.  The multilateral diplomats must constantly analyze how that complicated interaction can be made to further U.S. goals and have the technical skills to effect that interplay.  In sum, multilateral diplomats must have the political skills of a legislator.

Earlier, I mentioned that at the 1982 IAEA General Conference Israeli credentials were denied by a single vote, causing the United States to suspend its participation in this important U.N. agency.  Perhaps it is instructive to review some of the steps taken that helped turn that situation around for the 1983 IAEA General Conference.

When I arrived in Vienna prior to the 1983 General Conference, I asked for such rudimentary lobbying tools as profiles on each swing vote country to include all U.S. bilateral and multilateral nuclear cooperation over the past five years, outstanding requests for further aid, requests for U.S. export licenses for equipment to facilitate their peaceful nuclear programs, etc. Amazingly, no such information resource bank existed. It took months to glean the information from a variety of sources within the State Department, the Department of Energy, and our National Laboratories, and we were never confident that our information was complete.

Going into the conference we made the U.S. position perfectly clear in capitals and in Vienna posts early and reinforced our message repeatedly prior to and throughout the conference. In addition to our Western allies, I personally visited with the ambassadors to Vienna from every Arab, African, Asian, and Latin American state. I also spent considerable time with my Soviet and Eastern European counterparts. It was tremendously time consuming, as personal lobbying always is; but it also is an effective way to show respect, to make the U.S. position perfectly clear, and to ask for support. Understanding that political limits for some countries made support of the U.S. position impossible, I asked them for help in quieting the cacophony of debate and directing more militant states to seek some reasonable accommodation. Supportive member states that did not plan to send delegates were requested to do so. We worked with those supportive members who, because of one technicality or another such as overdue contributions, could not vote to perfect their position and ensure their right to vote. Procedural alternatives were developed and neutral states lined up to initiate actions as necessary to deflect the issue.

To make the U.S. position absolutely clear on Israeli credentials, President Reagan made reference to the importance of U.N. universality in his address to the U.N. General Assembly just weeks before the IAEA General Conference, and copies of his address with that section highlighted were delivered to every country's embassy in Vienna.31/ Leading the U.S. delegation to the IAEA General Conference was then Secretary of Energy Donald Hodel, the first cabinet member to lead the U.S. delegation in the 26-year history of the IAEA. This reinforced the message that the United States felt the IAEA was important and gave added weight to Hodel's opening address, in which he restated the U.S. position on Israeli credentials and universality.

We set up an elaborate whip system and boiler room that would have been familiar to any legislator in the United States. We established reporting assignments and procedures to ensure that full and timely information would be collected and acted upon accordingly just like any political convention or legislative body in the United States.

For these reasons and others, we won on a motion not to consider challenges to any credential by a vote of more than 2 to 1, just one year after having lost on the very same issue. By 1984, we had such overwhelming support that at the last minute Iraq decided not to even challenge Israeli credentials. The steps outlined here for the 1983 and 1984 IAEA General Conferences are important only as they illustrate routine legislative techniques that should be an integral part of U.S. multilateral diplomacy and, too often, are not.

### Reforms

Politics is an art, not a science. Legislative politics, such as that practiced in the United Nations, is among its most subtle forms. Nonetheless, there are skills, mechanics, and tactics of legislative politics that can and should be taught to FSOs before their posting in a U.N. center.

Today, there is too little training and orientation for foreign service officers who are rotated into U.N. posts. While the most able FSOs can learn from on-the-job training, others cannot. Even the most able FSOs lose valuable time and invariably make many mistakes which would have been avoided if they had been better prepared.

The Foreign Service Institute should provide the officers with detailed training on the rules of procedure and the unwritten U.N. general practices that control the ebb and flow of debate and negotiations. There should be more detailed training about how the various U.N. bodies interrelate, how to fight off intervention from other forums that might thwart U.S. objectives, and how to secure and exploit gains in one forum that can be translated into benefits in another. There should be orientation into the more complex arts of multilateral negotiations and logrolling. Courses should be provided in how to work within and outside caucuses and blocs. Coalition building should be studied. The case study method can be employed to help. In sum, drawing upon the ample experience and expertise of people now in the Foreign Service, better and more professional training in the multilateral diplomacy of the United Nations should be provided to FSOs at the Foreign Service Institute.

In addition to inadequate training for FSOs rotated into United Nations posts, the United States' performance at the United Nations suffers from inexperienced foreign service officers. When rotated to a multilateral post, many of the more able FSOs try to keep this "frolic and detour" to get the minimum two years so they can get on with their real careers back in bilateral diplomacy. If the United States is going to reverse its poor U.N. performance of the past, we need to develop a cadre of able FSOs who stay in multilateral diplomacy throughout their careers and stay at one posting for longer periods of time. Indeed, this is exactly what is done by the Soviet Union and others who excel in the U.N. system.32/

Experience comes from numerous postings at U.N. centers during a career. A full grasp of the system comes from participation in the United Nations' various forums: New York, Geneva, Vienna, Nairobi, Rome, and Montreal. Another valuable dimension would come from a tour or tours working in the International Organizations Bureau servicing the posts and resolving interbureau and interdepartmental issues related thereto.

The State Department should create a multilateral cone just as there are political, economic, and counselor cones. The United Nations matters to U.S. foreign policy interests. It requires unique skills. The United States would benefit from seasoned professionals intimately familiar with the intricacies of the U.N. process and its legislative politics. Recognition of these facts require the creation of a career path whereby an FSO can develop this experience so as to be better able to further U.S. interests in the U.N. system. Creation of a multilateral cone would provide such a career path.

There should be better promotional opportunities for multilateral diplomats. Historically, FSO promotions have heavily favored geographic bureaus and the political cone. Human nature responds to reward systems. Consequently, generally the best and brightest of FSOs are attracted to geographic bureaus and the political cone. The creation of a separate multilateral cone is one way to provide opportunities for FSO career advancement. The Foreign Service Director General and the annual Review Panels should be more sensitive to the need to recognize and promote FSOs who have demonstrated exceptional skill as multilateral diplomats.

The length of tours and particular U.N. postings should be lengthened. The minimum posting for an FSO is two years, and at most bilateral postings it is common to have a one- or two-year extension. Since at present multilateral postings generally are seen as nice frolics and detours rather than solid building blocks for a career, an unusually high percentage of FSOs fulfill the minimum two years at a U.N. post and then move on. This is too short. The cast of characters is too numerous and the tempo too frantic to assimilate and effectively act upon in a short period of time.

Again, we should learn from our more successful colleagues in the U.N. system and lengthen FSOs tours at U.N. posts.

The State Department runs an excellent program whereby approximately 30 FSOs a year are detailed from the State Department to state and local governments throughout the country. This can provide an excellent opportunity for FSOs to learn further dimensions of legislative politics by participating in city council or state assembly deliberations. This unique incubator can accelerate the learning process about techniques of legislative politics and provide first-hand exposure to the supple maneuvering of its best practioners. Foreign service officers in the multilateral area should be encouraged to have tours as Pearson fellows and be assigned to legislative areas in state and local governments. A foreign service officer should benefit in the annual review board process for having been a Pearson fellow. Similarly, some FSOs serve one-year terms on Capitol Hill. This too should be encouraged and rewarded for multilateral diplomats.

Finally, U.S. multilateral diplomats need better, more complete, and more timely data. Today we are still in the horse-and-buggy stage. There are no computerized data banks of all U.S. votes in the various U.N. forums and their implications for U.S. foreign policy, let alone how all other nations voted. There is no information center with profiles of other member states with respect to the many bilateral activities the United States has with them from aid to trade. Fundamental institutional information necessary for rational, well-organized, and well-executed lobbying is simply not available. To become effective U.N. multilateral diplomats, U.S. representatives need fundamental tools they now lack. Such tools should be developed and stored in a central computer at the State Department.

## Conclusion

The United Nations system matters to U.S. interests, but unfortunately the United States performs poorly there. In part, it is due to a failure to recognize fully the U.N. as a legislative political arena and to train foreign service officers accordingly. It is due, also in part, to a failure to provide U.S. multilateral diplomats with adequate and timely information.

The Reagan administration and Congress have recognized the value of the United Nations to advance or thwart U.S. interests. Under Ambassador Kirkpatrick's leadership, and now under Ambassador Vernon Walters', the Reagan administration is providing growing U.S. vigor and leadership in the United Nations system. With new resolutions such as those that call for the Department of State to provide it with an annual report on voting practices in the U.N.,33/ Congress is seeking better results.

The U.S. permanent representative to the United Nations, the assistant secretary of state for international organizations, the director general of the Foreign Service, and key members of Congress must continue to seek to improve our performance in the United Nations. The status quo is simply unacceptable. This paper has sought to outline some simple reforms that would better equip foreign service officers to achieve that goal. The time for implementation of reforms is now.

---

1/      Daniel Patrick Moynihan, A Dangerous Place (New York:    The Atlantic Monthly Press, 1975), p. 31.

2/      Jeane J. Kirkpatrick, "Standing Alone" (address given at Arizona State University, Tempe, Arizona, October 23, 1981), The Reagan Phenomenon (Washington, D.C.:  American Enterprise Institute for Public Policy Research, 1981), p. 80.

3/      Claiborne Pell, "U.N. at 40: Adjusting to Mid-Life," Los Angeles Times, October 6, 1985, p.1.

4/      See editorial, "Three Yesses for the U.N.," New York Times, October 24, 1985, p. 26; and Javier Perez de Cuellar, "The U.N. Simply Must be Made to Succeed," New York Times, October 20, 1985, p. E21.

5/      See Bertrand Goldschmidt, The Atomic Complex (LaGrange Park,
        Ill.:   American Nuclear Society, 1982); and The Nonproliferation
        Role of the International Atomic Energy Agency:  Proceedings of a
        Symposium (Washington, D.C.:  Resources for the Future, 1986).

6/      Gerald F. Tape, "Historical and Political Framework of Safeguards,"
        Nuclear    Safeguards:    A    Reader, report    prepared    by    the
        Congressional Research Service for the House Subcommittee on
        Energy  Research  and  Production,  Committee  on  Science  and
        Technology, 98th Cong., 1st sess., December 1983, p. 26.

7/      These percentages take into account all recoreded votes, including
        procedural motions and paragraph votes, which occurred in the
        UNGA Plenary but does not include issues approved without vote or
        by consensus.   U.S. Department of State, Report to Congress on
        Voting Practices in the United Nations, submitted pursuant to P.L.
        98-151 and P.L. 98-164, May 20, 1985 (Washington, D.C.:   U.S.
        Government  Printing  Office,  1985),  section  II,  tables  1-8  (page
        numbers not listed in publication).

8/      U.S. Department of State, Report to Congress on Voting Practices in
        the United Nations, submitted pursuant to P.L. 98-151 and P.L. 98-
        164, 1984 (Washington, D.C.:   U.S. Government Printing Office,
        1984), p. 7.

9/      Stanley J. Michalak, "U.N. Conference on Trade and Development:
        Cheating the Poor," The Heritage Foundation Backgrounder no. 348,
        May 3, 1984 (Washington, D.C.:  The Heritage Foundation, 1984).

10/     Jeanne J. Kirkpatrick, "Standing Alone," The Reagan Phenomenon,
        p. 80.

11/     Statement of the Honorable Edward Derwinski, Counselor, U.S.
        Department of State.   U.S. Congress, House Subcommittees on
        Human Rights and International Organizations and on International
        Operations, Committee on Foreign Affairs, U.S. Withdrawal From
        UNESCO:  Hearings, 98th Cong., 2nd sess., May 2, 1984 (Washington,
        D.C.:  U.S. Government Printing Office, 1984), pp. 259-303.

12/     Dean Acheson, Present at the Creation:  My Years in the State
        Department (New York: W. W. Norton & Co., Inc., 1969), p. 111.

13/     President Ronald Reagan, address to the 39th session of the U.N.
        General Assembly, New York, September 24, 1984.

14/     President Ronald Reagan, address to the 38th session of the U.N.
        General Assembly, New York, September 26, 1983.

15/     Kurt Waldheim, "The United Nations:  The Tarnished Image,"
        Foreign Affairs, Vol. 63, No. 1 (Fall 1984), p. 93; Abba Eban, The
        New Diplomacy:  International Affairs in the Modern Age (New
        York: Random House, 1983), pp. 237-287.

16/     Robert G. Wesson, "The United Nations in the World Outlook of the
        Soviet Union and the United States," in Alvin Z. Rubinstein and
        George Ginsburgs, eds., Soviet and American Policies in the United
        Nations - A Twenty-Five Year Perspective (New York:  University
        Press, 1971), p. 37.

17/     Daniel  P.  Moynihan,  "The  United  States  in  Opposition,"
        Commentary, Vol. 59, No. 3 (March 1975), p. 31. See also, Maurice
        Tugwell, "The United Nations as the World's Safety Valve," in Burton
        Yale Pines, ed., A World Without A U.N. (Washington, D.C.:  The
        Heritage Foundation, 1984), p. 168; Kurt Waldheim, In the Eye of the
        Storm (Bethesda, Md.: Adler & Adler, 1986), pp. 111-124, 93-95.

18/     Jeanne J. Kirkpatrick, "Standing Alone," The Reagan Phenomenon,
        p. 83.

19/     Richard Bernstein, "African Nations Show Tight Brotherhood at
        U.N.:  Whatever the Stresses at Home, Delegates Take Pride in
        Diplomatic Unity," International Herald Tribune, January 26, 1984,
        p. 3.

20/     The stated goal of the G-77 is to gather less developed countries to
        try to promote economic development.  The NAM includes all
        African and Arab states, most of Asia, and a few Latin American
        states.  The NAM deals with a broader range of issues.  See also,
        Karl  P.  Sauvant,  The  Group  of  77:  Evolution,  Structure,
        Organization (New York: Oceana Publications, Inc., 1981).

21/     Richard Bernstein, "Adept Soviet Envoys Gain Influence at U.N.,"
        International Herald Tribune, January 1, 1984, p. 1.

22/     The United Kingdom's skillful political use of its Commonwealth
        network in the United Nations was evident throughout the Falklands
        War.

23/     Yugoslavia is an active member of the G-77 and also caucuses with
        the Soviet Union and the Eastern bloc.

24/     At the U.N. Offices in Vienna and Geneva there is a voting bloc
        called Western and Other Countries (WEOG) in which the United
        States actively participates.  However, there is no WEOG in New
        York.

25/ Jeanne J. Kirkpatrick, "Standing Alone," The Reagan Phenomenon, p. 98. See also, Richard Bernstein, "The U.N. versus the U.S.," New York Times Magazine, January 22, 1984, p. 12; and Daniel P. Moynihan, "At 40, U.N. Needs A Firmer U.S.," New York Times, September 17, 1985, p. 23.

26/ Richard Bernstein, "Washington and the U.N.: What Went Wrong?," International Herald Tribune, February 1, 1984, p. 4. These numbers do not include meetings at the other U.N. centers in Washington, Vienna, Rome, Paris, Montreal and Nairobi.

27/ Jose Sorzano, "Restoring United States Influence in the United Nations: Five Proposals," to appear in an upcoming issue of Insight.

28/ Abraham Yeselson and Anthony Gaglione, A Dangerous Place: The United Nations as a Weapon in World Politics (New York: Grossman, 1974).

29/ Jose Sorzano, Insight.

30/ Otis Pike, "The U.N.: Forum for a Batch of Politicians," Chicago Sun-Times, October 20, 1985, p. 69.

31/ President Ronald Reagan, address to the 39th session of the U.N. General Assembly, New York, September 26, 1983.

32/ Richard Bernstein, "African Nations at U.N.," International Herald Tribune, January 26, 1984, p. 3.

33/ P.L. 98-151 and P.L. 98-164.

# UPGRADING SMALL-POWER DIPLOMACY

The United States is among the oldest continuous governments in the world. Our diplomatic relations reach back to Benjamin Franklin at the Court of Louis the 16th in Paris. As the U.S. emerged on the world stage, diplomacy was conducted country to country - bilaterally. Suspicious of broader multilateral entanglements, the U.S. rejected entry into the League of Nations after World War I.

A quarter-century later, the battles of World War II had ravaged the rest of the developed world while our industrial base went unscathed. And the closing days of the war witnessed the awesome destructive power of the atomic bomb, a new force held solely by the United States. We became the dominant superpower.

Quickly, however, the Soviet empire annexed Eastern Europe and acquired its own nuclear weapons. NATO was formed, the new containment theory dominated our thinking and our foreign policy and defense strategies focused on the Soviet-U.S. competition, the so-called East-West debate.

The Soviet Union remains our primary adversary and threat; the East-West debate properly is the dominant diplomatic concern of the United States and bilateral relations a major means of advancing our foreign policy interests. Yet the East-West debate cannot be our only concern nor bilateral relations the sole means of diplomacy.

We must become more sophisticated at multilateral diplomacy, too, because the world has changed in the last 25 years and the United States has not kept pace. Failure to respond to today's challenges will result in

---

Appeared in The Chicago Tribune, June 15, 1988.

the United States becoming more isolated and less effective in advancing our own national interests.

The world has become more multifaceted, and individual national economies, including America's, have become more interdependent on the global economy. While the threat of nuclear holocaust helps prevent a third world war, regional conflicts rage in the Middle East, Central America, Asia and Africa, each a tinderbox that could blaze out of control. And nation-states have proliferated enormously.

Developing countries can have a major impact on our vital interests: economic prosperity, war and peace. As sovereign nations, they deserve our respect. We must understand their interests and aspirations.

As the world's wealthiest economy, the U.S. has achieved a prosperity that can benefit the struggling economies of the Third World through example, expanded trade and direct investment. But too often there is resentment and hostility by developing countries toward the United States. Some of this is the unavoidable friction between different cultures and resentment of our size and wealth, but a good part of it results from the U.S. failure to show proper respect for their highest concerns in their preferred diplomatic forum: the United Nations.

The scores of new nations that gained independence in the 1960s often were relatively poor and struggling for an identity. They lacked the tradition of country-to-country diplomacy. They lacked an experienced diplomatic corps. And they lacked the resources to found embassies all over the globe. So rather than conduct their world affairs in the capitals of scores of nations, they did so through the United Nations.

The importance of the U.N. to the developing nations was explained in an apocryphal story a Third World ambassador told me a few years ago. It seems that in the early 1960s a certain African country attained its independence after a prolonged struggle. Two brothers had led the fight for independence. One became president of the new nation while the other went to New York to represent his country at the U.N. A diplomat from a neighboring African country asked the ambassador why he was not president. The new ambassador replied: "My brother and I agreed that one of us would be president, while the other would go to the United Nations. We flipped a coin and I won."

From the U.N.'s founding in 1945 through the early 1960s, the United States and like-minded Western democracies dominated the world body. With the proliferation of new members, however, we lost that controlling influence. The new majority of undemocratic developing nations shifted the agenda to development and related issues. With that shift, U.S. interest in the U.N. began to wane.

But if we recognize the importance of these new nations to our vital interests and also the importance these nations place on the U.N., then we should actively and constructively engage them diplomatically within the U.N. framework.  This means working with them on issues of importance to them as well as pushing our own agenda, constructively negotiating on resolutions and working for common ground.

On our fundamental values and basic principles we must be constant and uncompromising.  But to advance these values and principles we must be pragmatic and flexible where possible.  We cannot hesitate to have the courage of our convictions and stand alone if required.  But we must vigorously pursue multilateral diplomacy to constructively engage the issues before the U.N. that are of great importance to developing countries and work to build broad-based coalitions.

Too many important issues are not confined to bilateral answers. Broader multilateral solutions must be forged.  We must recognize the U.N. as an arena that can contribute constructively to finding these solutions.

## ADVANCING U.S. OBJECTIVES IN THE UNITED NATIONS

For many Americans the United Nations has become a focal point of our great dissatisfaction, frustration, and bitterness over what the postwar world has become. The United Nations was created under America's leadership with the hope that a future world order would emerge in which the old colonial empires would develop into independent and sovereign nation states which treated each other as equals. Just as Americans conduct themselves in their political affairs civilly and peacefully and according to the rule of law, it was hoped that the new countries would respect the injunction contained in the U.N. Charter to refrain from aggressive acts against one another.

Since the United Nations was founded, over 20 million people have been killed in well over 100 wars around the world. Today regional conflicts rage in the Middle East, Central America, Asia, Africa--each a tinderbox that could blaze out of control.

Once seen as man's last, best hope for international order and peace, the United Nations has fallen into severe disrepute among many Americans. Critics have pointed out many legitimate problems. Far from being just ineffectual or an expensive Turkish bath, they charge that the U.N. General Assembly (UNGA) exacerbates the world's problems by forcing nations to take positions on many matters on which they otherwise could avoid entanglements. Critics charge that the United Nations is rife with double standards. And many feel the United Nations is hostile to our values and interests.

---

Address before the Council of Washington Representatives on the United Nations, Washington, D.C., June 21, 1988.

Or as William F. Buckley has observed: "Obviously, our country attaches importance to the values and ideals of the United Nations. The question is whether the United Nations attaches any importance to the values and ideals of the United Nations."

The fact is that member states in the United Nations have greatly politicized this important body--politicized it in ways that harm the United Nations and certainly do no credit to the member states themselves. The 1975 UNGA resolution branding Zionism as racism is a disgrace. It is absurd. It damages efforts to bring peace to the Middle East. It properly brings discredit to the United Nations.

The double standards in the United Nations, especially on human rights, undermine the United Nation's moral authority and, some would say, its legitimacy. Name calling--while less--still persists in the United Nations. This, too, is unacceptable.

The fact is that the member states in the United Nations have supported, and for too long allowed to flourish, mismanagement and inefficiency. As the United Nation's largest financial contributor by far-- nearly $900 million this year in assessed and voluntary contributions paid by the U.S. Government--this is cause for profound concern.

Having pointed out some of these serious problems in the United Nations--problems the United States must diligently and forcefully seek to correct--let me now say categorically that the United Nations matters. It is important. It is important to the world community, and it is important to the United States.

The U.N. Charter reflects our fundamental beliefs, our basic values, and our aspirations for mankind. Further, the United Nations, in many of its activities, indeed does advance U.S. interests.

- At the International Atomic Energy Agency (IAEA), invaluable and near irreplaceable work is done on nuclear nonproliferation, assurance of supply, and nuclear safety. The IAEA responded fully and constructively to the Soviet nuclear accident at Chernobyl, helping to analyze the causes of the accident, contain the fallout, and draft international conventions to deal with future nuclear accidents.

- The World Health Organization (WHO) led the fight to eradicate small-pox. And today at WHO, international research on the AIDS [acquired immune deficiency syndrome] crisis is coordinated and advanced.

- At the U.N. Fund for Drug Abuse Control, programs to battle illicit drugs through crop eradication and substitution are advanced. New international conventions to strengthen legal sanctions and enhance cooperation to fight illegal drug traffic are moving rapidly toward ratification within the United Nations.

- The International Civil Aviation Organization promotes higher standards for aviation safety, as well as more effective aviation and airport security against international terrorism.

- The World Meterological Organization coordinates global weather reporting and forecasting.

At these and other specialized agencies of the U.N. system, important work goes on every day. And while there are continuing efforts by some member states to politicize these bodies, generally, such assaults have failed. Further, nowithstanding its serious faults, the General Assembly and the Security Council can--at times--effectively advance U.S. interests.

We see this today with the situation in Afghanistan. The General Assembly condemned the illegal occupation of Afghanistan--repeatedly. World attention focused on the issue, and pressure built for a remedy. Simultaneously, the Secretary General's personal representative, Under Secretary Diego Cordovez, worked to find a political solution. Now, the United Nations is not the cause for the present Soviet troop withdrawal. Events on the ground in Afghanistan and events and decisions in Moscow dictated the withdrawal. Nonetheless, the United Nations made a contribution. The United Nations helped facilitate the implementation of the political decision. The United Nations continues this role. And this is important.

The United Nations has a critically important role to play in the return of over 5 million refugees, assisting over 1 million displaced persons within Afghanistan, and reconstruction of a countryside devastated by nearly 9 years of brutal Soviet occupation. The demands for expertise, experience, and finance compel an international response to this problem, to which the United Nations and its technical and development agencies can provide special leadership. The United Nations has the capacity to coordinate and pool resources. Its agencies have the experience of managing major refugee programs. It can operate in areas where other individual countries may be unable to.

We are delighted the Secretary General has appointed Prince Sadruddin Aga Khan as U.N. coordinator for the effort. As President Reagan told the Prince last week at an Oval Office meeting, the U.S. Government wants to work closely, in full cooperation in this effort, with him and with the United Nations.

Prince Sadruddin has moved with record speed in developing a coordinated U.N. program. At a meeting to provide donors with information recently held in New York, Sadruddin provided an overview of his proposed program. It will be focused primarily on relief and resettlement of Afghan refugees and displaced persons, providing them with food, agricultural supplies, irrigation, and health care. Most importantly, the program will be decentralized and geared to provide assistance directly to the Afghan people rather than channeled through the illegitimate Kabul regime.

Further, the United States must recognize that the world has become more multifaceted, and individual national economies, including America's, have become more interdependent on the global economy. Newer nation states, developing countries, can have a major impact on our vital interests: economic prosperity, war, and peace. As sovereign nations they deserve our respect. We must seek to understand their interests and aspirations.

The Soviet Union remains our primary adversary: the East-West debate properly is the dominant diplomatic concern of the United States. Yet the East-West debate cannot be our only concern or bilateral relations our sole effective means of diplomacy.

With increasing frequency we should seek multilateral solutions. We must seek creative solutions for North-South as well as East-West issues. And to advance U.S. vital interests, we must work with developing countries. There are a variety of multilateral forums in the world today where such cooperation should be sought. And it is the United Nations which remains the primary multilateral arena. The United States must show proper respect for developing countries' highest concerns in their preferred diplomatic forum: the United Nations.

President Reagan has addressed the United Nations six times--more than any of his predecessors. In Dr. Jeane Kirkpatrick and Gen. Vernon Walters, President Reagan sent distinguished and very able ambassadors to New York to advance U.S. interests in the United Nations. Their selections reflected the importance Ronald Reagan placed on the United Nations and his commitment to improve it.

Ambassador Kirkpatrick took the "Kick Me" sign off the U.S. delegation. Her forceful eloquence advanced the U.S. agenda. In the United Nations, name calling has all but stopped. Efforts to delegitimize Israel unfortunately continue, but the momentum to challenge Israeli credentials within the United Nations and its specialized agencies has been reversed.

Following a 2-year campaign led by Ambassador Walters and the United States, this past March, the U.N. Human Rights Commission took a major step to correct the cynicism, hypocrisy, and double standards of the United Nations in the field of human rights. For years, Cuba has been the worst U.N. member of all in violating its citizens' human rights. Nonetheless, it remained free from careful scrutiny by the United Nations. This year, the United States succeeded in achieving a consensus decision at the U.N. Human Rights Commission to launch an investigation into Cuba's human rights abuses. Already Castro has begun to free some political prisoners, improve prison conditions, and allow greater religious freedom.

In 1986, under the able leadership of U.S. Permanent Representative to the United Nations Vernon Walters and of Ambassadors Keyes [former U.S. Representative to the Economic and Social Council] and Sorzano [former Deputy Permanent Representative to the United Nations], the U.N. reform effort really took off.

The U.S. efforts succeeded in the establishment of a "Group of 18 Governmental Experts" to look at the need for budget and program reform in the United Nations. The Group of 18 proposed some sweeping measures affecting personnel reductions, budgeting by consensus, and the need to establish program priorities. The United States worked tirelessly with other major donors to advance these proposals, both in the United Nations and in U.N. specialized agencies. Most of the specialized agencies now have adopted significant aspects of these reform proposals. The U.N. members are teetering on the brink of implementing these proposals, but whether the U.N. membership has the political will to fully implement these needed reforms is still an open question. U.S. resolute leadership during the rest of this Administration and the next will be necessary to achieve the reforms required to make the United Nations budgetarily responsible and programatically effective.

The Group of 18 recommendations are extremely important, not only because they offer hope for improved management and a rational budget process but just as critical, perhaps more so, because the CPC [Committee on Program Coordination] consensus decisionmaking offers hope that the importance of consensus decisionmaking can be relearned in the U.N. General Assembly.

The force and effectiveness of the United Nations lies in consensus, not polarization. The contentious balkanization within the United Nations today, driven in large part by regional blocs, hurts the institution and thwarts its potential effectiveness.

Some charge that the Reagan Administration has been too tough-minded toward the United Nations. But the facts speak for themselves. We are no longer in retreat within the United Nations. Thanks in large part to forceful, persistent, clear-headed U.S. leadership, the United Nations is a better place today than it was 8 years ago.

The United Nations is still an institution with serious flaws--a forum of great frustration for us. But it also is a forum of opportunity for us. The United Nations matters. It matters a lot. We must dedicate ourselves to working constructively in the United Nations to advance U.S. interests, and to help us achieve those interests, to advance U.N. reform.

## TOWARD THE 21ST CENTURY:
### The Future for Multilateral Diplomacy


I firmly believe that as we look toward the 1990s and on toward the 21st century, multilateral diplomacy will be of growing importance to the United States in pursuing its national interests and for other nations in pursuing theirs.

Profound changes are underway in the world--changes in virtually every subject from science to superpower relations. As a result, the "member state" itself has undergone a redefinition. That is because the issues confronting us, whether they be political, economic, or scientific in nature, transcend national borders.

A number of factors are increasing national interdependency. Scientific, economic, and political matters are global in dimension and enormous in extent. They are outstripping the traditional means by which governments dealt with them. The speed at which information flows-- whereby, in an instant, a computer in New York can exchange information around the globe by tying in with another computer--has already created a global marketplace. The amount of money that changes hands in the global financial market in 1 day exceeds $1 trillion--more than the entire annual budget of the U.S. Government. Such flows transcend national boundaries and can overwhelm rigid economic policies.

Facing every nation is a variety of emerging problems of great urgency which transcend the national borders. We can see this today in a number of environmental issues. Emissions from factories in one nation

---

Address before the Annual Conference of the Department of Public Information for Nongovernmental Organizations, U.N. Headquarters, New York City, September 16, 1988.

cause trees to die and lakes to be polluted in another nation. Floods in Bangladesh are caused by deforestation in upriver countries. Rain forests are cleared for development in one region, and the climate is changed throughout the Western Hemisphere. Chlorofluorocarbons are released in several countries, and the "greenhouse effect" in the earth's atmosphere is apparent.

Actions which were once viewed as strictly national or domestic are now being perceived as having international repercussions. Nations are becoming more aware that we must work together within the global community to better understand the many implications which our individual actions will have for all our societies in the decades ahead.

I believe that multilateral negotiations will inevitably become more important as we increase our awareness of interdependency; that there will be a growing need to develop and strengthen multilateral forums. And this will mean that each nation must further develop its skills at multilateral diplomacy. To do this, we must have a recognition of our past experience in multilateral diplomacy, face multinational fora with realism and an understanding of their limits and opportunities, and have a commitment to nurture their potential.

### The Importance of Political Groupings

The global nature of changes in science, in economics, and in technology must be matched by political developments, particularly the strengthening and closer association of like-minded nations.

With the increased awareness of national interdependency, the importance of regional country and functional groupings has been heightened. Regional, political, and religious blocs of nations--such as the OAS [Organization of American States], the Organization of African Unity, the South Asian Association of Regional Cooperation, the Nonaligned Movement, and the [Organization of the] Islamic Conference--now provide platforms for certain countries to exercise influence more effectively than when alone.

Other regional organizations are taking on growing economic and political importance. The Pacific Basin, for example--a region of phenomenal economic growth--has been developing a web of cooperative realities. ASIAN [Association of South East Asian Nations] is showing the way to regional cooperation and has been taking on more and more of a political dimension beyond its initial focus on economic affairs.

These developments in political cooperation are outgrowths of our efforts and aspirations for a better world. The United States led the way after World War II in advocating the importance of the regional approach to the recovery of a devastated Europe. Today, the institutions that resulted from this effort are thriving: regional organizations such as the NATO alliance, the OECD [Organization for Economic Cooperation and Development], the European Economic Community, and the Western European Union; and functional organizations such as GATT [General Agreements on Tariffs and Trade], IMF [International Monetary Fund], the World Bank, and regional development banks, as well as the effective functional organizations of the United Nations.

Over the past several decades, the United States has come to an increased recognition that, in many areas, we can be more effective in advancing U.S. objectives if we pursue these objectives in a multilateral context, which allows us to assert values that transcend narrow political interests. The United States recognizes that--in order to meet the challenges facing us as we look toward the next century--we will have to have recourse to a variety of multilateral forums, of which the United Nations is going to be just one. The group of 7, for example, is a vital multilateral forum today for the United States and the other most industrialized Western nations. Over the years since its inception, the Group of 7 has broadened its scope beyond just economic concerns. And it is an explicit example of how nations can overcome cultural differences or past difficulties to work together on issues--whether they be economic, political, or environmental--which know no boundaries.

### Upgrading Small-Power Diplomacy

Just as there is a need for nations to achieve an increased awareness of inter-dependency, as well as a realistic understanding of the limits and capabilities of multinational forums, so, too, is there a need to recognize that political, technological, and economic power have been dispersing horizontally. Ours is no longer a bipolar world. For far too long, too much of U.S. efforts and attention have focused on the Soviet-U.S. competition, the so-called East-West debate. The Soviet Union remains our primary adversary: the East-West debate properly is the dominant diplomatic concern of the United States and bilateral relations a major means of advancing our foreign policy interests. Nevertheless, just as bilateral relations cannot be the sole means of diplomacy, the East-West debate cannot be our only concern.

Developing countries can have a major impact on U.S. vital interests--economic prosperity, war, and peace. As sovereign nations, they deserve our respect. We must understand their interests and aspirations, just as they should try to understand ours.

The scores of new nations that gained independence in the 1960s often were relatively poor and struggling for an identity. They lacked the tradition of country-to-country diplomacy. They lacked an experienced diplomatic corps. And they lacked the resources to fund embassies all over the globe. So rather than conduct their world affairs in the capitals of scores of nations, they did so through their preferred diplomatic forum--the United Nations.

If we properly recognize the importance of these new nations to U.S. vital interests and also the importance these nations place on the United Nations, then we should actively and constructively engage them diplomatically within the U.N. framework. This means working with them on issues of importance to them while we work on our own agenda, constructively negotiating on resolutions and working for common ground.

Again, I would like to emphasize that broader multilateral solutions must be forged. And we must recognize the United Nations as an arena that can contribute constructively to finding these solutions.

### The Importance of the United Nations

When the United States emerged on the world state, diplomacy was conducted country to country, bilaterally. Suspicious of broader multilateral entanglements, the United States rejected entry into the League of Nations after World War I,

Following World War II, however, traditional American idealism heartily embraced the work in San Francisco in 1945 to create a world assembly. The U.N. Charter embodies the ideals and moral goals of our own Constitution. Despite frustrations with the organization, the United States has remained firm in its commitment to the United Nations as an important forum in helping governments take collective action for addressing global problems and challenges. We have demonstrated our commitment by consistently supporting the United Nations morally, financially, and politically.

The United Nations was founded to keep the peace, to promote political self-determination, to foster global prosperity, and to strengthen the bonds of civility among nations. By subjugating the individual interests of member states to the greater good of the world community, the United Nations was to speak with the voice of moral authority, its greatest power. Over the past 40 years, however, as the voice of the United Nations has become louder, its moral authority has been weakened by the trends toward double standards, loose rhetoric, bloc voting, and petty politicization.

Much progress has been made in addressing these problems, but there is still an important need to take a realistic look at the United Nations as it actually is. What are its limitations and its capabilities? What do we need to do in seeking broader multilateral solutions to the challenges of today so that the United Nations is better able to fulfill its mandate in the world of tomorrow?

I have tried to stress here important questions not confined to bilateral solutions. There are important issues that transcend national borders and must be considered in a global context. Two such issues--refugee assistance and human rights--are ones for which the United Nations has become a vital forum in addressing multinational interests and concerns.

Refugee Assistance. Throughout history, people have fled injustice, war, drought, and famine. More than 100 million people have been uprooted from their homes since World War I, making the 20th century what has been called "the century of refugees and prisoners."

Today conflict and repression on every continent have forced more than 11 million people outside their nations' borders as refugees. And, again, no specific national situation can be considered in isolation. Following the invasion of Afghanistan, millions of refugees poured into Pakistan. Thousands of Vietnamese were forced to find their way to countries throughout Southeast Asia as a result of the excesses of that government. More than a million Mozambicans have fled into neighboring nations to escape war and starvation in their homeland.

We must not forget that the root cause of mass refugee flows is the denial of fundamental human rights. The care of refugees is an international concern and the responsibility of every country and each individual, with equitable burdensharing.

While the initial focus of refugee assistance is on short-term material assistance for basic life-sustaining needs, an important element of assistance efforts is the search for more lasting solutions to refugee problems. Such solutions include the fostering of voluntary repatriation, when that is appropriate, local integration in the country or region of asylum and, finally, resettlement in third countries.

Refugees have no political influence. If the international community fails to speak for them, their cause will be lost in darkness, and the violation of human rights will go on endlessly. And it is in the United Nations that the international community can rise up and speak with one voice, a voice of moral and political authority. We, as members of the international community, have been tasked to share the burden of supporting multilateral, bilateral, or private efforts to achieve more durable refugee solutions wherever possible.

Human Rights. Another continuing challenge for U.N. member states as we look toward the 21st century is human rights. The protection and promotion of basic human rights and fundamental freedoms are among the principal purposes of the United Nations set forth in its Charter and in the Universal Declaration of Human Rights.

A reason for the primacy of human rights in the United Nations is that its founders recognized from the bitter experience of the Second World War that those governments that abuse the rights of their own citizens are more likely to abuse the rights of citizens of other countries. Promotion of the respect for human rights is thus linked to the United Nations' basic purpose of keeping the peace.

As we prepare to commemorate the 40th anniversary of the Universal Declaration, it is important to note the progress that has been made in seeking to restore these vitally important norms and standards, as well as the significant role which the United Nations continues to play in addressing human rights abuses around the world.

The United States uses its influence in favor of human rights and democracy bilaterally, both in public and in private, and in multilateral forums such as the OAS, the U.N. General Assembly, and the U.N. Commission on Human Rights. We see the United Nations with its various organs as the preeminent global organization in the area of human rights. The need to address human rights violations in multilateral forums is also linked to the efforts to help avoid new mass flows of refugees.

In our view, no state may hide behind the argument of national sovereignty in the area of human rights. The world community has made clear that human rights are matters of international concern.

As in the case of all manmade institutions, the United Nations often carries out its tasks in an imperfect way. But the United Nations can and does have an impact with respect to protecting human rights. It is like a hoe--by itself useless, but in the hands of the gardener, it can make the earth productive and help it yield fruit. Its principal tool is its ability to generate publicity and investigate a specific situation of human rights abuses or promote thematic human rights issues.

The problems I mentioned previously regarding the double standards, politicization, and bloc voting are particularly abhorrent with respect to the consideration of human rights within the United Nations. The message that is often sent is that countries with a powerful friend or popularity among the voting majority in the United Nations can be held to a different human rights standards than others. This double standard undermines that United Nations' moral authority--and its legitimacy.

Despite these serious problems, however, progress has been made. The achievement of consensus earlier this year in Geneva on concerns about human rights in our hemisphere was significant not only because it marked a departure from the United Nations' too frequent double standard but also because it demonstrated how, in this age of bloc voting, a country like the United States can strike a victory for freedom by carefully marshaling the full range of our multilateral resources to forge a coalition. And this initiative serves as another example of the unique capability of the United Nations to make an important contribution to the world community.

With all of its flaws, the United Nations remains the only body of its kind in the world. It is the only arena where the tortured and abused of the world have an opportunity to lay forth their cases and stand some chance of having the world community act on their behalf.

### The Role of the United Nations in Conflict Resolution

I know that over the past 2 days others have addressed this conference on the topics of U.N. peacekeeping and the role of the United Nations in conflict resolution. I would, however, like to address these issues as they relate to the broader topic of multilateral goals and efforts.

Since the first U.N. peacekeeping effort in Palestine in 1948, peacekeeping operations have become an important technique in international conflict management. Today we face a unique and exciting opportunity for the United Nations in the peacekeeping area. To quote the remark of one U.N. observer: "Peace seems to be breaking out all over." In Afghanistan, Iran-Iraq, Angola-Namibia, Cyprus, Western Sahara, and Cambodia, the United Nations is moving center stage in helping to resolve significant regional conflicts that have cost many lives and, in some cases, have been tinderboxes with the potential to explode into major power confrontations.

At a time of such major U.N. involvement in making positive contributions for peacekeeping, it is incumbent upon us to study the reasons events have joined to create this opportunity, and to learn the lessons of history and of these current conflicts, so that we may better understand precisely what the United Nations is able to contribute in resolving these conflicts. If we are unrealistic in our expectations, or fail to be hard-headed in our analysis of the apparent recent success and progress of U.N. peacekeeping, we will endanger future potential for the United Nations as a peacekeeping tool.

The fact of the matter is that the United Nations cannot and should not seek to impose solutions on parties. Rather, once the parties have-- through exhaustion, their own cost-benefit analysis, or other reasons-- reached a stage where it is time for the conflict to end, the United Nations can provide an invaluable role as a facilitator to this process. Whether by bridging a gulf of remaining differences or merely providing a graceful exit, and/or providing domestic justification that the respective governments can use with their own situation at home, the United Nations has a role. It does not impose peace. However, it can act as a midwife, a helpful facilitator, a promoter of peace. This is a limited role, but it is an enormously important role.

It is a result of U.N. efforts and this Administration's policies that the major players have agreed to come to the negotiation table in a number of these recent conflicts.

· In Afghanistan, for example, it was the steadfast support of Ronald Reagan and the strong bipartisan support in the U.S. Congress for the mujahidin that raised the Soviet costs of the brutal occupation of that country.

· It was the deployment of U.S. naval forces in the Persian Gulf, as well as the diplomatic isolation of Iran, that led Iran to accept the terms of Resolution 598 and agree to a cease-fire.

· The United States is taking the lead in trying to arrange among the parties a peaceful solution to the Angola-Namibia conflict. However, Assistant Secretary [for African Affairs] Chet Crocker, the mediator in these talks, has recognized from the outset the helpful role the United Nations can play in implementing the arrangements the parties eventually agree on concerning self-determination in Namibia and the end of civil war in Angola.

· In Cambodia, we anticipate that the United Nations will have to be involved in bringing about true self-determination for the Cambodian people following withdrawal of the Vietnamese occupation forces.

We strongly support the Secretary General's [Javier Perez de Cuellar] role in these recent peacekeeping initiatives, and we welcome the resurgence of the United Nations as a forum for the resolution of international disputes.

Pressure for new peacekeeping operations is likely to continue and perhaps increase in the years leading to the next century. Additional initiatives over the next few years could have several important consequences--political as well as financial--for our efforts in the multilateral arena. We must ensure that an expanded U.N. peacekeeping role is not manipulated in a way that would undermine the constructive and practical contribution the United Nations is making toward world peace.

### U.N. Role in Global Problem-Solving

As with conflict resolution, the U.N. system is uniquely able to help governments take collective action, when governments have a unity of purpose and political will. In recent years, the ability of the United Nations and its specialized agencies to respond quickly and effectively to global problems has taken on new importance.

At the International Atomic Energy Agency (IAEA), for example, important work is done on nuclear non-proliferation, assurance of supply, and nuclear safety.  The IAEA responded fully and constructively to the nuclear accident at Chernobyl, helping to analyze the causes of the accident, contain the fallout, and draft international conventions to deal with future nuclear accidents.

At the Secretary General's initiative, 138 countries met last year and declared the elimination of drug abuse and illicit trafficking a universal priority.   We are now moving toward a strong new antidrug trafficking convention.   With our collective commitment and with the Secretary General's support, this important law enforcement treaty will be completed in December 1988, and stronger U.N. drug control programs will follow to address this serious international problem.

Another excellent example of global problem-solving can be found in the World Health Organization (WHO).  WHO has led the fight to eradicate smallpox, developed programs targeting the health of children, and has been aggressively coordinating the global response to the problems of AIDS [acquired immune deficiency syndrome].

Finally, we should also note the significant problem-solving undertaken by other U.N. agencies like the International Maritime Organization and the International Civil Aviation Organization.  These have both been in the vanguard of the global fight against international terrorism.

We will need to continue our efforts into the next century to strengthen the U.N. specialized agencies and programs so that organizations like IAEA, U.N. Children's Fund, the U.N. Environmental Program, and the U.N. Fund for Drug Abuse Control can perform their essential functions-functions which no one country can perform alone.

## Conclusion

At this time of global challenge and change, our efforts in the multilateral arena will be of ever-increasing importance to the United States in advancing our interests and goals and to other nations in advancing theirs.   We must vigorously pursue multilateral diplomacy to constructively address issues of concern to the international community and work to build broad-based coalitions.

Among the foremost arenas for multilateral diplomacy is the United Nations.  The U.N. system is important to the world community and to the interests of its individual member states.  Debates in the United Nations set the international agenda for much of the world.   These debates legitimize and delegitimize issues on the world stage and focus world attention, often establishing the framework for progress.

In the areas of peacekeeping, human rights, and the vital work of the specialized agencies, we can see an increasing number of opportunities on the horizon for effectively utilizing the diplomatic benefits of the United Nations as a gathering place for the world.

At the same time, we must continue to take a realistic look at the United Nations as we approach the next century. We must not allow the present euphoria felt in some quarters to blind us to the political realities which are intertwined within the multilateral arena.

The Reagan Administration and Congress have recognized the value of the United Nations to advance U.S. interests. Under the leadership of Ambassador Vernon Walters and his predecessor, Ambassador Jeane Kirkpatrick, this Administration has provided increased U.S. vigor and leadership in the U.N. system.

We share with other member states a deep concern about the financial difficulties now facing the United Nations. There should be no doubt that the United States clearly recognizes its obligations to the United Nations, and it is because the work of the United Nations is so important that we care about reform. We also must avail ourselves of all means of influence to effect reform of the United Nations that is in all members' interest. This includes moral leadership, political and diplomatic persuasion, and financial leverage.

Much has been achieved, but much more remains to be done. In the first place, we must recognize that the United Nations simply cannot solve all the world's problems. To continue business as usual by piling committee on top of committee to deal with a handful of abstract issues is not only pointless but counterproductive. The issue of international security, for example, is important, and it does involve many things, but security can be maintained without creating a whole new structure or radically revising the U.N. Charter.

As member nations, we must strive to see that the United Nations focuses its resources on those areas where experience has demonstrated that it can make a difference - in facilitating real peacekeeping and real problem-solving in the real world.

In order to be forward-looking about the United Nations, we must be able to take a long look back - back to the United Nations as it was intended to be by its founders. The future of multilateral diplomacy, its promises and potential problems, can be glimpsed in the achievements and in the mistakes of the past and in the faith and commitment of today. We should renew that faith and understand that our goals for the future can only be attained by the steps we take today.

PART TWO

THE U.N. AS AN INSTITUTION

# THE IMPORTANCE OF THE U.N. AGENCIES

This is my first appearance before a congressional committee since my recent confirmation as Assistant Secretary of State for International Organization Affairs. It is a pleasure and an honor to be here.

My statement for the record today highlights the following three areas:

- My initial impressions of the substantive work undertaken by the major technical and specialized agencies of the United Nations, with particular emphasis on the extent to which they serve important U.S. national interests;

- The results of efforts encouraged by the U.S. Congress and the executive branch to achieve reform in the decisionmaking procedures on budgetary matters in these technical agencies of the United Nations; and

- Finally, the criteria-based interagency process used by the executive branch, in close consultation with the Congress, to allocate the limited funds available for fiscal year (FY) 1988 and 1989.

## The Productive Work of the U.N. Agencies

These subcommittees will be discussing the work of the United Nations during the hearing two days from now. We can go into more detail on the United Nations at that time. However, suffice it to say here that many believe that, for too long, the debate over the United Nations in New

---

Statement before the Subcommittee on Human Rights and International Organizations and on International Operations of the House Foreign Affairs Committee, Washington, D.C., February 23, 1988.

York and the need for specific changes in its administration have overshadowed much of the work of the smaller but very important technical agencies in the U.N. system.

In general, I believe that the technical agencies -- such as the World Health Organization and the International Atomic Energy Agency -- have received insufficient public attention.  Many Americans are not familiar with the important and constructive work being performed by many technical and specialized agencies in the U.N. system.  All of us here today are painfully aware of the global challenges resulting from acquired immune deficiency syndrome (AIDS), the tragic hijacking of the cruise ship Achille Lauro, the recent bombing of Korean Air Flight 858, and the widespread fear and legitimate concerns that followed the accident at the Soviet nuclear power plant at Chernobyl.

We also are familiar with less dramatic but important continuing problems, such as food shortages in sub-Saharan Africa and other places, the high incidence of disease and malnutrition among children of the developing world, the need for effective airport security in the wake of continuing international terrorism, the growing concerns about drug abuse and drug trafficking, and the ever-present threat that more countries will develop nuclear weapons, with all of the attendant insecurity and tension that will bring to the international community.

In dealing with such sobering problems, there is a clear need to work steadily to achieve effective international cooperation.  That is precisely what is happening in the majority of the technical and specialized agencies in the U.N. system today.  I would not pretend that those agencies present us with no problems.  They do.  These organizations, like the U.S. Government, are not perfect.  But the work they do in regard to these pressing international problems is impressive.  I would like to touch upon the activities of just a few of these agencies to illustrate their importance to U.S. national interests.  It was not by accident -- nor without good reason -- that the most recent economic summit looked to many of these organizations for leadership and critical followup on problems requiring a multilateral solution.

The World Health Organization (WHO), which led the fight that eradicated smallpox, is now leading the international effort to coordinate the attack on the pandemic of AIDS.  It has played a major role in the development of oral rehydration salts, which are used to combat diarrheal diseases, and it is working to ensure protection of children everywhere against six major childhood diseases. The successful completion of work on a new vaccine against malaria, carried out by WHO in cooperation with U.S. Government agencies and others, will have revolutionary social and economic impact throughout the world.

The International Atomic Energy Agency (IAEA) serves as the cornerstone of international efforts to prevent the further spread of nuclear weapons. IAEA serves as the focal point for efforts to improve nuclear safety practices around the world. Its safeguards constitute a unique international system of verification, providing essential assurance that nuclear material in peaceful nuclear programs is used exclusively for peaceful purposes. The United States is required by law to apply IAEA safeguards to U.S. nuclear exports, which currently total approximately $1 billion a year. If, for some reason, IAEA were not able to apply safeguards, the United States would have to either discontinue its nuclear exports or initiate a bilateral system of safeguards, which would be costly and possibly less effective than the current safeguards system. Neither approach would be beneficial to the U.S. taxpayer.

The International Labor Organization (ILO) mirrors to the world the U.S. democratic traditions of labor, management, and government working together. It is strongly supported by U.S. labor and employer organizations because it has been highly effective in setting minimum standards of employment for workers all over the world. Its work in the area of human and workers' rights is a role that was endorsed by the Senate just in the past few weeks as it agreed to the ratification of two key ILO conventions.

The World Meterological Organization (WMO) has pioneered new efforts to forecast the weather and to bring these benefits not only to farmers around the world but also to communities everywhere. Its work is essential to aviation, shipping, and agriculture, as well as to storm detection and warnings.

The Food and Agriculture Organization (FAO) and its related agencies are helping the world come to grips with food shortages and drought and to eradicate pests and animal diseases. Its fisheries and forests programs are of great importance to the U.S. private sector, and the work it does with WHO in setting international food standards is of great value to U.S. food industries.

The International Civil Aviation Organization (ICAO) promotes safety in air navigation by setting up commonly accepted standards for radio transmission, landing systems, and communication. Its pioneer work in combating international terrorism has led to creation of new procedures for dealing with airplane hijackings, bombings, and attacks on airports. ICAO continues to serve the international community by facilitating discussion of the outrageous bombings by North Korea of Korean Air Flight 858.

Similarly, the International Maritime Organization (IMO) is promoting, through a new convention, safeguards against terrorism at sea, such as the vicious attack on the passengers of the cruise ship Achille Lauro, which resulted in the murder of a U.S. citizen (Leon Klinghoffer).

The U.N. Industrial Development Organization (UNIDO) encourages private sector emphasis in the developing nations. This approach, in turn, stimulates the local economy and leads to increased markets for U.S. goods and services. UNIDO also promotes other goals pursued by the United States -- most notably, focusing on small enterprise and rural development in the Third World.

I could go on, because there are many agencies in the U.N. system which make vital contributions to America's national interests and to U.S. foreign policy. One of my purposes as Assistant Secretary will be to bring increased information about the work of these agencies to the Congress and to the American people. We cannot let their work go uncriticized, and I intend to remain vigilant. But our policy toward them needs to be constructive and supportive. I hope the Congress will assist in this effort.

### Movement for Change

Let me now turn to the efforts undertaken by this Administration, in concert with the Congress, to bring about improvements in decisionmaking procedures on budgetary issues. The relevant legislation -- that is, the Kassebaum/Solomon amendment and the modifications included in the State Department authorization bill adopted at the end of 1987 -- focused on these processes. The recent authorization legislation says that no payment of an assessed contribution can be made to any specialized agency if the payment would cause the U.S. share to exceed 20% of the budget, unless the President determines and reports to the Congress that the agency has made substantial progress toward the adoption and implementation of decisionmaking procedures on budgetary matters in a manner that substantially achieves the goal of greater financial responsibility.

On the surface the standard voting system in the U.N. agencies is one nation/one vote. But, in fact, the major donors have substantial influence in the U.N.'s technical organizations. We and the other major contributors are most outspoken on matters of budgetary concern. Indeed, representatives of the U.S. Government often are so outspoken that representatives of some of the agencies accuse us of being able to exert undue influence over their work simply because we are responsible for such a large portion of the budget. On programmatic matters, U.S. expertise on technical issues -- such as health, the environment, agriculture, labor law, copyrights, weather research, nuclear energy, aviation or maritime affairs, just to give a few examples -- is so pervasive and outstanding that we provide leadership in developing these programs. The United States exerts a major influence in shaping the direction and activities of these organizations, regardless of the one country/one vote situation.

In response to the Kassebaum/Solomon amendment, the United States pursued this financial issue first in the United Nations and achieved what appeared to be a promising victory in late 1986 -- the prospect of major decisions on budgetary questions reached in a relatively small committee, by consensus. President Reagan issued a statement commending the United Nations for this constructive action. Followup implementation of the major reforms in New York will be addressed in more detail at the congressional hearing on February 25.

In the specialized agencies, with the exemption of FAO, there has been a positive response to U.S. requests for reform. In fact, some of the agencies -- such as the International Civil Aviation Organization -- already had in place consensus-based decisionmaking procedures that exceeded even the standards of the agreement approved by the U.N. General Assembly. If we look at them one by one, the results of reform in the technical and specialized agencies of the United Nations are as follows.

The World Health Organization's Executive Board in January 1987, just two months after the U.N. General Assembly decision, adopted its own resolution on "cooperation in program budgeting." This resolution asked each of the WHO governing body units to work toward consensus in reaching conclusions on budget proposals. This commitment included even a 31-member Executive Board, which has the most significant impact on budget review.

The revised WHO procedure will help solidify the longstanding overall satisfaction of the United States with the WHO's administration and management. WHO staff have been open, cooperative, and responsive to U.S. interests. Our delegations have often held up WHO as a model for emulation by other U.N.-system agencies at the same time we have praised WHO programs that promote primary health care and coordinate the international effort against AIDS. The revised decisionmaking system is now in operation. In June 1987, the WHO Program Committee agreed on a planning ceiling for the 1990-91 program budget. And, during 1988, the regional committees and the program committee will be developing consensus proposals on the next budget and working out other mechanisms to ensure more effective and efficient operations.

At the International Labor Organization, the conference in 1987 adopted a key reform measure that provides an additional consultative step for the review of main program options and resource parameters in off-budget years. Like the WHO procedures, this approach will facilitate development of consensus at a key point in the budget development process. The new mechanism links ILO's medium-term plan with biennial programs and budgets and identifies program priorities for 1990-91 and subsequent periods within specific resource levels in real terms. In line with the new procedures, the Program, Finance, and Administrative Committee and the Governing Body of the ILO are considering the medium-term plan, including the identification of priorities and a budget ceiling for 1990-91, at their meetings this month (February).

At the International Civil Aviation Organization, the United States traditionally has been a major player in the review of the proposed budget. We have joined the customary consensus and have praised ICAO for both its good financial management and its important contributions to the safety and security of international civil aviation. Nevertheless, we promoted adoption of a decision at ICAO to ensure continuation of this consensus-based approach to budget and financial issues, and, in 1987, the ICAO Council reaffirmed the organization's commitment to the consensus principle.

I would note that, in terms of ICAO's substantive work, both the Tokyo and Venice summits endorsed ICAO's action on air traffic and airport security, which had been pursued despite the budgetary constraints on ICAO. Indeed, these constraints were so severe that ICAO not only sought to be responsive by lowering assessments for 1987 and 1988 but also found it necessary to institute a hiring freeze, still in effect in 1988. The organization also seriously considered giving notice to a number of staff when severe cash flow problems led to uncertainty about ICAO's ability to continue paying salaries.

The World Meterological Organization has been responsive to U.S. proposals for U.N. budget reform, particularly efforts to provide major donors with more influence in the organization. In response to U.S. efforts to cement into place the normal consensus-based decision procedures, the WMO Secretariat in 1986 -- even before action was taken by the U.N. General Assembly in the fall of that year -- proposed the establishment of a Financial Advisory Committee to advise the Secretary General on budgetary and financial matters. The WMO Congress, meeting in May 1987, approved the proposal and created a committee composed of the eight largest contributors (including the United States), the president of the Executive Council, and six regional representatives. The committee, which works by consensus, began its work immediately, holding its first meetings during the 1987 session of the WMO Congress.

The new Financial Advisory Committee will consider all WMO budgetary and financial matters when the WMO Executive Council holds its annual meeting in June 1988. The agenda will include recommendations on program expenditures for 1989, which must be within the overall four-year budget ceiling established by the 1987 Congress.

The U.N. Industrial Development Organization was created in 1966 to accelerate the process of industrialization in developing countries. It became a specialized agency of the U.N. system only recently, on January 1, 1986. The constitution and rules of procedure for the newest specialized agency, including many of the provisions that we are now discussing, were developed with major input from the U.S. Government. They already permit significant input by major contributors. To supplement that input, the General Conference in 1987 adopted by consensus a decision on improvements in the program budget process, following up on a proposal initiated by the U.S. delegation to the Program Budget Committee meeting in March 1987.

Among the results during 1986 and 1987, its first two years of operation, UNIDO has reduced staff; cut some programs and increased others, consistent with U.S. priorities and interests; adopted budget reforms urged by the United States; and achieved negative real growth in the budget. We still have problems with the orientation of some UNIDO program activity, but the operation of consensus-based decisionmaking on financial issues is coming along well.

Of the major technical agencies in the system, the Food and Agriculture Organization is the one that has not responded well to longstanding calls for reform from the majority of its largest donors, including the United States. For some time, the United States and other FAO member states have been asking for revisions in budget presentations in order to obtain a clearer view of proposed or actual expenditures. However, the Secretariat has refused to comply fully.

Specific reform proposals were made in 1986 and 1987 and rebuffed. For example, the U.S. delegation to the FAO Council in June 1987 was ruled out of order because we proposed discussion of needed decisions on reform in the organization. At the FAO conference in November 1987, the United States introduced a budget reform resolution, supported by other major contributors. But the conference voted overwhelmingly against the U.S. resolution. It also rejected overwhelmingly the reform proposals put forward by the Nordic nations, the United Kingdom, Canada, Australia, Japan, New Zealand, the Netherlands, the Federal Republic of Germany, and others. Representatives of 12 major donor member states of FAO (the so-called Camberley Group, named for the group's first meeting place) met in Helsinki in early February and reaffirmed their commitment to pursue reform in the FAO.

The likely result of the situation to date is that the President will not be able to provide for FAO the determination required in the recently revised Kassebaum-Solomon legislation. Nor can the FAO rank high among the 46 organizations in the CIO [Contributions to International Organizations] account, based on the criteria for distribution of scarce funds indicated by the Congress. We have, therefore, proposed that the funds for FAO be set aside in the hope that the FAO will make progress on reform in the near future. We are continuing longstanding efforts to work with other FAO member states and the FAO Secretariat to help assure that FAO serves the needs of those who require assistance most -- the hungry and malnourished in developing nations. The United States -- as demonstrated by the magnitude and range of its contributions in this regard

-- is strongly committed to reducing the needless tragedy that afflicts countless millions in the developing nations.

In sum, I would argue that, in the majority of the U.N. technical agencies, we have achieved the goal set by the Congress. That is, we have ensured that the major donors, especially the United States, have significant influence over budgetary and administrative questions. My intention, as I take over the reins as Assistant Secretary, is to maintain the momentum that has been established and to ensure that the new procedures put into place actually work.

Specifically, for this year, I will urge that U.S. delegations to meetings of U.N. organizations do the following:

- Continue to ensure that key budget decisions are taken by "consensus," at least in the forums subordinate to the chief governing bodies where there is a clear right to a vote;

- Continue to ensure "major donor" (i.e., U.S. Government) representation on the key committees in the budget process;

- Continue to work to ensure establishment of ceilings for development of the next budget, possibly with subceilings for subsidiary parts;

- Work to create new committee mechanisms to serve these purposes if the existing ones are not effective or cannot be modified adequately;

- Develop procedures for item-by-item review and decisionmaking on the components of budgets, rather than have delegations forced to deal with an entire budget package;

- Continue to use mechanisms or to develop new mechanisms, as needed, to require the organizations -- which now make their own internal decisions on the creation of new program activities and the elimination or curtailment of old ones -- to present decisions on priorities to a representative group of member states for review or revision;

- Reinforce efforts to make secretariat operations more transparent, where this appears necessary, in order to let member states have a clearer understanding of the real components of a budget proposal and on activities actually pursued during the preceding cycle (perhaps encouraging the establishment of new member-state evaluative mechanisms);

. Ensure that U.S. Government domestic agencies, and others involved in the substantive operations of the U.N. organizations, join officials at the Department of State in renewed efforts to evaluate the work of the U.N. organizations, so that we can make more concrete proposals for reducing, eliminating, or expanding specific activities or for starting new ones.

All of these steps are possible, as they always have been. U.S. representatives to the U.N.'s technical and specialized agencies have always advocated improved efficiency and effectiveness. There is no reason not to continue pursuing these goals. Indeed, there are important reasons, given the prospect for the foreseeable future of too few resources to meet seemingly unlimited needs, to press on with vigor in behalf of setting priorities more thoughtfully, employing budgetary discipline and planning ahead.

I understand that the purpose of the legislation of recent years was to help assure that the United States has major influence on important decisions within the U.N. system, including those made within the technical agencies. Now, by and large, we have done that. The opportunity before us now is to take advantage of the enhanced influence that we have in order to promote the substantive, technical program activities that we believe are in the best interests of the agencies themselves and, most fundamentally, in the best interests of U.S. taxpayers.

### Allocation of Resources

As you know, from the account for Contributions to International Organizations, we pay the assessed contribution for the United States to 46 different international organizations. Only one of those 46 organizations is the United Nations. The United Nations -- obviously the biggest of the agencies -- accounts for about 34% of the requirement for U.S. contributions. The other 66% goes to the U.N.'s technical agencies, as well as to other important organizations such as NATO, the OECD [Organization for Economic Cooperation and Development], and GATT [General Agreement on Tariffs and Trade].

But, when the overall appropriation falls below the total requirement for U.S. assessments -- as it has for the past three years -- a serious blow falls on the entire account, including the U.N.'s technical and specialized agencies. In FY 1988, the appropriation covered 84% of the request ($480 million out of $571 million), which was a substantial increase over that of the previous year, but it still left many of the specialized organizations hurting.

The question for all of us, Congress and Administration alike, is how we make payments to these organizations when the appropriations are not sufficient to meet the total requirements. As you know, the Appropriations

Conference Committee Report (for the FY 1988 Continuing Resolution -- PL 100-202) asked the Department of State to evaluate international organizations objectively, utilizing five specific factors, in order to rationalize the decisions made by the Department in making payment of assessed contributions to these 46 organizations.

We have sought to establish a disciplined set of criteria for use in assigning funding priorities. The criteria that were developed included the following:

- The level of direct benefit or substantive importance of the agency's work to the United States in political, strategic, or economic terms;

- To the extent to which the agency has achieved program budget reform or an effective budget process;

- The quality of the agency's resource management, including financial and personnel resources;

- Importance of current political and operational factors, such as key elections, Soviet influence, or placement of Americans in key positions;

- The level of domestic U.S. support for the organization and/or its programs;

- The possible negative impact on U.S. interests and on the organization, should there be shortages in U.S. funding; and

- Organization performance in fulfillment of its chartered mission.

The first decision was to pay in full the U.S. assessments to the 30 smallest organizations in the account. These are highly specialized and generally effective bodies requiring relatively small contributions. Their total requirements were $8.6 million for FY 1988. None was above $1 million, and most were well below it.

The next step was to apply the criteria I have just escribed to the remaining 16 agencies in the account, who receive 98.5% of the appropriation. These were the United Nations, Organization for Economic Cooperation and Development, the North Atlantic Treaty Organization, General Agreement on Tariffs and Trade, the World Health Organization, the Food and Agriculture Organization, the International Labor Organization, the World Meteorological Organization, the International Atomic Energy Agency, the U.N. Industrial Development Organization, the International Civil Aviation Organization, the Organization of American States, the Pan American Health Organization, the Inter-American

Institute for Cooperation on Agriculture, the International Telecommunications Union, and the Customs Cooperation Council.

As a result of careful study of the criteria, by the Department of State and other interested U.S. Government agencies, these 16 agencies were placed in four clusters, with each agency in each cluster to receive approximately the same percentage of the U.S. assessment. For example, the WHO and the IAEA will receive 100% funding, and the United Nations will receive 75%.

The results of this clustering exercise form the basis for the reprogramming letter that is being sent forward by the department. It is, of course, unfortunate that we cannot fund in full all of the organizations that we believe are serving us well, particularly considering the treaty obligations that attend our membership in each of them. But, in the circumstances, we believe the outcome is both reasonable and fair. We hope that the Congress will be supportive of our approach, which was, in fact, stimulated by the criteria suggested by the Congress.

I suspect that the committee might well ask why it is that the Administration has not requested funds for FY 1989 sufficient to meet total requirements. This is a legitimate question, particularly given my generally favorable attitude toward the U.N.'s technical agencies and my concern that they may be damaged by the shortfall in overall appropriations for the CIO account.

The financing question will, of course, be discussed before the appropriations committees in the coming weeks. But it can be noted now that the total U.S. requirements for funding from the FY 1989 budget is $657 million. The President's budget requests $490 million, creating a shortfall of $167 million. The shortfall will inevitably have a negative impact on the U.N.'s technical agencies.

The reason for the President's budget request, quite simply, is the agreement at the budget summit that occurred at the end of 1987. It was an agreement between the Administration and the Congress that, in order to achieve the Gramm-Rudman-Hollings ceilings, overall FY 1989 requests would be no more than 2% over the FY 1988 levels. Our FY 1989 request of $490 million for the CIO account -- 2% over the level approved for FY 1988 -- is in line with this agreement. We are now in the process of applying the same criteria-based approach used to allocate FY 1988 funds for distribution of FY 1989 funds.

## Conclusion

I hope that this review has been helpful in placing the U.N.'s technical and specialized agencies in the context of the overall U.N. system. My experience -- based primarily upon my work as Ambassador to the United Nations Agencies in Vienna -- is that the technical agencies are often misunderstood in the United States and too often caught up in questions about the New York-based United Nations. This is unfortunate. Their work in health, agriculture, aviation safety, nuclear energy safeguards, and many other areas is vital to this country and to our policy affecting the rest of the world, in particular the developing nations. How the U.S. Government treats those agencies is worthy of the deepest consideration.

# THE UNITED NATIONS:
## Some Parts Work

Once seen as man's last best hope for international order and peace, the United Nations has fallen into severe disrepute among Americans.1/ Critics have pointed out many legitimate problems. Far from being ineffectual or an expensive Turkish bath, they charge that the U.N. General Assembly exacerbates the world's problems, is rife with double standards, and harms U.S. interests.2/ Or, as William F. Buckley, Jr., has observed, "Obviously our country attaches importance to the values and ideals of the United Nations. The question is whether the United Nations attaches any importance to the values and ideals of the United Nations."3/

The U.N. General Assembly was created in the image of a deliberative chamber, a place openly to arrive at open covenants. But over the years it became a sideshow; awash in polemical propaganda, it lost most if not all of the authority it once commanded. The General Assembly grew obsessed with a few issues -- North-South relations,4/ the Arab-Israeli conflict,5/ apartheid6/ -- and deals with other issues through a U.N. prism defined by those three.

In contrast to the General Assembly, U.N. agencies were established for non-political purposes. Some act as international clearing houses; others advance international standards or provide technical assistance. But even these limited goals do not protect against a General Assembly-like politicalization. Some states repeatedly use the specialized agencies to introduce resolutions on the usual issues -- Arab-Israeli, South Africa, and so forth. As a result, battle lines were drawn between those who would broaden the debate and those would would keep it focused.

Appeared ORBIS (Foreign Policy Research Institute, Philadelphia), Spring 1988, Volume 32, No. 2.

The former won in the United Nations Educational, Scientific, and Cultural Organization (UNESCO), leading the United States government to withdraw from it in 1984. Some critics of the United Nations argue that the same failures contaminate the rest of the U.N. system, and, therefore, that the United States should get out of the main organization and all its divisions.

But before coming to this conclusion, it is important to recognize that some parts of the U.N. system do make a positive contribution in a professional, businesslike, and technically competent manner. As U.N. Ambassador Jeane Kirkpatrick commented when visiting the U.N. offices in Vienna in 1984, "I've always considered the United Nations as two parts: the political U.N. General Assembly which doesn't work, and the technical agencies that do."

I served as U.S. ambassador and permanent representative to the United Nations in Vienna during 1983-85. Some of the nine U.N. organizations located in Vienna are not serious. They ignore their charters and are for political posturing and the recycling of tired, sterile North-South and East-West debates. But three of them -- the International Atomic Energy Agency, the drug agencies, and (surprisingly) the U.N. Relief and Works Agency for Palestine Refugees -- are well-run and make real contributions. They deserve some attention and a little praise; they also offer some hints on how to redeem the failed U.N. agencies.

## Unusual Harmony at the International Atomic Energy Agency

Clearly, the International Atomic Energy Agency (IAEA) is the most important U.N. organization for the United States in Vienna, for the agency has a pivotal role in promoting the peaceful uses of nuclear energy and in halting proliferation of the bomb. I devoted over two-thirds of my time and the resources of my mission to IAEA matters.

The agency serves as the world center for research on the practical uses of atomic energy for peaceful purposes. It provide members with a variety of services and supplies materials, equipment and facilities. It promotes the exchange of information and scientists. The IAEA sets safety standards and enforces those standards. It produces feasibility studies and does useful work on the siting of power plants. Of special interest to countries too small for their own nuclear power stations, the agency offers assistance applying radioisotopes and radiation in agriculture, medicine, biology, hydrology, and industry. It also supplies poorer countries with radioactive material and facilities to develop nuclear energy for peaceful ends.

Following the April 26, 1986, accident at the nuclear stations in Chernobyl, the IAEA performed invaluable work analyzing the causes of the accident and containing the fallout. It became a clearing house for information and mobilized international expertise to deal with the accident. Following the disaster, the IAEA sponsored negotiations that culminated in two international conventions, one requiring immediate and detailed notification of nuclear accidents, and the other setting guidelines for prompt assistance to a country suffering from a nuclear mishap.8/

At the same time, the agency deters the misuse of nuclear material for military purposes through the application of international safeguards. In this, the IAEA acts as the vital linchpin of worldwide nuclear non-proliferation efforts. It has a predominant position in enforcing the 1968 Nuclear Non-proliferation Treaty (NPT), a role that has helped focus the IAEA by giving it greater purpose.9/ The safeguards system relies on the independent measurement of nuclear materials by IAEA inspectors during unannounced on-site inspections of nuclear facilities, as well as by independent IAEA record-keeping.10/ The safeguards system aims to detect diversion of significant quantities of nuclear material to military purposes, and during my tenure in Vienna, anomalies led to immediate corrective actions. This program offers an excellent example of multilateral cooperation achieving a vital objective that a matrix of bilateral agreements could not.

While membership is open to all states, the board of governors is a strong executive body. Ten seats are filled by permanent members who are designated those with the most advanced nuclear programs. The rest rotate on a geographic basis.11/ This guarantees continuity in the agency and a strong voice for those states most interested in its work. Unlike the U.N. General Assembly, where there is no "reason of the whole,"12/ this does exist within the IAEA Board of Governors due to indigenous nuclear programs, technology transfer and non-proliferation concerns. This permits the board to keep the agency closely focused on appropriate issues.

Further, the board of governors has only three regularly scheduled meetings a year, sessions not open to the public (and only summaries of discussions are published). Prior to each meeting the board chairman consults individually with each of the thirty-five IAEA governors. This allows him to identify problem areas early and to engage in quiet negotiations when they do appear.

During my tenure, all problems were either resolved prior to the actual board of governors meeting or, if they were not, the troubling issue received only limited discussions at the board meeting and was postponed to the next meeting (allowing more time to reach a resolution). There were no open confrontations or hostile votes. Members acted as the U.N. founders had dreamed they would -- they showed real dedication to reach compromises on legitimate issues and to advance the objectives of the agency.

IAEA also benefits from the convergence of interests between the Soviet Union and the United States. Both governments want the IAEA to succeed and make sure the agency stays focused on its proper functions. Indeed, the U.S.-Soviet consultations at the IAEA are unique among all international organizations. We worked to exchange information, improve international safeguards, develop plans for the storage of plutonium and spent reactor fuel, and coordinate the transfer of technology.

I kept in close contact, as had my predecessors, with my Soviet counterpart, Ambassador Oleg Klestov. Approximately one month before a board meeting, he and I had long meetings to review the agenda in detail. We exchanged views on every item. In consultation with our capitals, we sought to coordinate positions and coordinate tactics for debate. A day or two before each board meeting, after delegations had arrived from Washington and Moscow, the entire two delegations met to review the forthcoming meeting for a last time.13/

Such U.S.-Soviet cooperation discourages others from politicizing the agency's deliberations. When potential political flashpoints arise, the U.S. delegation works with its allies and the Soviet delegation instructs its clients to reach a compromise. Each delegation also meets with other states with which it has influence.

A good example of U.S.-Soviet cooperation occurred in September 1983 at the IAEA General Conference. Just before the conference was to begin, a Soviet fighter plane destroyed Korean Airlines flight 007, killing hundreds of civilians, including many Americans. Worldwide, tensions shot up between the superpowers. President Reagan and Secretary Shultz condemned the Soviets' unlawful brutality and U.N. Ambassador Jeane Kirkpatrick forcefully berated the Soviet leaders at the U.N. Security Council. Diplomatic contacts were reduced to an absolute minimum. Nonetheless, both governments made a conscious decision not to let this act hemorrhage into U.S.-Soviet cooperation in the IAEA, and it did not.

On instruction from our capitals, Klestov and I worked together to prepare for the general conference. We even discussed how we would handle the KAL 007 issue. Klestov suggested how the Soviet delegation might refer to the incident during the debate. I with the South Koreans and Klestov with the North Koreans worked to contain the issue. The United States did not back off from its firm condemnation of the Soviets' unprovoked brutality, but it did acknowledge that the IAEA was not the proper forum to pursue this issue.

### Two Test Cases: China and Israel

Close U.S.-Soviet coordination in the IAEA occasionally leads governments to accuse the superpowers of collusion. For the most part, however, the other IAEA members view this cooperation as helpful. For example, Peking indicated in July 1983 that it might wish to enter the IAEA. The Peoples Republic of China had been the only major country that had not long been a member of the IAEA, and its actions had for many years disturbed the nuclear non-proliferation regime.14/ It had exploded a nuclear device in 1964, then built a substantial nuclear arsenal. Not being a signator to the NPT nor having accepted limits on nuclear exports, the PRC remained outside the nuclear non-proliferation regime. Its entry into the IAEA would be a first step in their journey to partnership in the regime.

But this also created several problems. While no state wished openly to oppose China's entry, some did have concerns, especially India. India had become the leading voice of the developing countries in the agency and held a permanent seat on the board due to its advanced nuclear program. The PRC's entry into the IAEA threatened both these Indian positions. Other states worried that the facilities on Taiwan under IAEA safeguards would drop out of this arrangement once the PRC entered the agency.15/ The industrial states liked the total composition of the board of governors which allowed a fragile but satisfactory control on budget matters, and the PRC could disrupt that control.

Fifteen months after the PRC's original overture and after hundreds of hours of consultations in capitals and in Vienna, the PRC officially entered the IAEA in an unusual arrangement: the permanent membership of the board of governors was expanded by one.16/ This accommodated both the PRC and India. The many other states with advanced nuclear programs (and therefore legitimate claims to permanent membership) agreed not to force their claims at that time.17/ The full board also was expanded by a single seat, and the many states that repeatedly had called for even greater expansion agreed not to force their motions just then. IAEA safeguards on Taiwan were allowed to remain through a linguistic gimmick (unfortunately one that is at any time vulnerable to an inquiry).

Any single one of the then 117 members could have disrupted the delicate balance needed to arrange the entry of the PRC. Any state wanting to politicize the issue or press its own advantage at the expense of the agency could have ruined the process, but not one did. Today the PRC is an active member of the IAEA and has taken other steps toward entering the nuclear non-proliferation regime. (For example, a U.S.-China Nuclear Agreement now further restricts PRC nuclear activities.)

But the greatest challenge to IAEA's avoidance of passionate politics was in response to the June 7, 1981, Israeli attack against the Iraqi nuclear research reactor at Osirak, which was under IAEA safeguards at the time of the attack.18/ It was the first military action taken to prevent the development of nuclear power. The attack created controversy over Israel's justification, over the integrity of IAEA safeguards, and the whole non-proliferation regime.

Even the United States condemned Israel's action in the U.N. Security Council.19/ At its June meeting, the IAEA Board of Governors passed a resolution by 29 to 2 (with 3 abstentions) strongly condemning Israel "for this premeditated and unjustified attack on the Iraqi nuclear research center, which was covered by Agency safeguards," and recommending that the general conference "consider all the implications of this attack, including suspending the exercise by Israel of the privileges and rights of membership," and suspension of technical assistance. The United States opposed the resolution because it pre-empted prerogatives falling within the competence of the U.N. Security Council; because the United States opposed in principle the exclusion of any member from an international organization, except in strict compliance with statutory provisions, which did not exist in this case; and because all member states have the right to benefit from Agency technical assistance.

The Iraqi reactor having been under agency safeguards, the attack was relevant to IAEA interests. And since abuse of Israel is a foremost U.N. activity, the Israeli attack created a real danger of the agency being politicized. The "reason of the whole" for IAEA's principal members came under direct assault by the many states interested in isolating and delegitimizing the state of Israel.

Approaching the 1981 fall general conference, the United States led those states arguing against continued debate in the IAEA on the Israeli raid. But the Iraqi delegation led a heated political attack on Israel, and the agency's general conference, for years an elite and apolitical gathering place of the world's nuclear physicists, became obsessed with Israel. Eventually, the United States mobilized the necessary third to block Iraq's proposal to suspend Israel. When it became clear that Israel would not be ousted, this effort was deferred to the next general conference, a maneuver that kept the issue alive. In the meantime, a resolution was adopted by 51 to 8 (with 27 abstentions) that called the Israeli action "an attack on the Agency and its safeguards regime" and suspended technical assistance to Israel.20/

In September 1982, the IAEA General Conference was again dominated by the Israeli issue. The conference passed another resolution condemning Israel and narrowly voted to deny Israeli credentials. This provoked the United States to walk out of the conference and temporarily suspend its participation -- including financial -- in the IAEA. (The United States rejoined in the spring of 1983).

When I arrived in Vienna in June 1983, the Israeli issue still predominated. Only through extensive preparations and long negotiations could we put the genie back in the bottle. Gradually a coalition developed around the issue of the IAEA's value and the importance of the non-proliferation regime. When the Iraqis again moved to deny Israeli credentials, they met a counter-motion not to consider challenges to any credentials, and this passed by a vote of 54 to 24, with 7 abstentions.21/

By 1984, the United States had achieved such overwhelming support for its position, Baghdad decided at the last minute not to challenge Israeli credentials, though some limitations were imposed on Israeli rights and privileges of membership in the IAEA.22/ At the 1985 general conference, the consensus had grown further; that year participants not only rejected an Iraqi effort to impose sanctions against Israel, but found that Israel had provided sufficient assurance that it would not attack peaceful nuclear facilities. The issue did not come up in the 1986 general conference.

The story of the IAEA containing and purging itself of politicalization is perhaps unique in U.N. history.

### The Drug Agencies

Three U.N. organizations in Vienna deal with the control of narcotic and psychotropic drugs. They have generally avoided politicalization, open propaganda, or inflated expectations. While not the answer to illicit drugs, these U.N. organizations make a solid contribution.

The Commission on Narcotic Drugs (CND), which includes representatives of thirty states, deals with the implementation of international drug treaties23/ and sets U.N. policy on drug control. Throughout my tenure in Vienna, the CND avoided political issues and focused on its responsibilities. Although public, its meetings were businesslike and had none of the normal U.N. political rhetoric. The member states sent technical experts and all showed a strong interest in increasing the effectiveness of international drug treaties. While I was in Vienna the chairmanship rotated from Argentina to Hungary, with no change whatsoever in agenda, emphasis, or rhetoric.

The International Narcotics Control Board (INCB) is responsible for the supervision of governmental implementation of drug control treaties. It reviews and confirms annual estimates of narcotic drug requirements submitted by governments and evaluates statistical reports on legitimate manufacture and trade. If treaties are breached, the board can require governments to adopt remedial measures and bring treaty violations to the U.N. Economic and Social Council and the Commission on Narcotic Drugs. Thirteen experts sit on the board, and they serve in their personal capacities. An American has always sat on the board since its creation in 1968. Meetings are closed, so there is little reason for propaganda.

The United Nations Fund for Drug Abuse Control (UNFDAC), established in 1971, aims to reduce the supply and demand of illicit drugs. UNFDAC relies entirely on voluntary contributions and its research and training take place only in countries that invite its help. All countries involved with UNFDAC have a direct interest in its success and a commitment to its purpose. There are no open UNFDAC meetings. The UNFDAC executive director meets privately with ambassadors from major donor and recipient nations to review projects and work schedules. During my tenure in Vienna no issue was ever raised that did not focus entirely on the functional work of UNFDAC.

UNFDAC grew out of a realization that multilateral aid could succeed where certain bilateral aid would be politically unacceptable. In the early 1970s the United States sided with Greece against Turkey on the Cyprus issue. Therefore, even though Ankara wanted aid to encourage crop substitution from opium production to other crops, it could not take U.S. aid. But UNFDAC aid, however much of it came from the United States, was acceptable. The UNFDAC crop substitution project in Turkey has been a resounding success.

### UNRWA's Unlikely Success

The General Assembly established the U.N. Relief and Works Agency for Palestine Refugees in the Near East (UNRWA) to aid the Arab refugees who came out of the 1948-49 war between the Arab states and Israel. UNRWA begain work in 1950 and services refugees living in Jordan, Lebanon, Syria, the West Bank and the Gaza Strip.

UNRWA depends entirely on voluntary contributions, which it gets from governments, inter-governmental organizations, and private sources. Over the years, the United States has contributed over one billion dollars to UNRWA. But the agency has perennial financial difficulties in meeting its annual budget of over $250 million. UNRWA employs over 16,000 people, mostly refugees, of whom about 9,000 are teachers or instructors in the more than 650 elementary and junior secondary schools it runs. Education consumes over 60 percent of the agency's budget, with food and medical assistance taking most of the rest.

Many observers of the Middle East note that the continued existence of the Palestinian refugee camps after forty years, made possible in part by UNRWA's support, helps to perpetuate and exacerbate the problems. Without these camps, they suggest, the Palestinian refugees long ago would have assimilated into the Arab cultures of these neighboring states.

Even if one does not accept UNRWA's raison d'etre, its headquarters in Vienna does a good job. Member states take care of UNRWA business without polemics and the UNRWA secretariat rarely engages in political posturing. Several factors contribute to this constructive environment.

First, the states that contribute to UNRWA have an interest in its success -- the usual "reason of the whole." The work with the secretariat in Vienna is limited to voluntary contributors and host governments.

UNRWA's Advisory Commission (which meets annually in Vienna to review UNRWA's programs and performance and draft a letter to the U.N. secretary-general) contains only major donors and host countries.

Second, the advisory commission's real work is not open and, therefore, there is little temptation to grandstand for a home audience. After very brief introductory remarks, the commission recesses. Members of the advisory commission leave the official conference room with its translators, transcribers, and other secretariat personnel and go to a small conference room for long, informal talks. During my tenure in Vienna, we had intense ten- to twelve-hour sessions negotiating the exact language of the advisory commission letter, discussing each phrase, every word. All parties pressed their positions hard but demonstrated a willingness to compromise. Once a consensus document had been drafted, the secretariat was informed and the delegations returned to the official conference room. The UNRWA commissioner-general would receive the document, and after very brief remarks, the advisory commission adjourned for another year.

Third, all parties have realistic expectations from UNRWA. No one sees it as a vehicle to solve the Arab-Israeli conflict. Emphasizing its temporary mission, UNRWA's mandate must periodically be renewed by the General Assembly. Fourth, UNRWA's task is specific -- to aid Palestinian refugees with food, education, and medical help. It is not charged with the burden of resolving political problems.

## Conclusions

The U.N. agencies that succeed share certain characteristics. Expectations for these organizations are realistic. They have specific assignments. A "reason of the whole" exists and affects behavior. The agencies' controlling bodies have a strong interest in fulfilling their mandate. Closed debate permits useful dialogue, compromise, and resolution.

These elements offer guidelines for the reform of those U.N. specialized agencies that matter to the United States. But they are probably impossible to implement in the General Assembly, where noisy rhetoric, distorted priorities, and vote-trading appear to be beyond reform.

**1/** In 1985, just 51 percent of Americans in a New York Times/CBS poll felt the U.N. was doing a good or very good job. "5-Nation Survey Finds Hope for U.N.," New York Times, June 26, 1985. See also, Senator Christopher J. Dodd, "On Nuremberg and the United Nations," New York Times, October 8, 1986; and Senator Paul S. Trible, "U.N. Anti-Americanism Will Backfire in the Senate," New York Times, December 15, 1986.

**2/** Ambassador Jeane Kirkpatrick is amongst the thoughtful critics who have accused the United Nations of being "perverted by politicalization." Quoted in Burton Yale Pines, ed., "The U.S. and the U.N.: Time for Reappraisal," The Heritage Foundation Backgrounder, September 29, 1983, p. 10. See also Charles Krauthammer, "Why the U.S. Should Bail Out of the U.N.: Let it Sink," The New Republic, August 24, 1987, p. 18.

**3/** William F. Buckley, Jr., United Nations Journal: A Delegate's Odyssey (New York: G. P. Putnam's Sons, 1974), p. 58.

**4/** See Edward W. Erickson and Daniel A. Sumner, "The U.N. and Economic Development" in Burton Yale Pines, ed., A World Without A U.N. (The Heritage Foundation, Washington, D.C., 1984), pp. 1-21; and Stanley J. Michalak, "U.N. Conference on Trade and Development: Cheating the Poor," The Heritage Foundation Backgrounder (Washington, D.C., 1984).

**5/** A study by the Heritage Foundation concluded that in 1982 the UNGA and its seven main committees devoted over one-third of the delegates' time to debate on the Middle East. In that same year, of the 430 UNGA-approved resolutions and decisions, 41 were devoted wholly or partly to criticizing Israel. "The United Nations' Campaign Against Israel," The Heritage Foundation Backgrounder, U.N. Assessment Project (Washington, D.C., 1983). See also, Thomas M. Frank, "A Place Where Lies Are Told: Israel Before the General Assembly," Nation Against Nation: What Happened to the U.N. Dream and What the U.S. Can Do About It (New York: Oxford University Press, 1985), pp. 184-204; and Daniel Patrick Moynihan, A Dangerous Place (Boston: Little, Brown and Company, 1978), pp. 169-99.

**6/** See John Barratt, "South African Diplomacy at the U.N." in G.R. Berridge and A. Jennings, eds., Diplomacy at the U.N. (New York: St. Martin's Press, 1985), pp. 191-203.

**7/** Charles Krauthammer, "Why the U.S. Should Bail Out of the U.N.: Let it Sink," The New Republic, August 24, 1987, p. 18; Ernest van den Haag and Joseph P. Conrad, The U.N.: In or Out? (New York:

Plenum Press, 1987); and Burton Yale Pines, ed., <u>A World Without A U.N.</u> (The Heritage Foundation, Washington, D.C., 1984).

8/       <u>Final Document Resolutions and Conventions</u>, Adopted by the First Special Session of the General Conference, September 24-26, 1986, IAEA, GC (SPL.1)/Res. (1986).

9/       Article III of the Non-Proliferation Treaty requires non-nuclear members to accept safeguards on all nuclear energy equipment in which fissionable maerial is used.    Article III makes the IAEA responsible for managing the safeguard system.   See <u>The Structure and Content of Agreements Between the Agency and States Required in Connection with the Treaty on the Non-Proliferation of Nuclear Weapons</u>, (IAEA INFCIRC/153).

10/      International Atomic Energy, <u>Non-Proliferation and International Safeguards</u> (78-20707) 1978.

11/      According to IAEA Statute Articles VI, members of the board of governors are, as designated by the outgoing board, first the ten member states most advanced in the technology of nuclear energy, including the production of source materials; in addition, the board elects, from each of eight areas -- North America, Latin America, Western Europe, Eastern Europe, Africa, Middle East and South Asia, South East Asia and the Pacific, and the Far East -- the member state most advanced in the science of atomic energy, and whose geographical area is not represented by any of the above ten states.

12/      In his Speech to the Electors of Bristol, Edmund Burke outlined the importance of the "reason of the whole." He said: "Parliament is not a congress of Ambassadors from different and hostile interests, which interests each must maintain, against other agents and advocates; but Parliament is a deliberative assembly of one nation, with one interest, that of the whole -- where not local purposes, not local prejudices, ought to guide, but the general good, resulting from the general reason of the whole." (B.W. Hill, ed., <u>Edmund Burke on Government, Politics and Society</u> [London: Fontana, 1975], p. 156.)

13/      Similar U.S.-Soviet consultations in Geneva went on in connection with the Third NPT Review Conference.  And separate regular U.S.-Soviet meetings on more general peaceful nuclear matters have been established, rotating between Moscow and Washington.   Because IAEA activities are integral to these matters, I was a member of the U.S. delegations to such consultations throughout my tenure in Vienna.

14/  See Danie Horner and Paul Leventhal, "The U.S.-China Nuclear Agreement: A Failure of Executive Policymaking and Congressional Oversight," The Fletcher Forum: A Journal of Studies in International Affairs, Winter 1987, pp. 105, 107-109.

15/  The Republic of China (Taiwan) had been an active IAEA member until 1971. That year, when the UNGA voted Taiwan out of the United Nations and the PRC entered the United Nations, Taiwan also left the IAEA.

16/  The 27th session of the General Conference (October 11, 1984) approved the membership of the PRC in the IAEA and its membership became effective on January 1, 1985.

17/  A number of nations had repeatedly sought expansion of the board including Spain, Italy, Venezuela, Argentina and others. See, in this connection, General Assembly Res. 32/49.

18/  Prior to the Israeli attack there had been a pattern of suspicious events regarding this Iraqi research reactor which was being built by the French. In September 1980, Iraq temporarily evicted all French technicians, saying it could not protect them because of its war with Iran. Two months later, Iraq's government announced it would not permit IAEA inspection of its nuclear facilities until the war with Iran ended. The Iraqi government refused French entreaties to allow it to substitute less highly enriched uranium rather than bombgrade uranium for the research reactor. Nonetheless, in June 1981 when Israeli fighters attacked the reactor, it was under IAEA safeguards.

19/  On June 29, the Security Council unanimously adopted resolution 487 (1981).

20/  Later that fall, the UNGA considered the matter in three plenary meetings and on November 10, 1981, adopted an Iraqi-initiated resolution. It reiterated condemnation of "Israel's continued refusal to implement Security Council resolution 487 (1981)" and demanded that Israel withdraw "its threat to attack and destroy nuclear facilities in Iraq and other countries." The UNGA adopted the resolution by a vote of 123 to 2 (Israel, U.S.), with 12 abstentions (UNGA Resolution 38/9).

21/  See Richard S. Williamson, "U.S. Multilateral Diplomacy at the United Nations," The Washington Quarterly, Summer 1986, pp. 5, 13-14.

22/  IAEA GC (XXVII)/RES/407.

23/    The Single Convention on Narcotic Drugs was adopted in 1961. The convention requires each of the 108 states who are signators to punish all international violations of its control provisions regarding cultivation, production, manufacture, trade, distribution, etc., of narcotic drugs. The Convention of Psychotropic Substances was adopted in 1971. It sets up a system of control for psychotropic drugs which is more elaborate than that of narcotic drugs.

# THE UNITED NATIONS:
## Changing Its Ways


President Reagan's September 13 decision to pay $44 million in back dues to the United Nations could not have come at a better time for the ailing world body. Teetering on the verge of bankruptcy, the organization was slowly succumbing to its own excesses, squandering its resources and moral capital while antagonizing its principal contributor and benefactor.

The President's action is a determination that the U.N. has begun to mend its ways. In the words of the President, it has made genuine progress toward implementing crucial institutional reforms.

In legislating the suspension of U.S. contributions to the U.N. two years ago, the Congress demonstrated an indignation that was fully justified. The U.N.'s behavior in recent years had mortgaged its credibility and devalued its political currency. Not only was the U.S. not getting its money's worth from the U.N., worse still, it was being insulted in the process.

Were it not for sustained U.S. pressure on the international forum, it might still be sliding down the path to financial oblivion. In the face of considerable opposition by countries from the Third World and in the Soviet bloc, the U.S. pressed for the badly needed changes. In the end, our patience and persistence won out.

In the past two years, the U.N. has moved in the direction of adopting several important internal administrative and budgetary reforms. It is already in the process of cutting its bloated staff and introducing a

Appeared in **Diplomat's Journal** (United States Department of State), September, 1988.

new budget-making system to ensure that future budgets are approved by a consensus reflecting the genuine wishes of all member states. Revised hiring procedures promise to correct the problem of disproportionate numbers of Soviet personnel in the Secretariat.

Despite our serious reservations over its performance, the United States stood by the United Nations even when its fiscal behavior was less than responsible. Continuing to support U.N. resolutions on the Middle East, the Persian Gulf, Southern Africa, and Afghanistan, we never abandoned our faith in the ability of the world body to rehabilitate itself.

But the President's decision to restore U.S. funding goes beyond recognition that the U.N. is shaping up institutionally. It also is a tangible expression of renewed U.S. confidence in the peacemaking efforts of the world organization.

Scarcely a day goes by when one cannot pick up a newspaper and read about the U.N.'s involvement in a full range of global issues. In virtually every part of the world, the world body is actively engaged in its work for peace. U.N. peacekeeping forces dot the international landscape. Countries tired of war and groping for a solution to their disputes are once again turning to the U.N.

This is a time of great hope and opportunity for the world organization. It has shown that it is capable of internal reform and can play an important role in advancing peace and freedom around the world by serving as an invaluable facilitator in the settlement of longstanding regional conflicts.

However, there is still a long way to go. The U.N. is only now beginning to learn the hard lessons of financial austerity. Still greater challenges lie ahead of it. It will need to become more goal-oriented and adjust to living within its means.

The economic health of the organization is not the only abiding concern, however. In order to redeem itself in the eyes of the international community, the U.N. will need to adopt a new code of conduct. Eschewing politicization, anti-Western rhetoric, and double standards, it must accompany the progress it has already made on financial reform with a renewed dedication to the values and ideals set forth in its Charter.

The promise of the United Nations lies in the fulfillment of the values and ideals of its founders. As one of the architects of the U.N. system as well as its major contributor, we want to ensure that it lives up to the high principles contained in its Charter of a world of peace, security, and justice. Recent events suggest this goal need not be an elusive dream.

# THE UNITED NATIONS:
## Progress in the 1980s


In recent days there has been a resurgence of enthusiasm for the United Nations in some quarters. This is due, in large part, to the progress that has taken place with respect to U.N. actions on reform and the advancement of human rights, as well as the increased contributions of U.N. peacekeeping operations which led to the award of the 1988 Nobel Peace Prize to the U.N. peacekeeping forces.

At the same time, however, significant problems continue to plague this world body. For example, the 1975 resolution which branded Zionism as racism is an outrage. It is a cancer which continues to eat away at the moral legitimacy of this world body. The rhetoric within the United Nations is too often reckless. Sometimes the United Nations even serves to exacerbate problems rather than help to resolve them. Nevertheless, the past 8 years have witnessed an evolution within the United Nations.

When the Reagan Administration took office, the United Nations was hostile to U.S. interests, and the United States was in retreat. Name-calling was a common practice that many considered to be not only legitimate but too enjoyable to resist. Efforts to delegitimize Israel and even deny it credentials were accepted practices within the United Nations. A double standard existed in human rights whereby the clients of the Soviet Union avoided close scrutiny while weaker and isolated nations such as El Salvador and Chile were condemned. From the standpoint of its administrative practices, the United Nations was poorly managed and rife

---

Address before the American Academy of Diplomacy and the Woodrow Wilson International Center for Scholars, Washington, D.C., October 19, 1988.

with fiscal inefficiency.   And in many respects, the United Nations had become at best a marginal actor on the world stage.   While many areas still exist in which the United Nations has strayed from its original goals and objectives, there have been noteworthy improvements.

Name-calling, while still too frequent, has diminished.   The cacophony of reckless rhetoric has abated.   Israeli credentials are not in threat in the General Assembly nor within the U.N. specialized agencies. In human rights the double standard has been challenged, and we have seen Soviet human rights abuses within Afghanistan condemned and Cuba put under the scrutiny of a U.N. Human Rights Commission investigative team.   There has been recognition and gradual progress in the area of management and fiscal efficiency.   And finally, the United Nations is playing a worthwhile role in peacekeeping in Afghanistan, Iran-Iraq, and potentially in the Western Sahara, Namibia, Cyprus, and Cambodia.

Three distinct and separate elements have combined to contribute to this transformation within the United Nations.

First, President Reagan's firm leadership and consistent policies in the United Nations and elsewhere have had a salutory impact.

Second, the Third World is playing an increasingly constructive role within the United Nations.

And, third, the positive developments in U.S.-Soviet relations have increased the opportunities for the United Nations to play a meaningful role.

## U.S. Leadership in the United Nations

In 1981, when Ronald Reagan took office, the United States was in retreat within the United Nations.   It had become commonly accepted practice to challenge the United States through the most grotesque rhetoric and name-calling.   U.S. interests seemed to have become subjugated to a standard of moral legitimacy that was set by a vote of the United Nation's majority membership (undemocratic and unfree) rather than the constant values of freedom, human rights, and democracy which have been the hallmarks of our nation since its founding over 200 years ago.   By the late 1970s, we seemed to have accepted within the U.N. General Assembly a position of moral inferiority in the face of a hostile majority of middle nations and mini-states (often in collusion with the Soviets and the Eastern bloc).

President Reagan, through his first Ambassador to the United Nations, Jeane Kirkpatrick, took the "kick me" sign off the United States. We no longer passively accepted outrageous charges and name-calling. Those who had challenged the United States began to realize that such reckless accusations would be met by an equally forceful challenge and the truth.

With his appointment of Ambassador Kirkpatrick and later Ambassador Vernon Walters, President Reagan signaled a new determination with respect to the United Nations. It was not a frivolous body to be ignored but a serious forum to be engaged. The seven visits which Ronald Reagan himself made to the General Assembly - a record number of appearances before that world body by any President of the United States - further demonstrated the importance which he placed on it. As the United States evinced its own serious approach toward the United Nations, others began to take the world body and their own actions more seriously.

With respect to the double standards on human rights, the United States has agressively pursued the uniform application of the Universal Declaration of Human Rights. This document, which was crafted in 1948 largely by American delegates Eleanor Roosevelt and John Foster Dulles, reflected our own values about human rights as embodied in the U.S. Constitution. It reflected our understanding after World War II that countries which tend to abuse their own citizens' human rights will be more inclined to abuse the rights of their neighbors.

In selecting his first representative to the Human Rights Commission, noted theologian and political scientist Michael Novak, President Reagan elevated the consideration of human rights beyond the rhetoric and actively sought to push the United Nations to evenly apply universal standards. In achieving human rights scrutiny in Afghanistan and now Cuba, the United States' persistence and political handiwork were slowly rewarded. Just as the Reagan delegation sought to continue close scrutiny of Chile, we set out to achieve close scrutiny of the Western Hemisphere's most egregious abuser of human rights, Fidel Castro. At first reluctantly, but eventually with an overwhelming majority, the members of the United Nations recognized the importance of this initiative, not only for the United States but for all member states.

In the area of management and administration, under the leadership of Ambassador Walters, the United States started a multi-year campaign to bring some sanity to the reckless, spendthrift manner in which the United Nations had been operating. Joining first with other major donors such as Japan and the Federal Republic of Germany, and then eventually gaining support from the Soviet Union and from leading G-77 developing countries, the United States achieved a miraculous development: In 1986 a group of 18 government experts was formed to look at U.N. management.

The G-18's report was far-reaching and profound. It contained 71 recommendations that addressed four main areas of concern:

- The proliferation of intergovernmental bodies which had caused the U.N. machinery to become overly complex, noncohesive, and difficult to coordinate;

- The mushrooming of the number, frequency, and duration of U.N. meetings and the corresponding increase in paperwork;

- The tremendous growth in the size of the Secretariat, which had become top-heavy and inefficient; and

- The seemingly unending growth in U.N. budgets.

In order to address these problems, the G-18 proposed, among other things, a 15% reduction in staff and a reform of the U.N.'s budgetary process that would ensure that budgetary questions would be settled by consensus.

When I was serving as U.S. Ambassador to the United Nations offices in Vienna, Austria, in 1983 and 1984, I never would have imagined that General Assembly formation of a team like the G-18 would have been possible. If such a group of diverse nations had been formed, I never would have thought that it could have reached consensus recommendations. If recommendations had been forthcoming from such a group, I never would have believed that the General Assembly might largely adopt them. And even if their adoption were achieved, I never would have foreseen implementation.

But through the persistence of the Reagan Administration, the leadership of Secretary Shultz and Ambassador Walters, and the help of Secretary General Perez de Cuellar, these sweeping recommendations were adopted by the Group of 18 experts, endorsed by the General Assembly, and have now undergone the first phases of implementation. The process if not perfect. Our steps are only small ones when we consider the massive task ahead. But the reform process has begun and begun well.

The Reagan Administration's firm, uncompromising yet nonconfrontational approach has been a major contributor to this progress. Further, in the peace-keeping efforts of Afghanistan, Iran-Iraq, and Angola/Namibia, the United States has played a very strong, supportive role in the "real world" beyond the United Nations as well as within the United Nations itself to support the Secretary General and his good offices in seeking settlements and the resolution of regional conflicts.

- In Afghanistan, for example, it was the steadfast support of Ronald Reagan and the strong bipartisan support in the U.S. Congress for the mujaheddin that raised the Soviet costs of the brutal occupation of that country.

- It was the deployment of U.S. naval forces in the Persian Gulf, as well as the diplomatic isolation of Iran, that led Iran to accept the terms of Resolution 598 and agree to a cease-fire.

- Finally, the United States is taking the lead in trying to arrange among the parties a peaceful solution to the Angola/Namibia conflict. However, the mediator in these talks, Assistant Secretary for African Affairs Chet Crocker, has recognized from the outset the helpful role the United Nations can play in implementing the arrangements the parties eventually agree on concerning self-determination in Namibia and the end of civil war in Angola.

In all of these areas - human rights, U.N. reform, and peacekeeping - Ronald Reagan deserves significant credit not only for having improved the United Nations as a tool which can both help advance U.S. interests and the interests of all those serious-minded countries but also for having improved the United Nations itself as an institution.

## The Changing Role of the Third World

The majority of the nations of the developing world are former colonies. President Franklin Roosevelt played a major role in spurring decolonization. He began to confront this issue with both the British and the French during World War II when they found such a challenge offensive to their national interests. Nonetheless, the United States continued to push for decolonization after the war, and the United Nations served as an invaluable midwife in this process. The result was the end of traditional European colonization. Beginning in 1958 with the independence of Tunisia a cascade of new nations was founded where former colonies existed.

These new nations did not have a history in bilateral relations nor the financial resources to have embassies throughout the world. They did not have the wealth to impact world events through economic force. Nor did they have the military power to exert their independence. But these new nations desperately sought to proclaim their independence. The United Nations became their preferred forum.

Within the United Nations they could have one delegation which could deal with all the other countries of the world. Also, within the United Nations they had an equal vote with other members in the General Assembly. And within the General Assembly they could express their independence. In some ways this was constructive. However, it also distorted the General Assembly. The rhetoric of the newly independent countries became excessive.  Perhaps frustrated about the limitations of their power to have an impact on the real world, they issued sweeping and often reckless statements, whether hurling accusations against former colonial powers or other powerful nations such as the United States. Frustrated with their poverty versus the wealth of other nations, they condemned the wealthy.

These developing nations also found it very salutory to pass sweeping resolutions mandating great changes.  However, over a period of time they learned that excessive rhetoric in the United Nations did have a cost.  They were taken less seriously.  And the sweeping resolutions had little impact on their very urgent and real needs.

The developing world has begun to understand that passing a broad resolution calling for a new international economic order has not put more food on the tables of the citizens in their countries.  They have learned that passing a New Delhi declaration at the UNIDO [U.N. Industrial Development Organization] conference in 1974 has not created new jobs in their countries.   They have learned that passing a sweeping Lima declaration in 1978 has not created further markets for their products.

The result of these developments, nurtured by Secretary General Perez de Cuellar, has been a gradual yet perceptible movement of the G-77 nations toward more responsible behavior.   There has been a recognition that the spendthrift ways of the United Nations hurt their interests, which are so dependent on a viable and vital United Nations, more than any other group of countries.  Thus, by degrees, leading nations among the G-77 have embraced the reform process and helped advance it. To strengthen the United Nations is to help strengthen their own abilities.

In the economic fora, sweeping condemnations of industrialized countries have slowly diminished and are being replaced by responsible work programs for specific projects to advance economic development.

This transformation within the developing nation majority in the United Nations is terribly important.   It has created new responsible leadership among their ranks, as well as a receptiveness for greater responsibility.   It has created a new opportunity as we face the United Nations in the 1990s.

These changes have contributed mightily to the improvements within the United Nations. They are to be nurtured for the sake of the developing nations, for the sake of the United States, and for the sake of the United Nations itself.

### The Changing U.S.-Soviet Relationship

A third major element in the evolving real world beyond the United Nations, which has helped the United Nations mightily in its gradual movement toward an improved body, has been the changed U.S.-Soviet relationship. While the Soviet Union remains the United States' primary adversary and the East-West confrontation the primary threat, there is no question that the U.S.-Soviet relationship is in a period of adjustment.

President Reagan deserves credit for this in part by having provided a stronger America, both militarily and economically, in which to engage the Soviet Union. In part this is a result of General Secretary Gorbachev and his efforts and perestroika and glasnost.

There is no question that the softened rhetoric and the efforts to avoid direct confrontation by both superpowers have created a new environment and opportunity for the United Nations.

Furthermore, as the superpowers have exerted influence to resolve some of the serious regional conflagrations that have been waged, be they in Afghanistan, Namibia, Cambodia, or elsewhere, the United Nations has stood available as a convenient facilitator to help bridge the final gaps toward peace, to provide a buffer for graceful exits, and to provide a framework for reconstruction. Both President Reagan and General Secretary Gorbachev have provided political and moral leadership to nurture this process.

### Conclusion

All three of these elements - President Reagan's firm leadership, the modification and maturing of views in developing countries, and the changing U.S.-Soviet relationship - have contributed to this evolution. It is not a revolutionary change. The United Nations still does much that is undesirable. The "Zionism is Racism" resolution still lies as part of the U.N. General Assembly theology. The rhetoric is excessive. The double standards persist, whether on South Africa or on human rights. But the reckless ship cast out toward dark seas of oblivion has been steadied. Enough progress perhaps has been made even to say it has begun to change its course. This is good for the United States and it is good for the world. It is a process that the next Administration must engage, nurture, and advance - both for the United Nations' own interests and for the good of the world community.

Maintaining this progress will require continued firm, persistent leadership in the United States. This means using all resources available - political, moral, rhetorical, and financial - to advance U.S. interests and to fight those actions that profoundly offend our moral and political values. This is a challenge for the next Administration.

This also means working constructively with developing nations, both on a bilateral basis and in their preferred forum of the United Nations; to nurture recognition of the benefits of responsible action, reasonable rhetoric, and constructive joint endeavors to avoid confrontation; and seek the progress of gradualism, which is the only solution for their many problems of poverty and, too often, limited freedoms.

Finally, we must continue our steps on the path that was opened by President Reagan and General Secretary Gorbachev through their efforts to explore areas of mutual interest to the superpowers. In the INF [Intermediate-Range Nuclear Forces] Treaty we have seen the benefits of the cooperation between the superpowers. We have seen in the INF Treaty the benefits of peace through strength. In the INF Treaty we have seen a harbinger of opportunities. While recognizing our adversarial relationship and the serious threat to our values and standards, this path should be explored. And one arena in which it can, should, and must be explored is within the U.N. system. The United States and the Soviet Union have long cooperated within the United Nations on areas of mutual interest such as nuclear nonproliferation. We have now found areas of cooperation within the United Nations on peacekeeping efforts such as in Afghanistan. The Soviet Union remains our primary adversary. But President Reagan has taken valuable steps toward limited cooperation.

Secretary General Dag Hammarskjold once said that the United Nations was like a hoe. By itself it can do nothing. But in the hands of the membership it can till the garden and bear fruit. The three developments in the 1980s discussed above have contributed to a more constructive atmosphere within the United Nations and greater opportunities. As the leader of the free world and the founding force of the United Nations, the United States has an obligation to seek to use the hoe for the advantage of all mankind.

PART THREE

THE U.N. AND HUMAN RIGHTS

# U.N. PANEL EXPOSES A WORLD-CLASS BULLY

The United Nations Human Rights Commission ended its annual conference in Geneva recently. Something quite extraordinary had happened. One of the world's great bullies was exposed.

A man who has brutalized his people and lived off them largely free of careful scrutiny by world opinion for decades, was subjected to lengthy, methodical and irrefutable evidence from affidavits, documents and victims bearing witness to the human rights abuses of his totalitarian regime. These charges were never refuted nor was a substantive reply even attempted.

While he avoided official U.N. condemnation for human rights abuses by a procedural gimmick that passed by a single vote, Fidel Castro, who has betrayed his people and lived off their oppression, will never again abuse his people with impunity. And the thousands still held as political prisoners have been given new hope that continued abuses will no longer be hidden from world opinion.

In Geneva, the U.S. delegation sought to bring these transgressions to the court of world opinion. As the former Cuban diplomat Andre Vargas Gomez has described it, under Mr. Castro Cuba has become "a place without a soul."

It is a country that in thirty years has driven nearly 15 percent of its population into exile, and today holds another 15,000 of its citizens in jails or labor camps for political "crimes." Cuba is the single most flagrant case of systematic violations of human rights in the Americas.

---

Appeared in The Chicago Sun-Times, April 7, 1987.

The U.N.'s Universal Declaration of Human Rights defines as basic human entitlements such rights as those to life, liberty, security of person, freedom of religion, freedom of opinion and expression, and freedom of assembly. It proclaims freedom from torture, the right to a fair trial and equality before the law. It declares rights to freedom of movement within one's state, and freedom to leave it.

It is precisely these human rights that Fidel Castro denies the Cuban people.

When a former Cuban political prisoner -- one who had served 27 years in Mr. Castro's prisons -- arrived in Miami in September, 1986, he said, "When they opened the gates we still felt like prisoners. In Cuba, everyone's a prisoner."

Life in Cuba today is characterized by an aggressive, systematic, and institutionalized denial of human rights virtually in every form. Under Fidel Castro, freedom of expression does not exist. No criticism of the basic policies and Marxist-Leninist orientation of the government, party, or its leadership is permitted. Telephones are routinely tapped and mail opened. There are no guarantees for freedom of religion, assembly, or press.

Censorship is rigorous in Cuban schools and the right to choose one's occupation is practically non-existent.

But most egregious of all has been Fidel Castro's massive, systematic and flagrant abuses of the judicial process and his regime's inhumane treatment of political prisoners. Cuba is a place where political terror masquerades as law. The Castro regime seized power by force and retains it through terror.

Cuban courts are subordinated to the party. People accused of certain "counter-revolutionary activities" are tried and sentenced secretly by military tribunals. Sentences often are extended without trial or due process.

Conditions and treatment in Cuban prisons are absolutely wretched. Prisoners from Mr. Castro's jails have reported major, systematic abuses, including beatings by guards and officers, withholding of food and water, inadequate diet and withholding of medical care, fresh air and exercise.

Prisoners are confined in dungeon-like cells, without family visits and mail for years, with physical injury caused by electronic noise machines, the participation of prison medical staff in acts of torture, and suspected medical experiments carried out without the permission of prisoners.

Former political prisoner Eduardo F. Capote has testified, "I was put in a cell originally built to hold about 80 men. We were 230 prisoners heaped together there. A hole in the floor was the only sanitary installation. The water was rationed to such an extent that we often spent up to two days in appalling thirst. We were harassed by plagues of lice, cockroaches and mice. We spent 23 hours a day shut up, only going out to eat a little rice, bread and soup."

Raul Carmenate, was arrested at the age of 16 and spent nine years in prison. He has testified that " . . . we were beaten until we fell to the ground . . . and led to work completely nude. One of our companions was made to cut furrows of grass with his mouth."

It is simply unacceptable to remain silent in the light of such brutal oppression of fundamental human rights.

At the close of the Human Rights Commission meeting, the United States delegation pledged to come back, and back, and back again until the repression against the Cuban people by Mr. Castro's regime is brought to account and reforms achieved.

# DOUBLE STANDARDS ON RIGHTS

Earlier this month, the 44th session of the U.N. Human Rights Commission convened in Geneva. For six weeks, government representatives from around the world will debate issues on an agenda that includes religious intolerance, torture and summary execution, as well as particular problem areas such as Afghanistan, South Africa and Chile.

At last year's session of the U.N. Human Rights Commission, a U.S.-sponsored initiative to put Cuba's human rights abuses on the agenda was defeated when a procedural motion to take no action was passed by a single vote. That motion, introduced by India, came after extensive pressure from Havana, springing from Fidel Castro's fear of a vote on the merits of the case.

Making the outcome doubly bitter for the United States was the fact that several of our friends in this hemisphere, democrats themselves, failed to vote with us and thereby helped to stifle any meaningful debate on the ways in which Mr. Castro has brutalized his people.

We look to the Human Rights Commission as the primary body within the United Nations for establishing international norms of human rights and monitoring compliance with them. Much of the commission's work is based on the standards for conduct established in the Universal Declaration of Human Rights, which was adopted first by the UNHRC and then by the General Assembly in 1948.

This seminal document, much as the Bill of Rights does for our own Constitution, sets forth positively individual liberties and fundamental freedoms to uphold these rights for their citizens.

---

Appeared in The Washington Times, February 23, 1988.

Although looking back 150 years to the liberal tradition of the Enlightenment, the U.N. declaration also grew out of the immediate experience with World War II. A world in which totalitarianism flourishes behind national boundaries is a war-prone state system. We had learned that governments which abuse their own citizens will abuse those of other states, if given the chance.

Tragically, over the years, the UNHRC has departed from the role envisioned for it by the U.N. founders. Instead of carrying out its mandate for impartially upholding the norms of fundamental freedoms and individual liberty, the UNHRC too often has been exploited cynically in order to reflect the political whims of the U.N. majority.

The UNHRC has become distinguished by a double standard in which countries that enjoy good standing with the unfree majority of nations in the General Assembly are politically immune from scrutiny by the rights commission.

The implication is that in the United Nations human rights standards are only applicable to embarrass and isolate the weak and the universal application of human rights standards is undermined.

Those who charge that, by endeavoring to bring Mr. Castro's record before the Commission, the United States is politicizing its work must address the present imbalance of the UNHRC agenda. Recent years have seen Chile, El Salvador and Guatemala become fixtures on its agenda, while the single-largest abuser of human rights in this hemisphere, Cuba, not only evades scrutiny, but often is a principal sponsor of resolutions critical of other nations. It is morally offensive for a country such as Cuba to set itself up as an arbiter of international human rights.

It is vital to the credibility of the UNHRC that its members demonstrate a capability to consider the human rights conduct of governments and to expose serious abuses of human rights wherever they occur. It is because we share the human rights standards of the U.N. and believe that the Commission can contribute to advancing human rights that its failure last year to address the situation in Cuba is especially disturbing.

In his 29-year rule, Fidel Castro has institutionalized repression. One-tenth of Cuba's population at the time he gained power have fled the island. According to Amnesty International, Cuba under Mr. Castro has imprisoned more persons per capita for political reasons than any other nation. In Cuba, it is even a political crime to distribute the U.N. Universal Declaration of Human Rights. In 1986, a 17-year-old boy was arrested on that charge and later died in prison under unexplained circumstances.

At all levels of society, Cuba maintains a regimented repressive system enforced by all-pervasive local committees which report to the secret police.    Mr. Castro's Cuba is a place where political terror masquerades as law.

Although seemingly immune from quiet solicitations from governments to improve his human rights performance, Mr. Castro seems to have felt the heat from last year's UNHRC debate on Cuba.  Recently, he has undertaken such steps as agreeing to increase immigration of political prisoners and releasing members of an unofficial human rights Commission from jail, which he hopes will deflect further scrutiny by the UNHRC.  However, thousands of political prisoners still languish in Cuban prisons.

It is clear that Mr. Castro is responsive to the threat of public international censure, and accordingly, it is all the more imperative that Cuba's dismal human rights record be scrutinized formally by the UNHRC.

This year the U.S. delegation to the UNHRC is led by Armando Valadares, the distinguished poet and human rights activist who, as a political prisoner in Cuba for 22 years, has firsthand experience of Mr. Castro's repression.

Past persistent double standards have ratcheted down the moral authority and practical force of the U.N. Human Rights Commission.  This can be reversed only by demonstrating that it is capable of evenhanded treatment of human rights offenses wherever they occur.

We are convinced that by any objective standard the body of evidence of continuing and systematic denial of human rights in Cuba commands the Commission to put Cuba on its agenda.  To do less will be to confirm that the UNHRC is losing its ability to uphold the basic norms of human rights and will brand the UNHRC just another political tool of the undemocratic and unfree majority at the United Nations.

# REVIEW OF EVENTS IN ETHIOPIA

Thank you for the opportunity to meet with you today on the subject of Ethiopia. The Congress is to be congratulated for helping put a public spotlight on the needless human tragedy unfolding in eastern Africa.

In the joint statement submitted for the record by the AID [Agency for International Development] and the Bureaus of African and International Organization Affairs at the Department of State, we have expressed our shared concern about the general situation in Ethiopia. Given the specific role of the United Nations, I would like to complement that statement with a brief summary of the work of the U.N. system -- emphasizing three points:

First, international compassion for the starving people of Ethiopia;

Second, the status of U.N. efforts, encouraged by the United States, to help the Ethiopian people; and

Third, the determination of the Reagan Administration to assure that the United Nations helps avert more death and devastation in Ethiopia.

Famine and human suffering have been the lot of mankind throughout history. The people of Ethiopia have known more than their share, suffering from recurring droughts and famines. The callous and indifferent Government of Ethiopia has allied itself with nature to jeopardize the lives of more than 2 million people.

---

Statement before the Subcommittees on Africa and on Human Rights and International Organizations of the House Foreign Affairs Committee, United States House of Representatives, Washington, D.C., April 21, 1988.

We will not -- indeed, we cannot -- sit silent during such a time of shame. Rather, we are more than ever determined to make every effort and to pursue every channel to help the people of Ethiopia through this crisis.

Working within the mandate of my office, I have impressed upon the officials of the United Nations the urgency of the situation and our deep concern and complete commitment to helping the people of Ethiopia through all available means.

I met last week in Geneva with U.N. Secretary General Perez de Cuellar on the subject of Ethiopia. He, like us, is extremely concerned. I expressed to him our great anxiety over the possibility that the horrible prospect of millions dying from starvation may result from decisions by the Ethiopian Government to ban international relief agencies from operating in the most seriously affected areas of the country. I stressed that the U.S. Government considered this situation to be a matter of utmost urgency and that we supported his efforts and that of the U.N. system to ensure that compassion prevails over conflict and blatant disregard for human rights.

In this connection, I expressed our full support for the mission of U.N. Under Secretary Ahtisaari. This mission, which concluded yesterday, has resulted in a decision by the Ethiopian Government to permit U.N. representatives to resume relief operations in Tigray and Eritrea. We welcome this news. But we will be watching very closely to assure that the Ethiopian Government adheres to this reported agreement. We note that the Ethiopian Government is continuing its ban on the International Red Cross and other private voluntary organizations in northern Ethiopia. Thus, in our view, Mr. Ahtisaari's mission has been only partly successful.

We must continue to insist -- through the United Nations and with the active involvement of the diplomatic community -- that the Ethiopian Government respects its basic responsibilities to its own people. I myself have already talked with a number of representatives of countries able and willing to provide assistance and with other senior officials in the United Nations. I met on April 19 with James Jonah, Assistant Secretary General and Director of the Office of Research and Collection of Information for the United Nations, to emphasize American concerns and, on April 20, I reiterated U.S. determination to help restore international relief to Ethiopia with Joseph Verner Reed, U.N. Under Secretary for Political and General Assembly Affairs. My colleagues and I plan to follow up with Under Secretary Ahtisaari upon his return from Ethiopia. I have underscored -- and will continue to underscore -- the seriousness with which we view the situation and our belief that firm resolve on the part of the international community is critical to getting needed relief supplies to the people of Ethiopia. Our U.S. Mission to the United Nations in New York has been instructed to begin planning, on a contingency basis, for seeking further action in U.N. fora.

I would not want to leave the impression that nothing has been done heretofore. As you know, the U.N. system took the lead some time ago in coordinating the international effort to confront the emergency in Ethiopia. One of the first steps taken by the U.N. Secretary General was the designation of a Special Representative in Ethiopia, Michael Priestley, to deal with all aspects of this emergency. Mr. Priestley heads the Emergency Prevention and Preparedness Group (EPPG) which serves as a fulcrum for U.N. system-wide efforts in the country.

The U.N. Development Program (UNDP) has augmented the financing and personnel of the group. UNDP has also allocated U.N. volunteers to work with the Relief and Rehabilitation Commission of the Government of Ethiopia. These young and dedicated professionals, from a number of countries, are providing know-how to expedite receipt, storage, transportation, and distribution of foodstuffs, medical supplies, and other basic necessities. They not only know how to get the job done but also are committed to taking every conceivable step to ensure that the people of Ethiopia get the help they so desperately need.

Another U.N. approach to the problem has been through the U.N. Disaster Relief Organization (UNDRO) and the World Food Program (WFP). Together they have led the effort to move huge volumes of food from the ports to the devastated areas in the north of the country. Also, in response to a UNDRO-launched appeal, donors have pledged almost $10 million to the Emergency Transport Fund to pay for the airlifting of food to remote areas of Tigray and Eritrea. The United Nations has appealed for an additional $5 million to extend this operation until the end of June. In March, before the latest crisis, EPPG was responsible for airlifting some 11,000 tons of emergency supplies. WFP has a fleet of some 200 trucks, provided by donors, and is purchasing an additional 70 vehicles for use in the north. We are using every available channel to reach the various groups which have attacked these relief convoys in order to end the loss of transport, supplies, and lives. We also are supporting U.N. efforts to persuade the government to permit convoys to operate freely at their own risk.

The U.N. Children's Fund (UNICEF) has raised more than $10 million in response to its appeal of November 1987 for relief to drought-affected women and children. The UNICEF aid will cover health, supplementary feeding and relief items, water and sanitation needs, and cash for food for drought victims.

The Food and Agriculture Organization's (FAO) Food Information and Early Warning System project was instrumental in bringing the impending drought/famine to the attention of the world last June and July. FAO also has three crop protection projects in Ethiopia addressing the agricultural side of emergency needs, valued at about $0.5 million.

They focus on controlling army worm infestation, tse-tse flies and desert locusts.

We know that these efforts and those of the rest of the international community cannot compensate for effective action by the Ethiopian Government. Nor may they be sufficient to meet the magnitude of the need.

We thus appreciate all the more this opportunity to highlight the need for all, especially the Government of Ethiopia, to ensure that the people whose lives are at risk get life-sustaining relief. The Government of Ethiopia must adopt policies which are grounded in the recognition that the needs of its people are its foremost concern. I will be working actively with my colleagues from the Department's Bureau of African Affairs and from AID and elsewhere to keep pressure on the U.N. system. The Government of the United States believes that the United Nations can and must play a critical facilitative role, so that we may deflect what otherwise will be a catastrophe of monumental proportions. The strong outcry of the international community in behalf of the Ethiopian people may make the difference between life and death.

# A SHAME OF SILENCE ON ETHIOPIA?


The Economic and Social Council of the United Nations is second only to the General Assembly in the range of issues it must examine and on which members must have views. Its oversight role has made the ECOSOC into a major international forum for the discussion of the principal themes of our time: those of violence and peace, death and life, suffering and triumph.

The nations represented are all signatories of the U.N. Charter. As such, we have voluntarily assumed a responsibility to advocate the values and moral principles reflected in the Preamble and in Article I of Chapter I of the charter. It is our duty to stand up for these values and to call for actions which reflect the moral authority of this great organization. We must never leave ourselves open to the shame of silence.

In 1986, the United States went before the U.N. Commission on Human Rights in an effort to get that august body to take a stand on the situation in Ethiopia. Unfortunately for the people of Ethiopia, politics prevailed and the commission refused to act. And sadly, subsequent events in Ethiopia proved us correct. We will never know how many could have been saved had the commission acted at that time or how many were, in fact, saved merely by our raising the issue.

Once again we come before a body of the United Nations to plead for the people of Ethiopia. Once again, the United Nations and its members must face the issue of whether to remain mute and blind in the presence of actions which starve an innocent population.

---

Statement before the U.N. Economic and Social Council (ECOSOC), New York City, May 19, 1988.

Put bluntly, a body of the United Nations must face the issue of whether human lives are more valuable than narrow political interests. We have no doubt about our answer; we have no doubt about what the answer of the world community should be.

We call on the United Nations and its members, regardless of ideology or foreign policy, to recognize the tragedy occurring in Ethiopia and to use all available peaceful means to end it. Above all, we call upon the government of Ethiopia to respect the most fundamental rights of its citizens.

My government is motivated strictly by humanitarian concern for the people of Ethiopia. The United States has consistently demonstrated its concern for the people of Ethiopia. We are the largest donor of relief assistance to the people of Ethiopia and cannot quietly condone obstacles to essential aid.

While fully reliable information about what is actually happening in Ethiopia is limited -- and uncertainty is itself one of our greatest causes for consternation -- we do believe the following:

Of 3.2 million people at risk, only about 850,000 are now being fed. That contrasts with almost 2 million who were being fed in February this year. The remainder face a very real prospect of starvation.

War is the principal culprit in limiting access to hungry people. Military actions by both sides, compounded by misguided government decisions, have affected delivery systems, the number of people under government control, and the ability of relief organizations to operate.

The decisions of the Ethiopian government on April 6 effectively stopped international relief efforts in the north, thereby seriously undermining feeding operations. Although several U.N. personnel have been allowed back, only a massive undertaking can now save those at risk.

My government deplores this cold-blooded neglect of millions of Ethiopians in pursuit of military objectives in an intractable and unwinnable civil war. We also condemn the callous decisions, actions and warfare of the rebel forces, which have resulted in anarchy and chaos in the north, and have impeded feeding operations. We are not addressing politics but human decency. It is a profoundly moral issue. We must speak out against -- and try to stop -- this horrible affront by the belligerent parties to the U.N.'s charter and to civilization itself.

The apparent willingness of the Ethiopian government to allow innocent civilians to starve has an impact beyond Ethiopia's borders. It threatens the lives of other Africans and the stability of the entire region.

A new bout of starvation in northern Ethiopia could produce anew a mass exodus of refugees seeking food in neighboring countries, particularly in Sudan. We should not forget the enormous burdens placed on the people and government of Sudan during the famine of 1984-1985. Without a resumption of unhindered food deliveries in the north, hundreds of thousands of Ethiopians might have to flee again. Many, many may die in the process.

The great irony is that the international community, in particular the United Nations, is ready this time, with adequate stocks of food, supplies and experienced personnel, to avert mass starvation in Ethiopia. Yet, that same government which a few months ago came before the world seeking assistance now refuses to allow that assistance to reach its people. It cites concern for the security of expatriate relief workers. These concerns are not shared by most of those workers; they are willing to resume their relief efforts regardless of personal risk.

We take the step of raising this issue here only because other approaches have failed. We have contacted Ethiopian authorities and have been in touch with the regime's allies. We have supported strongly the efforts made by the United Nations to clarify and rectify the situation in Ethiopia, in particular during U.N. Undersecretary General Ahtissari's visit in April. Important first steps have been taken, but much more must be done.

This body should not permit yet another sad chapter to be added to the history of our time. We should register -- for all to hear and act upon -- that we have not forgotten the people of Ethiopia. This is the least, the bare minimum, to which the people of Ethiopia are entitled.

## CUBA HELD ACCOUNTABLE:
### A Victory for Freedom at the United Nations


Earlier this year in Geneva, the United Nations Human Rights Commission agreed by consensus to launch an investigation into Cuba's human-rights record. The decision marked a dramatic departure from the U.N.'s too frequent double standard of pointing an accusing finger at only a handful of countries, especially Israel, Chile, and South Africa, while ignoring the gross human-rights violations of the Communist world; and it may lead, at least temporarily, to a partial relaxation of Fidel Castro's totalitarian grip over the Cuban people. The Geneva victory also is an example of how, in this age of bloc voting by developing countries, the United States can successfully advance important national values and interests at the U.N.

In the face of repeated attacks on American interests by U.N. bodies, the U.S. has scored isolated yet significant triumphs in recent years. In 1982, thanks to a strong effort by Jeane Kirkpatrick and her team, the General Assembly ceased referring to Puerto Rico as a "non-self-governing territory." In 1983 and 1984, moves to expel Israel from the International Atomic Energy Agency were blocked. In 1986, the General Assembly adopted a series of reforms proposed by 18 high-level experts, including a reduction in the number of U.N. staff by 15 percent, and agreement that budgetary levels would be adopted by consensus.

These victories taught us that to succeed in the U.N., the United States needs to identify precise goals, to make our concerns known to other countries, and, most important, to persevere in the face of initial defeat or protracted conflict. This approach guided the U.S. decision to seek to restore the norms and standards contained in the Universal Declaration of

Appeared in <u>Policy Review</u>, Summer 1988, No. 45.

Human Rights, by using Cuba as a test case for overturning the double standard in U.N. human-rights attention.

## Rebuff on Ethiopia

The U.N. Human Rights Commission (UNHRC), consisting of 43 members, meets every year in Geneva in February through early March to determine whether governments are complying with the Universal Declaration of Human Rights, adopted by the General Assembly in 1948 after being drafted under the leadership of Eleanor Roosevelt and John Foster Dulles. The UNHRC also studies thematic human-rights issues such as religious intolerance and the abuse of psychiatric medicine.

In recent years the UNHRC has focused primarily on countries in Latin America friendly with the U.S., such as Guatemala, El Salvador, and Chile. Only in 1984, five years after the Soviet invasion, did the UNHRC agree to investigate the situation in Afghanistan. It also agreed that year to investigate Iran. But apart from Afghanistan, no ally of the Soviet Union has ever been subject to a UNHRC investigation.

In 1986 at the UNHRC, the U.S. delegation informally circulated a resolution criticizing the Ethiopian government's resettlement policies, which had resulted in the death of at least 100,000 people. The U.S. resolution failed to attract any support. African countries rallied around their fellow African government. Our Western allies felt that the groundwork, particularly consultations and lobbying for support from other nonaligned countries, had not been sufficiently prepared. In any case, our allies argued that the world was preoccupied with the plight of the starving Ethiopian people, and that open criticism of the Ethiopian government might jeopardize the ongoing efforts of the international community to relieve their desperate plight. Our resolution was withdrawn.

## Cuba's Naked Prisoners

Following the rebuff our Ethiopian resolution received in early 1986, the State Department bureaus of International Organization Affairs, Inter-American Affairs, and Human Rights conferred with the U.S. Mission in New York to come up with another approach to the U.N.'s human-rights double standard.

We realized that for tactical reasons we had to focus on a single country rather than on all major human-rights violators in order to enlist the support of Western and other like-minded countries. A decision was quickly reached to bring Cuba to the attention of the UNHRC. Because almost all the major international human-rights organizations have denounced the violations of human rights in Cuba, this could not be construed as the U.S. government vs. Castro. The Organization of American States, Amnesty International, the International Commission of

Jurists, the European Parliament, the European Community, and the Spanish government had all expressed concern about human-rights abuses in Cuba.

A 1986 Amnesty International report cited the barbaric conditions imposed on Cuban political prisoners (more political prisoners per capita than any other country): crowding them naked into small, windowless cells for months, withholding proper medical treatment, and intentionally degrading them (for example, by throwing buckets of excrement over them).

In the summer of 1986, members of an unofficial Cuban human-rights committee, headed by Ricardo Bofill, were detained and imprisoned after meeting with French journalists. Bofill fled to the French Embassy in Havana where he remained in hiding until January 1987. During this same period a 17-year old boy was arrested while distributing copies of the U.N. Universal Declaration of Human Rights. He later died in custody under unexplained circumstances.

### Terror Masquerading as Law

Our decision to target Cuba was facilitated by the availability of new and up-to-date information furnished by political prisoners released in the early '80s by the Cuban government. The release of these prisoners, many of whom had served sentences since the early part of Castro's rule, was accompanied by a tightening of controls on Cuban society. We learned that in 1983 the Cuban government tried three individuals for the crime of sabotage. Merely for discussing the possibility of forming an independent Solidarity-style union, these Cubans were put on trial for their lives. When the guilty verdict was returned against them, the judge refused to comply with the political directive to impose the death sentence. The judge herself was removed, tried for incompetence and political bias and sentenced to 80 years. Another judge then imposed the death sentence, which was subsequently reduced to 35 years after an international outcry.

The complete subservience of the Cuban judiciary allows terror to masquerade as law and is only one aspect of the Cuban dictator's pervasive system of repression. Brutality is employed to dehumanize the regime's opponents. Raul Carmenate was arrested at the age of 16 and spent nine years in prison. He has testified, " . . . we were beaten until we fell to the ground . . . and led to work completely nude. One of our companions was made to cut furrows out of grass with his mouth."

Through the infamous Committees for the Defense of the Revolution, Castro's secret police turn child against parent, neighbor against neighbor. Daily life is closely monitored by these committees, which exist on practically every block in Cuban cities and towns. Members are expected to observe and report anything "unusual," including strangers in the neighborhood, reception of foreign radio or TV broadcasts, or critical comments about the government.

There are no guarantees for freedom of assembly or association in Castro's Cuba. All group meetings are monitored by the Committees for the Defense of the Revolution or State Security. A 1983 OAS report stated:

> Membership in the people's organizations -- including the large union and peasant associations -- is practically a prerequisite for any routine activity, since membership affects admission to universities, promotions, access to certain kinds of vacation or recreational activities, the obtainment of non-perishable products that require that a union certify that the buyer is an "advanced worker."

There is no freedom of the press, as all outlets of the media are controlled by the state and operate strictly according to party guidelines. Artistic and cultural freedoms are nonexistent in Cuba. Many of Cuba's most distinguished literary and artistic figures have been "erased" from cultural outlets. Religious broadcasts are completely prohibited, except for news of foreign clergy defending the Castro regime. Only 200 priests remain in Cuba compared with 720 before the revolution.

### India's Cynical Ploy

U.S. Ambassador to the United Nations Vernon Walters introduced our first resolution on Cuba at the U.N. General Assembly in 1986 to test the water and to lay down a marker for the 1987 UNHRC, which was to meet two months later in Geneva. As soon as the U.S. resolution was tabled in New York, the Cuban delegation also tabled two hastily drafted resolutions alleging violations of the rights of blacks and native Americans by the U.S. government. These Cuban papers, intended only as a foil to our own, did not take us by surprise. The United States, as an open society, is always prepared to defend its human-rights record, especially against countries such as Cuba. However, the Cuban resolutions provided the General Assembly with the means of avoiding the issue. The members of the UNHRC agreed to an Indian motion to take no action on either the U.S. or the Cuban resolutions.

In what turned out to be a full dress rehearsal for our successful campaign in 1988, our first UNHRC resolution on Cuba was circulated in Geneva in early 1987. It expressed deep concern over "serious human-rights violations in Cuba, particularly the rights to freedom of expression and association, freedom from arbitrary arrest and detention, and freedom of thought, conscience and religion," and appealed to the Cuban government "to release all those detained for their political views and activities and to allow any Cuban who might wish to leave or to return to

Cuba to do so without hindrance." The resolution also called for an investigation of human-rights violations.

The United States made a major effort to build support for its resolution. The U.S. Delegation in Geneva extensively lobbied other UNHRC delegations. President Reagan sent personal notes to heads of state. The State Department sent more than 400 cables urging support. Victims of Castro's prisons -- some lame or blinded as a result of their incarcerations -- came to Geneva to personally testify to the inhuman brutality they experienced as Cuban political prisoners. And Ambassador Vernon Walters himself went to Geneva to present the resolution and eloquently address the Commission.

### Latin American Double Standard

Nonetheless, the UNHRC in 1987 voted by 19 votes to 18 with 6 abstentions to adopt procedural motions again put forth by India to take no action on either the U.S. resolution or Cuban resolutions aimed at the United States. The U.S. had expected the procedural gimmick to be used again and in all our contacts had emphasized the need to allow our resolution to receive fair consideration on its merits in an up-or-down vote. We let it be known that we could not understand the motives of countries who voted to "muzzle" us on this issue. Among those countries voting for the Indian motion were Colombia, Peru, Mexico, Argentina, and Venezuela, countries that profess a belief in and respect for democratic principles and fundamental human rights.

The closeness of the vote on the Indian procedural motion made us all the more determined to redouble our efforts to have Cuba placed on the UNHRC agenda at its next session. Our experience impressed upon us the need to begin our campaign early, immediately following the 1987 UNHRC session.

Following the vote in Geneva, a member of the Indian delegation approached me on the floor of the assembly to discuss the disappointing result. I told her that I was unable to understand why India, the world's largest democracy, would side with Cuba on a question of the applicability of objective human-rights standards. She laughed as if I were unusually naive and said, "After all, Ambassador, it's only politics." Presumably, she was reflecting the imperative of bloc voting within the U.N., where members of the so-called nonaligned movement band together to protect each other from international criticism and scrutiny.

## 1988 -- The Strategy for Victory

Our strategy for 1988 counted upon the support of allies such as Britain, France, and the Federal Republic of Germany whose views on human rights coincide with our own. They would provide a diplomatic base for our effort with the developing country majority in the UNHRC who would have to be convinced through hard lobbying. In the course of routine consultations in New York within the Western group we repeatedly raised the subject of Cuba to solidify our support base.

Members of Congress were briefed and enlisted. They were asked to use their influence with contacts in other countries to support our effort at the UNHRC. The Congress adopted a resolution urging the U.N. to look into Cuban human-rights practices. Another congressional resolution said that countries' positions on our Cuban resolution were to be taken into account in setting foreign assistance levels. Both were adopted unanimously. The level of bipartisan support for this diplomatic undertaking was unusual and certainly reinforced the point that all Americans are concerned with the situation in Cuba.

We devoted a great deal of attention to public outreach because our strategy was to focus publicity upon the situation in Cuba so that even if we lost within the U.N., the word would be spread about the true nature of Castro's regime. The U.S. Information Agency (USIA) helped to disseminate the new details we had learned from former Cuban political prisoners about human-rights abuses.

The issue of Cuba was placed on the agenda of meetings between State Department and foreign diplomats whenever appropriate. We made it clear we would again bring up Cuba's abuse of human rights at the 1988 UNHRC session. This served to shore up support from those countries that had voted with us in 1987, and to remind those who had not that we would keep coming back on this subject until we were satisfied that they fully understand its importance to us.

### Lobbying Venezuela

The efforts of our ambassador in Venezuela, Otto Reich, exemplified our work in capitals. Ambassador Reich went to the Foreign Ministry immediately after the 1987 vote to register our serious concerns. Every few months he went back to talk to both Venezuelan President Jaime Lusinchi and Foreign Minister Simon Alberto Consalva to say how disappointed the United States had been by their vote on this issue. He used trips to Caracas in 1987 by both Jeane Kirkpatrick and Vernon Walters to hammer home the issue to government officials. Ambassador Reich gave interviews to local papers and sent copies of Armando Valladares' book, Against All Hope, to 20 opinion leaders in Venezuela. He lit a fire in both major political parties about the need for UNHRC action on Cuba. All these steps helped set the environment for Venezuela's dramatic turnabout on this issue in 1988, a change of position that broke the pro-Cuba South American bloc and helped us win.

During this period, the State Department remained in close touch with supporters in Congress. As a result of the bill calling for cutbacks in foreign assistance to the countries who had disappointed us in 1987, India lost a grant of $15 million. The Latin American democracies that had voted against us on the procedural motion were informed that the United States viewed their action as hostile to our common values of democracy and respect for human rights. Members of Congress raised the issue with their counterparts in the Latin American democracies and the legislatures in those countries became a positive force in pressuring the foreign ministries to support the U.S. initiative.

Our Trump Card -- Valladares

In October 1987, President Reagan appointed Armando Valladares, the renowned former political prisoner, human-rights advocate, and poet, to head the U.S. delegation to the 1988 UNHRC Session. This decision ensured that the U.S. delegation could muster the voluminous and detailed evidence of Castro's human-rights practices possessed by the Cuban exile community. The appointment of a man who bore the physical scars of Castro's torture was a public relations coup that paid large dividends when the UNHRC began its 1988 meeting.

Even before the 1988 session Valladares traveled to Geneva to introduce himself to other delegates based there. He held a well-attended press conference, which set the stage for the opening of the UNHRC. In his preliminary meetings Valladares made clear his interest in the full spectrum of human-rights issues before the UNHRC, including violations in the Middle East, Chile, South Africa, and religious intolerance, which helped deflect the expectation and criticism from some corners that he was a single-issue man, interested only in Cuba.

Of course, Ambassador Valladares gave powerful personal accounts of Castro's abuses of the human rights of his political prisoners:

> I had many friends in prison. One of them, Roberto Lopez Chavez, was practically a child. He went on a hunger strike to protest abuses. The guards denied him water. Roberto, on the floor of his punishment cell, delirious and in agony, asked only for water . . . water. The guards entered his cell and asked: "You want water?" They urinated into his mouth and onto his face. He died the following day.

> I remember when they had me in a punishment cell, naked, my leg fractured in several places -- fractures that were never

treated and eventually fused into a mass of deformed bones. Through the wire mesh that covered the cell, the guards would pour over me buckets of urine and excrement that they had collected earlier.

Castro views Valladares as one of his biggest enemies. Valladares' role as an official representative of the United States proved such a distraction to the Cuban dictator that, in the end, Castro made serious errors of judgment. The Cubans countered the hard evidence of their human-rights abuses with only a personal attack upon Valladares. Most other delegations and observers in Geneva saw through the Cuban campaign to defame Valladares. We believe the Cuban effort was weakened by not trying to refute the evidence itself. It is a common and transparent Communist ploy that when facts are incontrovertible the man presenting them should be impugned.

Valladares was not the only former political prisoner Castro had to contend with. Several prominent Cuban Americans, including ex-Castro prisoner Jorge Mas, traveled to Geneva at private expense in 1986 and again in 1987 to present to the delegates their own stories of the vicious nature of Castro's regime. The involvement of these private individuals and a powerful lobby in Washington helped keep attention focused on the issue. These people who had endured so much under Castro were not to be denied the opportunity to indict him before a court of world public opinion such as the UNHRC.

### Congressional Pressure on the Philippines

A bipartisan congressional delegation of House Foreign Affairs Committee Chairman Dante Fascell, who does not always support the administration, and ranking Republican William Broomfield went to Geneva to lobby other delegations. This impressed other delegations who realized that this was not just a Reagan administration vendetta, but a policy with broad bipartisan support.

Members of both the House and Senate, from both sides of the aisle, sent numerous letters to heads of state and foreign ministers. More than 25 telegrams from the Hill were sent to Philippine President Aquino alone, and the Philippine Embassy in Washington was overwhelmed by phone calls from congressmen on the day the U.S. resolution was to have come up for a vote. Partly as a result, the Philippines, which had abstained on the procedural motion of 1987, was very supportive of American efforts in 1988.

Maureen Reagan, who has close ties to several African countries because of her work as U.S. representative on the U.N. Commission on the Status of Women, came to Geneva as well. She had recently returned from a visit to Senegal on behalf of President Reagan where she had raised the

Cuban issue with Senegalese President Abdou Diouf. Her presence during the crucial last days of the UNHRC session was extremely important. Thanks to her personal intervention, no African country misunderstood that the highest levels of the U.S. government were personally involved in our effort.

In the final days, Ambassador Walters again traveled to Geneva. He movingly addressed the Commission:

> Mr. Chairman, I am old enough to remember those who apologized for Hitler and Stalin; I remember the cries of shock and betrayal when the truth of what those dictators had done filtered out to the world. I think that sooner rather than later the same cries will go up when the world finally acknowledges the horrors of life under Castro. Let us not let this Commission continue to participate in the silence -- for silence makes us the accomplices of oppression.

As the showdown vote on the resolution drew near, it was our assessment, and probably Castro's, too, that the United States would prevail. Our diplomatic work after the rebuff in 1987 had clearly paid off. The Latin American group was divided. The Africans had either been driven to sit on the fence or side with us because of their resentment of heavy-handed Cuban attempts to lobby them. Toward the end, large numbers of Cubans could be seen working the corridors in Geneva in a last-ditch attempt to intimidate delegates they could not otherwise persuade. The Cubans resorted to such techniques as spreading defamatory stories in the domestic press of countries whose representatives in Geneva were not cooperative. The representative of one country in Central America was bluntly reminded about his country's vulnerability to a domestic insurgency. These threats and blandishments had no effect. There was no country willing to put forward a procedural motion to deflect consideration of our resolution. Cuba therefore was forced to adopt another ploy.

## Castro's Miscalculation

Two days before the expected vote on the U.S. resolution, Castro invited the UNHRC to send an investigative team to visit Cuba, talk to Cuban government officials, and interview prisoners. He even offered to pay for it. Up to this point Castro had consistently refused to consider permitting any kind of international scrutiny of Cuban practices. The International Committee of the Red Cross had experienced repeated rebuffs to its requests to visit Cuban prisons and interview prisoners. Castro had previously referred to a U.N. investigation as an act of war. As recently as February he had told NBC's Maria Shriver that he would never permit a U.N. investigation of Cuba.

Castro and his envoys clearly miscalculated if they hoped their invitation would put the subject to rest and prevent Cuba from being formally placed on the UNHRC agenda. The chairman of the UNHRC, Senegalese diplomat Ambassador Alioune Sene, in consultation with the U.S.; several Latin American delegations who were brokering the invitation for Cuba (Cuba was not then a member of the UNHRC); and other members, crafted a decision that the UNHRC finally adopted by consensus. The decision in effect took Castro's cynical invitation and turned it against him.

Instead of accepting the offer on Cuba's terms, the decision adopted in Geneva called for an investigation of Cuba according to standard U.N. procedures that had been used to investigate and help correct human-rights violations in other countries, including Afghanistan, Iran, and Chile. Rather than being limited to the treatment of political prisoners as Castro intended, the investigation will look into the full range of human rights, including freedom of speech, press, religion, association, and emigration.

The decision reached in Geneva truly outstripped our own modest expectation that Cuba would be placed on the agenda of next year's UNHRC session. Most important, it was a victory for the Cuban people, who may now experience a relaxation of Castro's totalitarian grip on their homeland as he prepares for the U.N. team's visit. For instance, following the decision in Geneva the Cuban government announced that it would for the first time permit the International Red Cross to visit and inspect the prisons. The long-suspended Cuban immigration agreement with the U.S. has been reactivated and more than 200 recently released political prisoners now have been granted permission to depart for the United States.

## A Bulgarian in the Chicken Coop

Careful follow-up on our part will be essential. Representatives from Ireland, the Philippines, Bulgaria, Nigeria, and Colombia will serve on the UNHRC investigative team. The Bureau of International Organizations has assembled a State Department working group to monitor and to provide information for the investigating team. A week after the decision, I traveled to Geneva and met with UNHRC chairman Sene to discuss the importance of a strong and objective investigative team. I indicated to Ambassador Sene that the U.S. had great faith in his commitment to human rights and looked to him to ensure that the UNHRC lived up to its responsibilities.

Meanwhile, Castro is hastening to improve his image prior to the UNHRC team's visit, which is scheduled for late summer. As many as 300 political prisoners will be released in the near future. And Castro recently allowed Cardinal O'Connor to visit Cuba as a guest of the Roman Catholic Conference of Bishops. These dividends of our success in Geneva confound the argument that the glare of publicity cannot affect Castro's behavior. However, the leopard has not completely changed his spots. Castro's thugs are still trying to intimidate and discredit Ricardo Bofill, the unofficial Cuban human-rights advocate in Havana.

What implications on how to successfully implement multilateral policy may be drawn from our Cuban initiative?

· A firm decision must be made within the U.S. government that the issue has top priority and should engage fully all parts of the government.

· We must begin our effort early and be prepared for a long-haul endeavor.

· The entire spectrum of the U.S. bureaucracy must be used to communicate the importance of the issue to other countries.

· A solid diplomatic base of as many like-minded countries as possible should be established and used to attract more support.

· We must be tenacious and not accept initial rebuffs as final defeats.

The points above should be the rules of the road for U.S. multilateral diplomacy. Other areas that now present themselves as a focus of future multilateral efforts include:

· Overturning the infamous provision that Zionism is racism, which is a smear intended to delegitimitize the state of Israel.

· Promoting the positive linkage between human rights and economic development, for example, the connection between the right to own property and economic growth. The point that economic growth depends upon the enjoyment of fundamental human freedoms is absent from the U.N. debate on economic and human-rights issues. The U.S. needs to take the lead in restoring the appropriate perspective to the U.N.'s treatment of economic development.

· Continuing the budgetary and management reform process at the U.N., which began with the adoption of General Assembly resolution 41/213 in 1986. The United States seeks to ensure that the U.N. remains faithful to the terms of that resolution, which requires that budgetary questions be settled through consensus rather than through the vote of the majority of the General Assembly, who contribute less to the U.N.'s budget than the minority.

As a founding member of the U.N. and its largest financial contributor, we owe it to ourselves and to the U.N. itself to restore the original values and beliefs that its founders had hoped the institution would instill for the world.

## U.S. COMMEMORATES 40TH ANNIVERSARY
## OF THE UNIVERSAL DECLARATION OF HUMAN RIGHTS


In September of this year, the United Nations took another important step for advancing human rights: Despite firm, public statements by Fidel Castro that he would never allow a U.N. investigation of Cuba's human rights practices, a U.N. team visited Cuba. While it was there, the team met with Cuban human rights activists, interviewed political prisoners, and explored the systemic nature of human rights violations in that country. It is fitting that during this year of the 40th anniversary of the Universal Declaration of Human Rights, the U.N. Human Rights Commission (UNHCR) has finally gained access to a country which has committed the worst human rights violations in this hemisphere.

For years, Cuba has been a blatant violator of its citizens' human rights. Nonetheless, it remained free from careful scrutiny by a United Nations that consistently refused to acknowledge human rights violations by the left. We witnessed a significant victory for freedom, and for the United Nations itself, when the U.S. initiative regarding Cuba succeeded earlier this year in pushing the U.N. Human Rights Commission toward a consensus decision to launch an investigation into Cuba's human rights abuses. In anticipation of the team's arrival, Castro began to free some political prisoners, improve prison conditions, and tolerate the existence of a small, independent national human rights group.

The Geneva victory also was significant in that it marked a departure from the United Nations' too frequent double standard of pointing an accusing finger at only a handful of countries (especially Israel,

_____

Address made at ceremonies commemorating the 40th anniversary of the Universal Declaration of Human Rights at the United States Department of State, December 8, 1988.

Chile, El Salvador, and South Africa) while ignoring the gross human rights violations of the communist world. It also is an example of how, in this age of bloc voting by developing countries, the United States can successfully advance important national values and interests at the United Nations. It is important that objectivity be restored to the consideration of human rights by the United Nations.

Among the principal purposes of the United Nations, set forth in its Charter, is the promotion of respect for basic human rights and fundamental freedoms. The Universal Declaration of Human Rights, adopted by the U.N. General Assembly in 1948, offers a common standard against which individuals and nations can measure treatment of citizens and it remains the philosophical basis of our human rights efforts in the United Nations and throughout the world. Americans will recognize the basic provisions of our Bill of Rights as the root elements of the declaration. It underscores, for example, the right to self-determination and the right to choose freely one's government.

A major reason for the primacy of human rights in the United Nations is that its founders recognized from the bitter experience of the Second World War that those governments which abuse the rights of their own citizens are, if given the opportunity, more likely to abuse the rights of citizens of other countries. Promotion of the respect for human rights is thus linked to the United Nations' basic purpose of keeping the peace. In both of these areas, the United Nations is making an increasingly important contribution.

### The U.S. Emphasis on Human Rights

For the United States, no issue has surpassed in importance the protection and promotion of basic human rights and fundamental freedoms. This concern for human rights is interwoven in the national experience and beliefs of Americans. It is what has differentiated the United States from so many other nations in history. It is profoundly fundamental to our character and values. Our belief in the rights of the individual has led to the creation of our own economic, social, and political system. Our foreign policy, which seeks to secure our national interest, is inextricably bound to our belief in the inalienability of human rights and fundamental freedoms for all people.

We view human rights as limitations upon the power of the state. Based on the principles set forth in the Bill of Rights of the U.S. Constitution, our view of human rights is centered on defenses from the state, accorded every individual and protected by an independent judiciary. These rights are timeless, unalterable, and not subject to the intellectual or political fashions of the day. They establish the state as the servant of the people and not the other way around.

One clear example of the difference in approach between the United States and most of the rest of the world regarding human rights is the topic of the right to self-determination. For most of the world, self-determination is a one-time act, which ends when a country achieves political independence. Once the colonial flag has been lowered and local rulers take power, the issue is closed: The country has achieved self-determination. The United States, however, sees self-determination as a continuous process that need not include political independence. For example, the relationship between Puerto Rico and the United States illustrates how a country can freely exercise the right to self-determination by electing to associate itself with another country. For us, true self-determination results from individuals, on a regular and periodic basis, exercising their human rights, in particular, the right to choose their government. In other words, the essence of self-determination is the existence of genuine and periodic elections that will reflect the will of the people.

It is in the U.N. Charter's emphasis on human rights that this organization bears the greatest resemblance to the American approach to the relation between the individual and the state. The United Nations is essentially a body of constituent national governments. But just as the Bill of Rights in our own Constitution delineates the limits of the U.S. Government to compel American citizens, the Universal Declaration is intended to set forth similar limits on the powers of all governments over the conscience of the individual. The Universal Declaration sets forth the same principle contained in our own Declaration of Independence that the legitimacy of rule can only flow from the consent of the governed. Only by observing the human rights and fundamental freedoms contained in the Universal Declaration can the members of the United Nations fulfill the Charter's highest purposes.

The United States has been very dissatisfied when the United Nations has departed from its original purposes, particularly in regard to the promotion and protection of basic human rights. The past 25 years have seen a tendency to redefine human rights to include a new category of "social and economic rights," such as the right to education, the right to food, or the right to housing. The Soviets have even been bold enough to sponsor a "right to life" in their drive to secure a disavowal of nuclear weapons on the part of the rest of the planet. Recently the developing countries have decided to preempt the discussion on the appropriate strategy for development by asserting a "right" to development. In contrast to our notion of human rights as limitations upon the power of the state, these "rights" would augment the power of the state, make individuals more dependent, and could not be enforced by an independent judiciary..

The United States sees these socioeconomic "rights" as the goals of sound policy rather than as true human rights. A government should help create the environment that will permit its people to have adequate housing, food, medical care, and living standards. Beyond this, however, lies the fact that in many cases these new "rights" tend to be merely a smokescreen put up by those with no intention of honoring human rights regardless of the definition.

Dictatorships traditionally justify the denial of civil and political rights by asserting that these rights are predicated upon the achievement of certain social and economic goals. They will argue, for instance, that assuring the right to vote or the right to worship freely will not feed the hungry or house the homeless. The historical record shows, however, that those states that most energetically protect civil and political rights achieve the most in the social and economic spheres. One can see this by contrasting the social and economic achievements of countries with similar cultures--for example, the Federal Republic of Germany with East Germany, Austria with Hungary, Thailand with communist Indochina, and Botswana with most other African countries. Wherever the state fears and oppresses the individual, we see political prisoners, refugees, and economic stagnation.

The record of the United States in defending human rights is an excellent one. At home, we are engaged constantly in the struggle to ensure that all Americans enjoy the full protection of the law. Abroad, we have made human rights a top priority in our foreign policy.

The United States has more credibility on human rights issues than any other country. The State Department's annual report on human rights practices around the world is cited by many delegations at the United Nations as the best work of its kind. Because of the power of our media, the United States has the ability to turn an issue into one of global concern. When the United States speaks, other countries listen.

### The Unique Role of the United Nations

The seminal document in the United Nations pertaining to human rights is the Universal Declaration of Human Rights. This document was painstakingly drafted during 1947 and 1948 by a U.N. committee headed by Eleanor Roosevelt and on which former Secretary of State John Foster Dulles also served. The declaration was adopted without opposition by the General Assembly on December 10, 1948. Before casting the U.S. vote on that historic occasion, Mrs. Roosevelt told the General Assembly that she hoped the declaration might become "the international Magna Carta of all men everywhere."

The Universal Declaration of Human Rights represents the first global statement providing an objective standard for measuring the human rights performance of governments. Its adoption by more than 50 governments in 1948 is an affirmation of the word "Universal" in this document's title.  It also is an affirmation of the fact that human rights are of international concern and not merely an internal matter of sovereign states.

Although there are several U.N. organs that deal with human rights--including the General Assembly, the Commission on the Status of Women, and the Economic and Social Council--the U.N. Human Rights Commission is the United Nations' principal human rights body.  The UNHRC is one of several commissions mandated by the U.N. Charter.  It is composed of representatives from 43 member states who are elected for a 3-year term by the Economic and Social Council.  The commission meets every year in Geneva in February through early March to determine whether governments are complying with the Universal Declaration of Human Rights.

Seats on the Human Rights Commission are allocated on the basis of U.N. regional groupings:  the West European and others group, the Asian group, the East European group, the African group, and the Latin American and Carribean group.  The UNHRC has a crowded agenda, focusing on the Middle East, southern Africa, Chile, Afghanistan, Iran, El Salvador, Guatemala, Cyprus, and now Cuba.  The issues addressed by the UNHRC include religious intolerance, torture, summary and arbitrary executions, mercenaries, and disappearances.

When the United Nations was founded 43 years ago, the Western countries set the tone of the debate.  Most of the 51 member nations were democracies with a commitment to liberal principles.  Today there are 159 members of the United Nations.  Of those, 32 have fewer than 1 million citizens each.  Two-thirds of the vote in the General Assembly speak for less than 10% of the world's people, and 30 practicing democracies pay two-thirds of the bills.  According to one analysis, the proportion of prodemocratic countries in the United Nations has dropped from 60% to 40%.

The Human Rights Commission is a flawed organization.  The trend toward politicization has been a major problem faced by the commission in its handling of human rights issues.  One need only look at the tremendous changes which have taken place in U.N. membership over the past two decades to understand the drastic change which has occurred regarding the fundamental character of the United Nations and the U.N. agencies themselves.

This transformation has had a profound impact on the area of human rights and on the U.N.'s role in protecting human rights.  Human rights issues which initially were considered from mainly a technical and legal perspective have become a target of opportunity to be transformed by the Soviet bloc or radical Third World nations to a means of furthering their own political goals.  In following the imperative of bloc voting, UNHRC members like the Soviet Union and its allies band together to protect each other from international criticism and scrutiny.

The double standard in the United Nations, especially on human rights, undermines the United Nations' moral authority--and some would say its legitimacy. There are numerous examples of how this double standard is at work: The UNHRC spends an inordinate amount of time on human rights violations in the Israeli occupied territories but ignores the much greater and systematic violations that have taken place elsewhere in the region. Listening to the debate on human rights in Africa, one might believe that only South Africa violates human rights there. A 1986 U.S. resolution critizing the Ethiopian Government's resettlement policies was prevented from coming to action on the floor of the UNHRC by a procedural motion. In the case of Uganda, only now, thanks to a British grant to the advisory services fund, has the commission begun to get around to addressing the situation there.

Having pointed out some of these serious problems in the United Nations--problems which the United States must diligently and forcefully seek to correct--let me now say categorically that the United Nations matters. It does advance U.S. interests and it does make an important contribution to the world community, particularly in the area of human rights.

The concern of the United States for human rights is an integral part of our bilateral and multilateral relations. At the United Nations, our credibility on these issues has given us an advantage which helps compensate for our minority status. Regardless of how we do on votes on specific resolutions, no country wants to have its human rights record criticized by the United States. The fact that the United States raises a human rights issue is often enough to provoke a positive reaction from the country criticized. Our tough and consistent stance on human rights in the Soviet Union, for example, has undoubtedly contributed to the recent, though still too gradual, improvements in the human rights situation in that country--the world's most systematic and longest-lived violator of human rights.

Despite our credibility and sound record, however, the United States must face the need for political realism in addressing human rights at the United Nations. We are outnumbered; we represent values that too many states fear. Yet a large part of our weakness within the institution has stemmed not from the distribution of voting strength but rather from our failure to recognize international organizations for what they are: highly political arenas. Often when we have taken a position, we fail to gain support from other nations, fail to build coalitions, and many times fail to get even our closest bilateral allies to join us.

There is a real need to seek, with increasing frequency, multilateral solutions.   And, as we learned in the case of our Cuba initiative, the successful implementation of our multilateral policy depends on our ability to identify precise goals, make our concerns known to other countries, and most important, persevere in the face of initial defeat or protracted conflict.  We must be able to marshal carefully what multilateral resources we have.  When we do, we win.  When we win, the oppressed people of the world win.

## Conclusion

The Reagan Administration's activist policy in the United Nations on human rights issues owes profound thanks to Ambassador Vernon Walters and his predecessor, Ambassador Jeane Kirkpatrick, whose insistence on evenhanded treatment of human rights violations everywhere in the world set a clear standard for this government.  They have argued, sometimes against great odds, that the United Nations must ignore the regional and political alliances of its members in order to protect those who suffer at the hands of violent and oppressive governments.  They also have insisted that the United States must be willing to stand alone, if need be, in defense of impartial and universal justice.   Their respect and admiration for Armando Valladares, the U.S. representative to the UNHRC who was himself a prisoner in Castro's jails for 22 years, has been a consistent theme of their major statements before the United Nations.

Over the past several years, we have struggled to make these goals a reality.   In 1984, the Western countries succeeded in gaining a special rapporteur, Felix Ermacora of Austria, to examine the human rights situation in Afghanistan.  His early hard-hitting reports on Soviet violations of human rights in that war-riddled country finally forced the Kabul regime to allow him entry.  As the Soviet forces withdraw from Afghanistan, the United Nations will continue to monitor the extent to which human rights are respected by any new government which attempts to bring order out of chaos.

In the case of Iran, the United States has provided strong political momentum in support of a special rapporteur and in defense of minority groups persecuted by the Iranian Government.   President Reagan has spoken out on behalf of the Bahais, and we believe that his remarks, together with pressure from other governments, have helped defend the defenseless.  We will continue our watch, however lonely and unpopular, as long as the need remains.

We also take great pride in a U.S. Government initiative in the U.N. Human Rights Commission which succeeded in winning a special rapporteur on religious intolerance.   This kind of thematic approach--in this case a rapporteur empowered to report on specific instances of intolerance anywhere in the world--allows the United Nations to address problems in countries otherwise protected from criticism.  Similar approaches are taken by rapporteurs on torture and summary and arbitrary executions. The very titles of these rapporteurs underscore the urgency of the need for a continued focus on these barbaric practices still common in secret places throughout the world.

In closing, I would like to stress that, with all of its flaws, the United Nations remains the only body of its kind in the world.  It is the only arena where the tortured and abused of the world have an opportunity to lay forth their cases and stand some chance of having the world community act on their behalf.

As we commemorate the 40th anniversary of the Universal Declaration of Human Rights, I think it only appropriate to remind ourselves of the duties and responsibilities which the United States has as a founding member of the United Nations and as its largest financial contributor.  We owe it to ourselves and to the United Nations to continue our efforts to restore the original values and beliefs set forth in both the U.N. Charter and the Universal Declaration of Human Rights and to call for actions which reflect the moral authority of this great organization. When we see a situation developing which is contrary to these values, we are obligated to speak out.  We must never leave ourselves open to the shame of silence.

## A GLOBAL BEACON OF HOPE TURNS 40

December 10 marks the 40th anniversary of the adoption of the United Nations Universal Declaration of Human Rights.

Emerging from the ashes of World War II, the declaration was the first international attempt to codify basic human rights and fundamental freedoms. As "a common standard of achievement for all peoples and all nations," it lists numerous rights--civil, political, economic, social and cultural--to which people everywhere are entitled, and has become the global yardstick by which the human rights practices of governments are measured.

Anyone familiar with the U.N. system can only marvel over this remarkable achievement. In less than two years, members of the fledgling world organization were able to agree on and adopt a text on a subject which goes to the very heart of national sovereignty and the essence of ideological differences between East and West.

In remarks before the opening session of the U.N. General Assembly in Paris 40 years ago, Secretary of State George Marshall observed that "governments which systematically disregard the rights of their own people are not likely to respect the rights of other nations and other people and are likely to seek their objectives by coercion and force in the international field."

No U.N. action before or since has had as profound an effect on contemporary thinking and the lives of as many people throughout the world. The declaration's influence is arguably deeper and more enduring

---

Appeared in The Chicago Tribune, December 9, 1988.

than any other political document or legal instrument. Its political authority is second only to the U.N. Charter.

The United States takes special pride in commemorating the declaration's 40th anniversary. The declaration is rooted in the strong tradition of human rights and freedom which form the foundation of this nation. It elevates to the international level the most cherished principles and ideals enshrined in our Declaration of Independence and Bill of Rights. The words in its preamble, which proclaim that freedom of speech and belief and freedom from fear and want are the highest aspirations of all people, were inspired by the vision of President Franklin Delano Roosevelt in his four Freedoms speech during World War II.

The U.S. also played a leading role in the formulation and adoption of the declaration. President Roosevelt's widow, Eleanor Roosevelt, was head of the drafting committee and the primary force behind the declaration. Mrs. Roosevelt, who conceived of the document as "the international Magna Carta of all men everywhere," was instrumental in assisting its drafters to translate their noble ideals into simple, everyday language which could be understood by people everywhere and pressed strongly for the declaration's adoption.

Since 1948, the U.N. General Assembly has adopted more than 50 instruments on human rights intended to implement the principles of the declaration. Among the most important are the Genocide Convention, Convention on Racial Discrimination and two International Covenants on Civil and Political Rights, and Social, Economic and Cultural Rights. It is the declaration itself, however, which remains the cornerstone of a developing international consensus on human rights.

Since the declaration was adopted, countries that respect human rights have moved toward democracy, while human rights abusers have found that totalitarian rule is the only way to remain in power. The lesson is clear. The best way of assuring that governments respect the rights of the individual is to make sure they are accountable to the people.

The 40th anniversary of the adoption of the declaration is an appropriate time to reaffirm this country's commitment to the promotion of universal respect for human rights. No one can doubt the depth of this commitment. It is at the core of U.S. foreign policy and central to America's concept of itself. Over the years the U.S. has led the world in speaking out against human rights abuses and promoting steps to strengthen worldwide observance of human rights. We will continue to do so.

Regrettably, for millions of people around the world, respect for human rights is still far from reality. For them, the Universal Declaration of Human Rights remains a set of ideals whose fulfillment is a continuing quest. A long and difficult road lies ahead before these ideals are fully realized. Forty years later, the declaration continues to light that road and give strength to all those who would follow it. It remains a beacon of light and hope for all peoples.

# UNITED NATIONS CREDIBILITY REQUIRES HUMAN RIGHTS

The United Nations Human Rights Commission opens its 44th session today in Geneva. Forty-three countries elected from all of the five U.N. regional groups to three-year terms compose the UNHRC. It is the focal point of the U.N. human rights agenda, which includes review of the situation in specific countries ranging from Chile to Afghanistan, and discussion of important thematic human rights questions such as torture, religious intolerance and abusive psychiatric practices.

According to the U.N. Charter, promotion and protection of human rights are a principal purpose of the United Nations, second only to the maintenance of peace.

In 1948, a committee formed by the General Assembly under the chairmanship of Eleanor Roosevelt drafted a document which has become known as the Universal Declaration of Human Rights. In many ways it resembles America's Declaration of Independence, in that it provides for the right of self-determination and the right of individuals to choose freely their form of government. It also reflects many of the values contained in the U.S. Bill of Rights, in that it sets forth fundamental rights to freedom of expression, assembly and worship.

The architects and founders of the United Nations recognized the intrinsic role that human rights plays both in ensuring a peaceful world political order and in social and economic development. The frightful experience of World War II taught the statesman of the 1940s that governments which trample on the human rights of their citizens are prone to international aggression. Leaders of the free world understood from

---

Appeared in The International Herald Tribune, January 30, 1989.

their own national experience that countries which protected individual rights and liberties enjoyed a much greater rate of economic growth and social stability than those which did not.

U.N. human rights activities during the 1960s and '70s gave rise to concern that instead of objectively applying the standards set forth in the Universal Declaration, the U.N. majority sought to use human rights as another means of furthering political warfare. In the United Nations during that period, there was a double standard which meant that if you were a politically well connected or powerful country you were virtually immune from scrutiny of your human rights practices, but if you were relatively weak or not very popular with the U.N. "establishment" you could very easily find yourself as a nation hauled before the "bar" of the UNHRC. Those circumstances made a mockery of the objective standards for measuring human rights performances contained in the Universal Declaration.

Notwithstanding the obvious bias in the handling of human rights issues by the United Nations in recent years, several countries have demonstrated a marked improvement in their record after U.N. scrutiny. In Latin America, Chile, Guatemala and El Salvador have brought about dramatic improvements in their human rights performance, thanks partly to advice and prodding from U.N. experts.

The major U.S. objection to the United Nations' handling of human rights has been that the major violators have too often avoided the spotlight glare of publicity that is the chief U.N. weapon in reducing human rights infractions by governments. Countries like Ethiopia, Vietnam, Romania and, until last year, Cuba had avoided being subjected to U.N. resolutions and investigations. This seriously undermined the Universal Declaration and international adherence to the norms for human rights that it contains.

Last year the United Nations reached a major watershed in international human rights when it decided to undertake an investigation into the human rights situation in Cuba, including a visit by a UNHRC working group in September.

The UNHRC report is expected to indicate that the Cuban government does indeed deprive its citizens of most of the basic human rights contained in the Universal Declaration. Despite many recent acts by Fidel Castro in response to the UNHRC spotlight--acts intended to influence world public opinion, including the release of some political prisoners (which he had hitherto denied holding), permitting visits by the Red Cross and representatives of the Catholic Church, and even the toleration of a small independent human rights group in Cuba--the overall situation remains grim, and what Mr. Castro has granted under duress in the recent past he can take away tomorrow. After the UNHRC team's visit, Mr. Castro renewed his campaign of intimidation against several members of the unofficial Cuban human rights committee.

The efficacy of the United Nations in bringing about improvements by governments in their human rights record clearly lies in continuing to shine the glare of unwanted publicity upon them. A crucial test for the UNHRC therefore will lie in whether it will continue its scrutiny of Cuba, as it has continued similar scrutiny of El Salvador, Chile and Guatemala, among other countries, over a period of years.

The handling of human rights is a crucial indicator of the overall effectiveness of the United Nations. Lacking armed might, its principal force is its moral authority. Thus it must abandon political expediency and cynicism in its treatment of issues which directly affect the lives of all people. It must demonstrate consistently an ability to face up to the grave and systematic abuses of fundamental human rights which far too many people face daily.

In so doing, the United Nations will become a true champion. U.N. human rights investigations already carried out have made the difference between life and death in many individual cases. The United Nations has the capacity to be the court of last resort for the countless individuals who have no hope of due process at the hands of their own government.

If the United Nations proves unable to act in this capacity, its credibility will be damaged, perhaps irretrievably. But by demonstrating that it can uphold universal human rights standards, it can build on the upsurge in its standing resulting from recent successes in helping to arrange the end to the brutal Soviet occupation of Afghanistan and the cessation of hostilities between Iran and Iraq.

## CUBA LET OFF HOOK ON HUMAN RIGHTS ABUSES

The United Nations is held in disrepute by many because its membership too often perpetuates double standards. A few weeks ago we saw this again. Presented with overwhelming, irrefutable evidence of Cuban human rights abuses, the U.N. Human Rights Commission (UNHRC) denied the Cuban people the full victory they deserved, and gave hope to Fidel Castro that he again could hide his shameful human rights behavior. The United States cannot let this happen.

Following U.S. leadership a year ago, the UNHRC agreed to send to Cuba an investigative team composed of members of each regional group. This marked the first full U.N. human rights investigation of any Communist country (apart from Afghanistan). The investigation resulted in a 400-page report, including some 1,600 individual testimonials to human rights abuses, one of the largest ever presented to the UNHRC. The document was presented as a unanimous report from the team, including representatives from Bulgaria and Columbia.

Over the past three years the U.S. government, under Presidents Reagan and Bush, had waged an important crusade at the United Nations for Cuban human rights. Also leading this effort has been Armando Valladares, the distinguished U.S. representative to the U.N.'s Human Rights Commission who has first-hand experience of Cuban human rights violations as a former political prisoner of Castro. Thanks to their dedication, the cause of human rights in Cuba has been advanced.

This year, the report on Cuba was subject of vigorous debate. I was present in Geneva for the day-and-a-half-long debate and was impressed that only the delegation from Cuba itself denied the human rights abuses

Appeared in <u>Human Events</u>, May 13, 1989.

documented in the report. Neither their political sponsor, close allies nor Latin neighbors were so brazen as to deny the irrefutable evidence.

In the last hours of this year's UNHRC session, members were faced with two resolutions dealing with the question of how to follow up on the report on Cuba.

One, principally sponsored by the U.S., called for a continuation of the investigative team and another visit to Cuba this year.

The other, sponsored by Panama, merely places faith in the Cuban government's willingness to respond to United Nations inquiries on human rights. We sought an action-forcing mechanism as an appropriate follow-up. The Cuban government, through the Panamanian resolution, sought a more passive follow-up. Their proposal places all the burden on the U.N. Secretariat.

The U.S., West European and Morroccan proposal lost in a 17-to-17 tie, a result that was a great disappointment to those who had worked on this issue over the years. It is a sad example of the failure of the U.N. membership to confront clear, convincing evidence of massive human rights abuses. Especially disappointment were the votes of some of our friends.

Colombia is a country that prides itself on the democratic processes which guide its own government. A Colombian diplomat served on the investigative team and joined in the unanimous 400-page report that documented Cuban human rights abuses. Yet Colombia broke ranks with some other Latin American democracies to vote against us.

Mexico, as well, often spearheads efforts to ensure strict U.N. monitoring of human rights abuses in other countries. Yet on this issue, Mexico acted behind the scenes to defend Castro from the same scrutiny with it insists on for Chile and El Salvador.

The United Nations report on Cuba, a remarkable achievement in itself, contained information of widespread human rights violations. Although no final conclusions were drawn in the report, the debate indicated that no country, apart from Cuba itself, had any doubts of the repressive nature of the island prison. Examples of the trampling of human rights in Cuba abound, and I would refer the reader to the U.N. report.

Plainly, there is enough smoke arising from the Cuban human rights situation to justify ringing fire alarms. Instead, the forces of darkness chose to shield Castro from the invaluable spotlight that the United Nations alone can shine upon deplorable human rights situations such as Cuba.

The resolution ultimately adopted this year falls short of what is necessary to guarantee lasting progress on Cuban human rights.    As Armando Valladares said following the vote in Geneva on March 9, "I do not believe that Cuba will fulfill any of the terms of the resolution.  And that, in turn, will deeply affect the credibility of the commission."

Despite the setback which occurred to the cause of human rights progress in Cuba at this year's U.N. human rights meeting, the effort over the past three years has produced results.  Following last year's UNHRC session, many Cuban political prisoners were released and allowed to emigrate.  For the first time, a Communist country in this hemisphere has been subject to a full-blown human rights investigation.  Castro is now on the defensive.

The ball rests in the U.N. secretary general's court.  The credibility of the U.N.'s ability squarely to confront human rights violations anywhere in the world is again in question.  We cannot let the Cuban people down. We must continue to wage a crusade for human rights in Cuba.

We expect the United Nations to make every effort to obtain access to all aspects of Cuban society to inspect the extent to which applicable human rights are enjoyed.  This will necessarily require access to individual Cubans in order to be fully credible.  The secretary general must himself be the beacon which certain members of the UNHRC were reluctant to illuminate on their own behalf.

## THE U.N. PUTS CASTRO ON THE RUN

In 1948, an extraordinary thing happened. The member states of the United Nations adopted the Universal Declaration of Human Rights. This magnificent document set forth principles of fundamental human rights and fundamental freedoms, values embraced in our own Declaration of Independence and Constitution.

As a "common standard of achievement for all peoples and all nations," it lists numerous rights -- civil, political, economic, social and cultural -- to which people everywhere are entitled.

This document was intended to protect the weak against the strong. It set minimum standards of decency for every government to meet in dealing with their own citizens. And the U.N. Commission on Human Rights (UNHRC) provided a process by which callous governments that transgressed the human rights of their own people could be brought before the court of world opinion.

Unfortunately, over the years the U.N. Human Rights Commission fell from an objective court intended to judge human rights performances to a smoke filled room of petty politics. In the process, the member states debased the Universal Declaration on Human Rights themselves, and, worst of all, turned their back on the oppressed.

By the mid-'60s, many members of the United Nations began to organize themselves into blocs: the Islamic bloc, the Communist bloc, the developing countries (G-77), etc. These blocs serve as political parties for

---

Appeared in Human Events, March 24, 1990.

most nations within the U.N. They provide a vehicle for countries to organize, to gain strength in number and to protect themselves.

While the U.S. is not a member of any bloc, and, arguably, as a super-power does not need the benefits of participation in a bloc, one can certainly understand legitimate reasons why membership in a bloc can benefit a country, especially a smaller one. But in the arena of human rights, the blocs have worked to subvert the U.N. Universal Declaration on Human Rights.

Tragically, notwithstanding the noble intent of the drafters of the Declaration, abuses of human rights have continued to be a constant reality in many parts of the world. Nonetheless, generally the U.N. Human Rights Commission has turned a blind eye to abuses by the strong or those countries protected by bloc support.

At the same time some nations that are medium or small powers isolated and not members of blocs, such as Israel, are repeatedly challenged by the Commission, even when the facts do not sustain the allegations.

I well remember an incident a few years ago that captured for me this rise of politics over substance at the U.N. Commission on Human Rights. At the time, I was a member of the U.S. delegation to the Commission.

By a single vote, the membership had voted to avoid the substantive evidence and not consider well-documented human rights abuses of a member state. In essence, they voted not to vote on the charges.

After the vote I went over to a member of the Indian delegation that had made the motion. I asked how could representatives of India, a nation founded upon the moral courage of Mahatma Gandhi, turn their back on these clear violations of human rights. The response was revelatory.

The Indian delegate said that I shouldn't take it so seriously. "After all, Ambassador, it's only politics," she said. Those words are little comfort for the oppressed.

In recent years, there have been occasions when the commission rose above petty politics. In 1984, the Western countries succeeded in gaining a U.N. special rapporteur to examine the human rights situation in Afghanistan. The results were hard-hitting reports on Soviet violations of human rights in that war-torn country. In the case of Iran, another U.N. special rapporteur was appointed in an effort to protect minority groups persecuted by the Iranian government.

And in 1988, the commission finally acted on Cuba.

Ambassador Vernon Walters has joked that Fidel Castro has made Cuba one of the world's largest nations: its government is in Moscow, its army is in Angola, and its population is in Miami.

Well, the fact is that hundreds of thousands of Cubans have left their homeland for the United States. They have come here to flee the tyranny of Fidel Castro. According to the State Department's Bureau of Human Rights, throughout the 1980s Cuba was the single worst violator of human rights of any U.N. member state. The documentation to such an assertion is overwhelming.

In 1988, behind the leadership of Ambassador Armando Valladares, the United States delegation pressed for a UN Human Rights Commission resolution on Cuba. The Eastern Bloc and most developing countries were acutely uncomfortable with this initiative.

While the case of Castro's human rights abuses was irrefutable, it cut against fundamental internal U.N. politics to challenge the conduct of one of their own bloc. But the power of overwhelming facts coupled with vigorous lobbying by the U.S. delegation resulted in passage of a resolution calling on the Commission to undertake an investigation into the human rights situation in Cuba. In September 1988, a multinational UNHRC working group visited Cuba.

The investigation resulted in a 400-page report, including some 1,600 individual testimonials to human rights abuses, one of the largest ever presented to the UNHRC. The document was presented as a unanimous report from the investigative team, including representatives from Bulgaria and Columbia.

In 1989, at the annual UNHRC meeting in Geneva, the report on Cuba was the subject of vigorous debate. Only the delegation from Cuba itself tried to deny the human rights abuses documented in the report. Neither their political sponsor, close allies nor Latin neighbors sought to deny the irrefutable evidence. Their silence spoke volumes. Presented with overwhelming evidence, no one had any doubts about the repressive nature of that island prison.

At the end of the commission meeting, the U.S. delegation sought a resolution that called for a continuation of the investigative team and another visit to Cuba. But having slapped Castro's wrist once, the developing countries and Eastern bloc nations were reluctant to follow through on the path dictated by the evidence.

Instead, a majority favored a more passive resolution asking U.N. Secretary-General Javier Perez de Cuellar to discuss the accusations with Cuba. The resolution went on to say that "these contacts and their results will be taken up by the secretary-general in an appropriate manner."

The United States government and others repeatedly made it clear to the secretary-general that the resolution called on him to submit a report on human rights abuses by Cuba to this year's meeting of the commission.

On Dec. 11, 1989, Vice President Dan Quayle met with the secretary-general and, among other things, discussed the Cuban human rights situation. At that meeting, de Cuellar assured the Vice President that he would submit such a report if any member nation asked for it. The United States followed up with a formal request for a report.

But just before the commission meeting, the secretary-general reneged. He refused to submit a report on the human rights situation in Cuba, notwithstanding last year's resolution, unless the commission formally instructed him to do so this year. In late January, Vice President Quayle sent a strong letter of protest to Secretary-General de Cuellar for his decision to turn his back on those Cubans brutalized by Fidel Castro.

Even on an issue of fundamental human rights embraced in the Universal Declaration the secretary-general was unable to rise above the quagmire of internal U.N. politics, concerns over the possible discomfort such a report would create for the Cuban government and the balance of bloc interests of member states.

Last year's UNHRC investigative team report made clear that the Cuban government deprives its citizens of most of the basic human rights contained in the Universal Declaration. The situation is grim. And following the investigation, there are reliable reports of renewed intimidation and reprisals against witnesses and members of the unofficial Cuban human rights committee.

Violations of the UN Universal Declaration on Human Rights continue in Cuba, yet the U.N. remained silent.

The power of the United Nations to bring improvements by governments in their human rights record lies in shining the glare of unwanted publicity upon violators. Faith with the countless individuals who have no hope of due process at the hands of their own government compels action. Fidelity to the Universal Declaration requires no less.

As a tidal wave of history is bringing freedom and basic rights to millions in Eastern Europe, Panama and Nicaragua, Fidel Castro stands astride his island and shouts, "No, not in Cuba, not here!" The United Nations met its best instincts 42 years ago in drafting the Universal Declaration on Human Rights. It is ironic and sad that this year the U.N. Secretariat became Fidel Castro's co-conspirator in his efforts to isolate the Cuban people from this new wave of freedom.

Fortunately, earlier this month the member nations themselves stood tall and said to Castro that he could try to run but he could not hide.

This year's meeting in Geneva of the U.N. Human Rights Commission just completed its work. Close observers of the U.N. felt there was very little chance for progress on the Cuba issue this year. As noted, Secretary-General de Cuellar ducked the issue. And, not only had the Castro government managed to retain a membership seat on the 43-nation commission, the Cuban representative served as its vice-chairman. Nonetheless, the promise of the U.N. Declaration on Human Rights prevailed.

By a 19 to 12 vote with 12 abstentions, the commission adopted a resolution to keep Castro's human rights record under scrutiny. It states clearly that the secretary-general will submit a report at next year's meeting. It calls on Cuba to respond formally on the issue. And it urges Havana to keep its promise not to retaliate against individuals who have spoken with U.N. representatives.

Eastern European nations that in the past have opposed efforts to call the Castro regime to account supported the Cuba resolution this year. Poland and Czechoslovakia, observers at the Commission, helped sponsor it. Bulgaria and Hungary voted in favor.

Within days, Castro's security police made a series of early-morning raids rousting at least 11 human rights advocates, searching homes and confiscating papers and books. Granma, the Cuban Communist Party newspaper, said seven of the dissidents were arrested because they sent a congratulatory letter to the U.S. delegation to the U.N. Human Rights Commission. Other anti-Castro dissidents have been roughed up and spat upon in this latest crackdown.

Americas Watch, the New York City-based human rights monitoring group, said this brought to 31 the number of people detained without trial or sentenced for political crimes in Cuba since September 1988. This brings to over 200 the number of political prisoners held by Castro's government.

Clearly, the period of tolerance that began in the fall of 1988 was just an act that the Cuban government put on for the United Nations.

Castro's citadel of repression lives on. But it is becoming more and more isolated.

PART FOUR

THE U.N. AND ECONOMICS

# THIRD WORLD NEEDS FREE ECONOMIES

We gather in Vienna at the fourth general conference of UNIDO [United Nations Industrial Development Organization] mindful and painfully aware that today economic stagnation in some countries, high energy prices, extensive natural calamities, and wars that have displaced millions -- have ravaged people. These problems are painfully aggravated by the heavy debt burdens of many countries, burdens that need urgent attention.

This uncertain and troubled climate compels us to sober reflection and, hopefully, drives us to realistic and constructive results.

First, and most important, world-wide economic growth and prosperity are important on fundamental humanitarian grounds. The misery of need -- need of food, need of shelter, need of opportunity -- must be eliminated on this earth. Human decency prescribes it. Divine Providence commands it.

Second, economic progress is integral to political stability. Our thirst for worldwide peace is great, and that thirst cannot be quenched without global economic growth.

Third, in a world economy ever more subtle, complex and interrelated, each country needs others for valuable supplies to fuel the engine of its own domestic economy, and each country needs others to sell its goods. The United States, with the most successful economy in history, is no exception. We recognize the great benefits to us from global economic growth.

---

Address before the fourth General Conference of the United Nations Industrial Development Conference, Vienna, Austria, August 7, 1984.

We recognize that a key to such growth is the industrialization of the developing countries.  While critical of some aspects of UNIDO's past performance, the United States remains hopeful that UNIDO can realize its mandate to assist the industrialization of the developing countries.

We meet in Vienna at an auspicious time.  The long-sought goal of transforming UNIDO into a specialized agency now appears attainable. This provides a unique opportunity for a fresh start, a rebirth where we learn from our past experiences and re-make UNIDO with a clear eye on practical results, not blinded by the glare of dazzling polemics or succumbing to the temptation of counter-productive political declarations, but rather sobered by the real need and committed to forging partnerships for practical results.

The United States has made and continues to make an enormous contribution to worldwide economic growth and industrialization:

First, as a result of sound policies at home, regulatory relief, cutting excessive domestic spending, stable monetary policies and the supply-side stimulant of tax-rate reductions, the United States is experiencing a strong recovery, as are a growing number of other countries that either already had the proper climate for such recovery or have made the necessary policy adjustment.  Thereby, today the United States is leading the world out of global recession.

As set forth in the London economic declaration this past June: "We need to spread the benefits of recovery widely, both within the industrialized countries and also to the developing countries, especially the poorer countries who stand to gain more than any from a sustainable growth of the world economy."

Second, the United States has been and remains the most generous nation on this earth in giving economic and humanitarian aid, both bilateral and multilateral.  In the past 20 years alone, the Unied States has given over $60 billion in economic assistance to countries in all parts of the world.  This year the United States has helped revitalize the important U.N. development program through a sizably increased contribution.

In the area of assistance to developing countries, there has been dramatic progress.  In 1970, the total net flow of assistance to developing countries from the developed countries stood at $15.9 billion.  By 1981, this total had climbed to $87.9 billion.  This figure includes all direct economic assistance, grants, loans, multilateral aid, investments and export credits. Of that total, the United States provided the developing countries approximately one-third of all assistance.

In that same year, 1981, OPEC countries transferred $9.9 billion and centrally planned economies transferred just over $2 billion to developing countries. In other words, the United States alone provided approximately 13 times more resources to developing countries than all centrally planned economies combined.

But, as Lloyd George said, "You cannot feed the hungry on statistics." It is not the abstract numbers alone that are important, however generous the United States may be, but it is concrete results that matter.

Today, we face a watershed. After years of assistance money flowing to the developing world, my government and indeed the American people are becoming more and more concerned with the need for better results from development assistance contributions and are insisting on improved accountability.

The record is clear. The transfer of resources alone does not bring industrialization and economic development. Massive infusions of foreign aid alone have proven not only ineffective in stimulating economic development in the Third World; in many cases they've actually been counterproductive.

The sound premises for United States development assistance are as follows:

One: Sustained economic progress and development has not come to the Third World as the result of the transfer of resources alone. The key to progress is internal policies that promote broad-based growth, induce domestic investment, encourage private sector involvement and release the productive energies of people. In fact, resources not carefully directed to enhance the base can discourage productivity.

We believe in order to accelerate industrial growth, we need to build on the solid bedrock of personal freedom that allows individuals to reap the rewards of their efforts. Where this principle has been applied, we hve witnessed dynamic economic growth. U.S. economic assistance must be carefully targeted and must make maximum use of the energy and efforts of the private sector.

In countries such as Thailand, Singapore and South Korea, some resources were judiciously combined with sound domestic policies designed to promote broad-based growth. These policies stimulated the private sector involvement, the development and adoption of practical technologies, education and training, diversification of agriculture and industry.

Two: A principal limiter to growth has been the general environment in which the chronically poor are obliged to live. The lack of skills, education, technology, a voice in the selection of leadership are all limiters.

Three: Statism--the building of and reliance upon powerful central bureaucracies--hasn't worked. The truth is, top-heavy government structures are inefficient. Moreover, they divert scarce resources from productive purposes.

The creativity of the free enterprise system has been central to the most positive industrialization and economic growth. Whenever countries of comparable resources have run the race together -- Austria and Czechoslovakia, West and East Germany, South and North Korea--the economy with a significant private sector clearly has done more in fulfilling the economic aspirations of its people than has its statist counterpart. This is a matter of record.

As President Ronald Reagan has said, "Economic freedom is the world's mightiest engine for abundance and social justice."

Four: Poor people will change long-standing behavioral patterns when presented with an opportunity to improve their lives.

Balkanizing political declarations that establish redeployment goals are not helpful. The United States views restructuring and structural adjustments in the industrial sector as a global phenomenon occurring continuously on a massive scale primarily as a result of market forces. The United States favors policies that facilitate the increased processing of primary commodities and the evolution of industrial production in response to market forces. The United States stands ready and anxious to help provide and today does provide technical assistance and training, to help this process.

It is up to each government to take into account the structure of its own economy as well as its national plans and priorities. While each sovereign country has a right to develop in its own way, it does not have the right to expect that there will be a growing level of funds to finance whatever policies it chooses. Recipients, donors, and implementing experts alike demand that aid efforts achieve their goals.

During the fourth general conference of UNIDO, we must be practical-minded or we will miss our opportunity. President John F. Kennedy once said, "If we cannot now end our differences, at least we can help make the world safe for diversity."

Let us hope in the days ahead during this conference we can be mindful of President Kennedy's words. We can strive to appreciate our differences while being attentive to our common goal of industrialization in the developing countries and prosperity worldwide. Let us avoid confrontation on political documents and forge practical partnerships on specific programs for technical assistance.

In the words of Franklin Delano Roosevent, "The only limit to our realization of tomorrow will be our doubts of today." Mindful of the opportunity for a new, improved, strengthened UNIDO as a transformed specialized agency and sobered by the importance of our task, let us not succumb to the doubts of today.

President Reagan has said, "Expanding opportunities for economic development and personal freedom is our challenge. The American concept of peace is more than absence of war. We favor the flowering of economic growth and individual liberty in a world of peace."

We are now engaged in a worldwide war against poverty and misery, the war for industrial development worldwide. It is truly mankind's war of liberation.

# POLICIES FOR THE AMERICAS IN THE 1990s

I would like to take just a minute to note this 40th anniversary of the founding of the commission. This organization has the ability to provide clear, analytic, and insightful work to the countries of Latin America and the Caribbean. The need for such guidance has never been greater. We wish you great success over the coming years of your service to our hemisphere.

This 22d session of ECLAC is an opportunity to review the past four decades and the wide swings of the economic pendulum which have occurred. As ECLAC embarks on its fifth decade, we hope a consensus can emerge on the approach we must take to even out some of the economic swings and begin a steady climb of sustained economic progress. ECLAC can help solidify this consensus. ECLAC can help all of us to focus our efforts toward the difficult adjustments critical to economic development, toward greater private sector contribution to growth, and toward the development of strong capital markets in debtor countries.

## Relationship Between Economic and Political Freedom

Underlying the strictly economic issues which we will discuss in this 22d session is the direct relationship and interplay between economic and political freedom. This is a basic tenet of U.S. Government policy.

For Latin America, the decade of the 1980s has been marked by profound political change. It is a decade where freedom has been on the march in Latin America. Democratically elected governments have come

---

Address before the Economic Commission for Latin America and the Caribbean (ECLAC), Rio de Janeiro, Brazil, April 26, 1988.

to power in 11 countries, replacing dictatorships or military regimes. Over 90% of the peoples of Latin America and the Caribbean now live under democratic regimes, as compared to only one-third in 1976. This profound advance for democracy is tremendously encouraging.

The acceleration of democratization in Latin America is exciting and vital. But it is not in itself sufficient. Even some believers in political democracy have misguidedly infringed upon economic and personal freedoms in the service of statist or other restrictive theories of economic life. The United States is committed to the proposition that economic freedom and political freedom are inseparably linked. President Reagan is personally dedicated to this principle, which is founded on the lessons of hard experience. The evidence of the failure of the statist model is seen whenever and wherever it is compared with one based upon individual freedom of economic choice.

This connection is clear in the experience of Latin America in the 1980s. The shift to democracy coincided with a period of economic difficulties that made the job of elected governments harder. Economic gains, particularly in per capita income, were eroded by falling commodity prices, global recession, and by internal debt servicing costs. Above all, democracies were beset by lack of confidence in their own economies by citizens who withdrew huge amounts of capital from the region. It became clear, more than ever before, that fiscal deficits could not be covered by foreign borrowing. Deficiencies in the economic policies of most governments in the region were identified as the root cause of economic instability, of the massive capital flight, and of stagnation.

The task of newly elected democratic leaders in consolidating democracy consequently has been complicated by the need to reduce and reorient the government's dominant role. Governments have begun to see the need to begin to shift to market-oriented policies in order to permit their citizens to produce at levels closer to their true potential. We should never underestimate the ability and resourcefulness of our citizens to work toward a better future. As governments, we must be sure that we don't stand in their way.

Sustaining Economic Growth

The serious debt problem is symptomatic of the general economic difficulties confronting debtor countries. However, a narrow focus on the debt burden alone too often has obscured and distracted attention from the underlying and more important issue--how to put our economies on a path of noninflationary economic growth which is sustainable over the long term. For this reason, the "international debt strategy" places emphasis on the measures needed to achieve that kind of growth. The meetings of the Interim Committee and the Development Committee of the World Bank, just concluded in Washington, reaffirmed the importance of continuing a case-by-case approach to debt problems.  The Interim Committee stressed the importance of maintaining open and growing markets for debtor countries' exports and timely financial support to facilitate the pursuit of growth-oriented adjustment policies in debtor countries.

Clearly, the debt problems of the region remain of fundamental concern to us, and we recognize that a strong cooperative approach must be continued to address these problems.  Economic growth is the basis of that approach in the context of comprehensive programs of reform supported by adequate financing to support the reform process.    The international strategy to address debt problems of the region is a dynamic and evolving one.  The development of a "menu" approach to commercial bank financing packages provides additional flexibility for both new financing flows and new debt conversion techniques.   And while all of us would wish for faster progress, the results to date have been greater than generally realized.  According to the World Bank, growth last year for the five major debtors globally averages 2.5%-3% versus 3% negative growth in 1983.   Export earnings rose sharply last year to 13%, and imports were up 7%.  Debt service ratios have fallen, and, in some cases, capital flight has begun to be reversed.   And while growth in a few countries faltered last year, we expect the implementation of sound economic reform programs will allow for sustained growth in the period ahead.   We expect the international environment to remain supportive with another year of solid global growth; near 3% in industrial countries and 3.5% or more for non-oil LDCs [less developed countries].   Industrial country inflation will remain low, and global trade volumes will continue to expand.

In this context, the policy prescriptions which we make here today are based on the recognition that a free marketplace is the most efficient and productive model.  The functions of a dynamic market require a sound macroeconomic setting:  realistic exchange rates, greater fiscal discipline, market-determined pricing of goods and services, control of inflation, more liberal trade policies, and reducing other distortions which impede the function of the marketplace.  We believe ECLAC should devote much more of its efforts to studying the introduction and implementation of these tried and true prescriptions. The market makes choices based on efficiency and effectiveness.  A free market is the answer to achieving significant and lasting long-term benefits, particularly in terms of more efficient use of resources, sustainable and broad-based growth, and greater flexibility in response  to  external  change.    No  caring  government  can  avoid responsibility for the future, for the well-being of the next generation and the one after that.  Time and again, the removal of such price controls has resulted in increased supplies, and initially higher prices have then fallen-- as one would expect from the operation of free markets.

Bureaucratic and legal constraints on investment protect the firms presently operating in a market.  However, relaxation of such constraints will permit entry of new firms and in this way create far greater economic benefits. Greater employment, increase in worker skills, increased tax revenues, and a wider choice of goods and services for consumers are the result.

The hard experiences of the 1980s have prompted most countries in our hemisphere to take steps toward a consensus that economic growth requires a fundamental shift away from the statist approach. It is this emerging consensus which I believe will set the policy framework for the Americas (North, Central, and South) in the 1990s. For example, Mexico, supported by World Bank trade policy loans, has significantly reduced both tariff and nontariff barriers to trade, even surpassing Bank loan targets. Bolivia has undertaken a fundamental restructuring of its economy. Colombia, Chile, and Uruguay eliminated many price controls and impediments to private sector activity. Costa Rica, the Dominican Republic, Dominica, and Jamaica have adopted more export-oriented policies which have enabled them to take advantage of the benefits of the U.S. Caribbean Basin Initiative.

Over the past several years, the Central American democracies have adopted macroeconomic policies and programs designed to stimulate exported growth generated by the private sector. The fact that the average real growth rate of these five countries improved from a negative 4% in 1982 to a positive 2.5% in 1987 is a remarkable achievement. Argentina, Chile, and Guyana have taken steps to make state-run enterprises more efficient and in some cases to convert them to more dynamic and productive private sector management.

Despite these and other examples, the process toward free market and growth-oriented policies has been slow and there has been some backsliding. It is difficult. This process forces hard choices and requires governments to tell some special interest constituents that favorite programs cost too much. However, evidence shows that where governments encourage, rather than hinder, the development of entrepreneurship, private initiative will point the way toward economic growth. The role of the government needs to be carefully limited and defined to provide a clear and level playing field for business activity. Privatization of state-owned enterprises is only one, but an increasingly important, means to achieve this end.

As we have seen many times, private investment--whether domestic or foreign--shies away from climates of instability an1 overregulation. The massive capital flight experienced by Latin American countries in the last decade was the result of unfavorable and shifting investment climates. It will be reversed only if the owners of capital believe that the rules have changed for the long haul. Likewise, foreign investment will follow adoption of sound economic policies.

The United States is prepared to assist in efforts to encourage flows of foreign investment capital, where investors are attracted by favorable domestic policies and business potential. We have ratified the newly created Multilateral Investment Guarantee Agency and support the agency in its efforts to direct equity capital to developing countries. We encourage those governments of the region who have not yet done so, to take a careful look at the potential benefits membership could offer to their economies.

Liberalization of financial markets and the development of strong capital markets in developing countries are essential areas in which increased focus can reap large, significant, long-term benefits. For economic development to be self-sustaining, the financial sector must operate on a market basis and be capable of functioning efficiently, free of excessive regulation. Mobilizing savings, domestic as well as foreign, and the efficient allocation of these savings are critical to sustaining economic growth.

### The Need for an Open Trading System

Finally, economic growth is strongly dependent upon international competitiveness. Developing country leaders are recognizing the costs and limitations of inward-looking trade policies. The benefits of import substitutions are quickly exhausted. Such policies leave as their inheritance high-cost industries which are confined to small domestic markets and dependent on high levels of protection.

Such a waste of economic potential is particularly tragic at a time when new technologies in production and information are revolutionizing the world economy. Our capacity for producing and distributing goods and services is changing and growing in ways unimagined just a few years ago. Technology is creating an increasingly interdependent and specialized world economy. The benefits of participating in such an economy are large and growing. Attempts to live quietly and securely behind protectionist walls are a harsh sentence to economic stagnation, strangulation, and poverty.

The countries of Latin America and the Caribbean have the natural and human resources to play a major role in the world economy. Fortunately, a number of them have begun to take the steps necessary to fulfill their potential--more rational, more market-based, and more open trading regimes. Reduced protection and greater transparency in policymaking and administration of trade regimes will encourage more efficiency and innovation in production, improved competitiveness internationally, and improved allocation of domestic resources. There are costs to these policy changes. They disrupt entrenched interests and force adaptation and change. But the benefits are enormous. Real lasting economic growth will be achieved that far exceeds any transitory dislocation costs.

It is fortuitous that the current series of global trade negotiations is designated by the name of an ECLAC country. The Uruguay Round serves as a symbol of the contributions made by the region to the world economy and of the need for greater participation in the international trading system. As countries of the region achieve greater development and trade competitiveness, they have both the right and the obligation to participate more fully in the shared responsibility for the international trading system.

The Uruguay Round is aimed at a major liberalization of trade barriers, both in industry and in agriculture--a sector which is of crucial importance to so many countries of the region. Clearly, developed countries have a responsibility to lead the international progress toward trade liberalization. At the same time, the countries of Latin America and other developing regions also have an increasingly important responsibility in this process, commensurate with their growing importance in the world trading system.

Another major objective of the round is to increase the effectiveness of the GATT [General Agreement on Tariffs and Trade], so that its rules are not only improved but also are respected more fully. Again, the advanced developing countries will have a crucial role in ensuring the implementation of agreed rules negotiated in the round.

Finally, the round is aimed at adapting the international trading system to the profound changes which technology has brought and will continue to bring to international economic exchanges. Trade used to be defined in terms of "a barrel of port and a bolt of cloth" moving between London and Lisbon. It now includes such exchanges as an electronic impulse sent by a computer in Kuala Lumpur to a computer in San Francisco or a set of technical specifications from an engineer in Sao Paolo to an engineer in Rome. The rules of the international trading system must adapt to these new dynamic types of trade. Developing countries have an enormous stake in ensuring that the benefits of technological innovation are exchanged as freely and as competitively as possible.

The United States has long been a leader in the drive toward a more open and integrated international economic system. We remain strongly committed to resisting protectionist pressures, not only because we believe such a world best serves our own long-term interests but also because it is the surest and fastest route to long-term, self-sustaining growth for the developing world.

### Conclusion

My delegation came to the 22d session of ECLAC because we remain concerned, engaged, and optimistic about the economic future of our hemisphere. All of us have long pointed to the great potential which exists for many countries in the region and for the hemisphere as a whole. The

United States is committed to help realize this potential in our bilateral relations and through multilateral institutions and organizations. We will continue our support for the international financial institutions as evidenced most recently by the agreement on a general capital increase of the World Bank. We will continue to support and further the objectives of our international institutions as we strive to maintain a domestic market open to the exports of developing countries.

Our hope is that the governments of our Latin American and Caribbean neighbors will be able to use the available support to develop the untapped human, material, and financial resources of the hemisphere. To succeed, critically important economic policies to support sustained growth must be put in place. However, if we work together, we can look forward to realizing the potential for dynamic, sustained economic growth too long unfulfilled.

It is up to us, the members of ECLAC, to insist that our organization meet the needs of the present and of the future--not those of times past. This can be an important forum for intellectual leadership to spur economic growth and advance human dignity.

I began my talk with a reference to the 40 years which have passed since the founding of this organization. I will conclude with the observation that the first inter-American conference, called by Simon Bolivar, met more than 160 year ago. There is no more fitting time to rededicate ourselves to the dream of the Americas.

# U.N. ECONOMIC RHETORIC MOVES TOWARD THE REAL WORLD

The contentious debates that marked most efforts to use the United Nations to help set a broad framework for international economic cooperation in the '60s, '70s, and early '80s have largely ended. Now, we are beginning to see indications of change forced by the reality of unsuccessful economic policies in LDCs. Many developing countries appear ready to put aside "quick fixes" in favor of more serious and practical approaches to economic development.

In some cases, the changes are found in nuance only, but in others there are important changes in direction and orientation. The voices that heretofore would have shouted down any talk of entrepreneurism, the role of free markets or the costs of capital flight as attempts by the West to impose "foreign systems" on their economies, now venture forth, even if tentatively, to look for more dynamic means to spur industrial growth. In many instances, this has meant a new look at the role of the free market.

A case in point is the U.N. Commission on Transnational Corporations. The Commission on TNCs has been a forum for confrontation between the developed and the developing countries regarding jurisdiction over multinational corporations, their value to host countries, and the need for domestic and international regulation. In debate, statements frequently compare the private sector to the public sector as a engine for development. Egged on by Soviet-bloc spokesmen, developing countries have sought to strengthen their moral bargaining power with TNCs through accusations of past exploitation, indifference to development objectives, support of apartheid and similar charges. Theorists from developing countries assumed that their economic

---

Appeared in The International Economy, October, 1988.

bargaining power was strong because the multinationals urgently needed to exploit the resources and markets of the developing countries. They had only to put up a unified front in order to gain foreign investment on better terms.

Expectations of greater investment flows, however, were frustrated by diminishing demand for basic commodities. Compounding the effects of lowered volumes and prices, the data on declining and stagnant economies among the developing world frightened away new investment. The newly industrializing countries of Asia, on the strength of free-market policy prescriptions and models, attracted significant foreign investment, and many developing countries suffered by comparison. The sudden and unexpected reversal of economic policy, first in China and then in the Soviet Union, created two new competitors for direct investment. In fact, at the most recent meeting of the Commission on TNCs, one developing country delegate criticized the U.S. for competing for growing amounts of investment capital from Japan and elsewhere.

The chairman of the Commission, Victor Gbeho of Ghana, in opening the recent session, remarked that the era of confrontation between the TNCs and the developing countries had given way to a new pragmatism and that there had been a shift "from denunciation to negotiation." Reflecting a sense of this change, the staff director declared at the beginning of his report to the Commission that the question now is not whether the TNCs are good or bad, but rather, how to take advantage of their potential contribution to development.

Belatedly, developing countries have begun to realize that they have to compete for foreign investment. At a time when foreign debt has become an overwhelming concern, many developing countries appreciate that foreign direct investment is one means to lessen their debt burden in addition to providing its traditional benefits of diversification, technical progress and other aspects of development.

This is not to say that the developing countries want the Commission to become a model of free-market economic thinking. On the contrary, delegates have continued to use the forum offered by the Commission to push North/South issues on debt, apartheid and alleged TNC shortcomings on environment and social policy issues. It is important, however, to differentiate between developing country views on TNCs and their views on the private sector in general; the latter seem to be enjoying a higher acceptability or even preference. Even the Soviets used the meetings to seek endorsement of joint ventures. It also is important to differentiate between the way that developing countries behave in political forums like the Commission, as opposed to their conduct in direct bilateral negotiations with TNCs, where investment, transfer of technology and jobs are at stake. Perhaps the Nigerian delegate best expressed the new thinking of developing countries when he said that times have changed and that the

Commission should examine how LDCs can attract foreign investment and how transnational corporations can contribute to development.

We have seen even more striking evidence of change in the international financial institutions.  Only a few years ago developing-country officials generally rejected the concern and economic advice offered by banking and Western government representatives.  In contrast to the developing-country foreign ministry representatives who participate in international economic meetings, these officials generally bear major responsibility for the economic decisionmaking in their countries.  More recently there has been a sea change in attitudes towards the "advice" they receive from these institutions.  This has been most apparent among African representatives whose countries often have been the worst hit by the depressed commodity prices and poor domestic management.

Further evidence of this change is borne out by African views expressed during the 1986 Special Session on Africa and views reportedly expressed within the Organization for African Unity.  The African ministers, who had met in Addis Ababa to draw up their report for the conference, described it as a critical self-examination of the nature of the African development crisis.  Such an inwardly critical analysis by developing countries was unprecedented in international organizations.

Furthermore, discussions with African officials reveal an emerging pragmatism.  There is increasing evidence that those countries willing to support structural reform to reduce the role of the state in the economy now show the best chances for viability.  By contrast, those countries that took the socialist path to development now number among the poorest of the poor.  Cameroon, an early pioneer in this new pragmatism, has been followed by Ghana and Senegal, which, after taking stringent restructuring measures, including a reduction of the public sector and an expansion of private enterprise, have begun to reverse the earlier deterioration of their economies.  Tanzania, which had been a leading proponent of African socialism, has begun to examine ways to give the private sector a new start.  In a more dramatic turn, Guinea, a country that endured more than two decades of stringent and severely debilitating socialism under its charismatic founder, Sekou Toure, has seen a sharp change in economic policies under new leadership.

As a result, some U.S. companies are showing renewed interest in investing in countries that have demonstrated this new pragmatism.  In the Congo, a consortium of American interests composed of Skaarup Petroleum, National Rural Electric Cooperative Association and Johnson & Towers has invested in a formerly government-owned forestry project to produce telephone poles for the region. Dupont is investing in a titanium project in Senegal and Heinz has invested in a tomato-paste plant in Zimbabwe.

Today, some members of the G-77 refuse to give up what they perceive as a political advantage by continuing the ideological confrontation between North and South. India, Brazil and Cuba invariably are found among the leaders of groups that pursue such confrontational tactics in the U.N. Depending upon the issue and the forum, other leading contributors often include Mexico, Zimbabwe and, somewhat less frequently, Tanzania. Unfortunately, within G-77 councils disagreement on a course of action is generally resolved in favor of the most radical or hard-line position, often argued as a necessary response to a threat from the West.

But, with the exception of Cuba, these countries act differently in these political forums than they do when their own interests are truly at stake. India has a very strong free market, Brazil is attempting to develop one and Mexico has taken major steps to privatize many of its key industries.

We must work toward eliminating the contentious politicization that remains in the economic debate between developed countries. We should focus on development issues and thereby support our overall international economic interests. This requires a more closely coordinated U.S. policy in economic forums. It requires more consultation with like-minded governments and use of their strengths in seeking our common goals. If this is successful, U.S. initiatives would less frequently become the focal point against which to rally G-77 resistance. A great deal of the current G-77 resistance to private sector programs is a negative political response to U.S. leadership, rather than hostility to the ideas themselves. We must encourage others to take the lead on contentious issues from time to time-- some would be happy to do so.

It is important that the U.S. government enlist the assistance of business and other non-governmental organizations, especially those with a multinational base. Finally, we should fully support the idea of helping create a healthy new class of entrepreneurs in the less advanced developing countries, largely apart from the traditional business community and the government. A successful effort in this regard, over the long run, would consolidate any success we may achieve in international and regional organizations.

If initiatives such as these are successful, we will be able to claim with justification that "North/South" debates are relics of the past. We may look forward to a reduction of the shrill and counterproductive confrontation that has characterized discussion of economics in U.N. agencies and to a new, more constructive and responsible role for these agencies in shaping approaches and international consensus on solutions.

PART FIVE

THE U.N. AND PEACEKEEPING

# STATUS REPORT ON AFGHANISTAN

I welcome this opportunity to appear before this committee for the first time since Secretary Shultz asked me to assume the job of Coordinator for Afghan Affairs. I look forward to working closely with this committee as we move forward with the implementation of the Afghan accords, which were signed in April in Geneva.

Under Secretary Armacost has given you a comprehensive overview of the political-military situation in Afghanistan. As he indicated, I will focus on our bilateral and multilateral effort to aid the refugees who fled from Afghanistan and the displaced persons within that country.

## The Objective: Return of the Afghan Refugees

For years the safe and honorable return of the Afghan refugees has been a major objective of the United States and the international community. Their return, as well as that of the displaced persons, will enable them to participate in the political and economic reconstruction of their country. It will help carry forward the process by which the Afghan people exercise their right of self-determination and establish their own government.

As the Afghan people return home, they hope to begin rebuilding their lives after enduring almost 9 years of Soviet occupation and the destruction of much of their country. However, as Prince Sadruddin Aga Khan, the newly appointed U.N. Coordinator for Humanitarian and

---

Statement before the Senate Foreign Relations Committee, United States Senate, Washington, D.C., June 23, 1988.

Economic Assistance in Afghanistan, has pointed out, this expectation of better things to come can turn into a crisis of hope.  As he notes: "Unless the essential needs of normal life can be quickly met, hope may be just as quickly followed by despair and renewed suffering."

The refugee and related issues pose a daunting challenge to the international community.  The demands for expertise, experience, and finance compel an international response to which the United Nations and its technical and development agencies must provide leadership.  This is one of the principal functions for which the United Nations was created - to help put into place the building blocks of peace and create the conditions "to give peace a chance."

The Afghan people are hardy and capable.  Their valor and self-reliance are impressive.  But despite their resilience, self-reliance, and downright toughness, the Afghan refugees need our help.  The international community must rise to the occasion to assist the refugees as they return to homes in rubble, fields laced with mines, and destroyed irrigation systems - so vital in an arid country such as Afghanistan.

### Organizing To Achieve the Objective

In recent months, we have put a great deal of energy and effort into assuring the creation of a U.N. relief and resettlement program for the Afghan people that runs efficiently, effectively, and without duplication. Beginning in March, I spoke with the Secretary General on several occasions, urging him to appoint a special coordinator who could organize and manage this type of U.N. effort and obtain the necessary contributions from the donor nations.  Secretary Schultz raised the issue with U.N. officials when he signed the Afghan accords in Geneva on April 14.  We continued to campaign for such an appointment right up to the announcement on May 11 that Prince Sadruddin Aga Khan had been selected as the special coordinator. We strongly applauded his selection.

We have already had extensive contact with Prince Sadruddin.  I spoke with him immediately following his appointment and consulted with him in Geneva at the end of May following his visit to Afghanistan, Pakistan, and Iran.  At that time, I shared with him our ideas on the U.N. assistance effort and ascertained how his thinking was evolving.  On June 13, 3 days after the Secretary General announced the U.N. appeal, Prince Sadruddin came to Washington for meetings with President Reagan, Vice President Bush, and Secretary Shultz - an indication of the importance which we place on Prince Sadruddin's role and coordinated U.N. action.  On June 14, I attended the first donor's meeting in New York, which was chaired by Prince Sadruddin.

Because Prince Sadruddin's office is in Geneva, we have appointed Ambassador Petrone, U.S. Permanent Representative to the U.N. offices in

Geneva, to serve as his principal U.S. Government interlocutor with that office.  As his work progresses, Prince Sadruddin is committed to provide frequent briefings to us and other donors on his planning and interaction with the various U.N. agencies.

Within the executive branch, we have also moved to organize ourselves so that we can administer the Afghan relief program in a coherent and effective manner.  As always, major decisions will be taken by the President or Secretary Shultz or by Under Secretary Armacost as the Secretary's designee.  I, of course, participate in the policymaking process.  The additional role the Secretary recently asked me to undertake was to serve as coordinator of our Afghan policy, with particular emphasis on the follow-up to the Geneva accords.  I have established an interagency working group, which meets every day, to help me with this complex task. In addition, Under Secretary Armacost chairs a weekly meeting to review all aspects of our Afghan policy.   For the indefinite future, we will continue these daily and weekly meetings, monitoring the situation closely in Afghanistan and continuing close coordination and consultations within our own government and with Prince Sadruddin.

## The U.N. Assistance Program

Prince Sadruddin has moved with record speed in developing a coordinated U.N. program.  Less than a month after his appointment, the Secretary General was able to issue his appeal to donors and supply them with an outline (to be refined later) for the cooperative work of the various U.N. agencies.  Other meetings will be scheduled after donors have had time to study the relevant documentation.

I am submitting to the committee a copy of the report [U.N. document SG/CONF. 3/1] distributed at that meeting, which you may wish to include in the record.  The report provides an overview of the proposed relief and resettlement program, with details about the structure and phased sequencing in the various sectors of food, agriculture, irrigation, health, and in logistical backup.   The report emphasizes that, as the refugees return home, the focus must be on immediate and basic support - e.g., providing food and aid and agricultural supplies (seed and tools), repairing local irrigation canals, and delivering basic health care.

In its introduction, the report acknowledges that what is presented is "no more than the first outline of a picture"--a picture that will have to be refined in the coming months as more information becomes available and circumstances evolve.  Even the estimated total cost for the first phase of the program (approximately $1 billion) is subject to revision.

Nonetheless, the underlying philosophy upon which the program is predicated will not change.  The Administration supports that approach.  As developed in the report, the program is based on these key principles.

Humanitarianism. The report explicitly states that the relief effort must be seen as being a humanitarian effort and notes that the Secretary General has clearly distinguished it from his political good offices.

Decentralization. The report states that it would be unrealistic to attempt a nationwide rehabilitation effort at the present time. Rather, program efforts will be focused at the regional level as conditions permit.

People to People. Aid will be channeled directly to the refugees as they return.

In summary, the report states that "the fundamental purpose of this programme is to link people back to their homes and engender self-reliance in order to avoid institutionalizing relief." We could not agree more.

There are basic principles that must underlie the U.N. effort to ensure the success of its program. The United States opposes U.N. financial assistance flowing through the Kabul regime. It must not be administered in a way that permits that illegitimate regime to enhance its political standing within the country. This position is firmly held by the United States. Secretary Shultz has emphasized this point on several occasions. I stressed the idea at the June 14 donors' meeting, insisting that "the U.N. assistance should be provided directly to the refugees and displaced persons as they return home, that the agencies involved must ensure that the aid indeed gets to the intended recipients and that humanitarian goals alone drive the effort." Other donors, such as Great Britain, the Federal Republic of Germany, and Japan, also voiced on that occasion their opposition to the Kabul regime obtaining any control over U.N. financial assistance.

Prince Sadruddin and other senior U.N. officials have assured us that they understand the strength of this shared concern and that they hold a similar view. We have made clear--and will continue to do so--that we will be watching this matter very closely. Working with Prince Sadruddin, we are confident that the U.N. effort will be directed in ways supportive of the interests of the Afghan people.

## U.S. Contributions

Let me now turn to our contribution and role in this relief effort. In fiscal year (FY) 1988, the United States budgeted $119 million in humanitarian assistance to the Afghan refugees. Approximately $49 million of this assistance goes through multilateral channels - specifically, the U.N. High Commissioner for refugees and the World Food Program - to assist the more than 3 million refugees in Pakistan. The remainder, consisting of food and agricultural equipment, medicine and medical supplies, and educational training and materials, is provided bilaterally, primarily to people still within Afghanistan.

Not only does the bilateral program assist needy Afghans, it has encouraged them to remain in their country rather than fleeing to Pakistan and placing and additional burden on the Pakistani Government and people.  Throughout the years of conflict in Afghanistan, Pakistan has earned the admiration of the world for its courageous stand against Soviet intimidation and the provision of refuge for millions of homeless Afghans. Our bilateral program, initiated with strong and bipartisan congressional input and support, has been generously funded.

Despite budgetary constraints, we intend to maintain an overall level of bilateral and multilateral aid around $119 million in FY 1989. We are also seeking--within existing funding--additional resources, particularly food aid, to contribute to our Afghan assistance effort. We have recently identified for this fiscal year an additional 80,000 metric tons (MT) of wheat and 3 million MT of dried skim milk for the multilateral effort and 20,000 MT of wheat for our bilateral assistance--approximately $23 million in food and transportation charges. Hence, our overall assistance for FY 1988 will total about $142 million. Consistent with the agreement last fall with the Congress, however, we do not intend to seek a supplemental for Afghan assistance.  Our continuing programs are consistent with, supportive of, and will be closely coordinated with the U.N. effort. As the refugees return home, an increasing proportion of our aid will follow them into Afghanistan.

We are encouraging other donors to contribute substantially to the Afghan assistance effort. In our appeals, we point out that we are by far the largest donor of humanitarian assistance to Afghans and that others should now assume a major share of the new burden as the refugees begin their return home.

We are making clear to the Soviet Union that it should make a major financial contribution to the special international assistance effort.  It destroyed the country of Afghanistan; it is obligated to pay a major part of the bill to rebuild it.  But its contribution to the United Nations must come without strings or any requirement that the funds be used to bolster the illegitimate Kabul regime.  Soviet and U.N. officials understand our position clearly.

The U.S.S.R. should certainly assist in eliminating the danger to the refugees of the millions of mines Soviet and Kabul forces have sown across the roads and fields throughout most of Afghanistan.  No humanitarian task is more important than the removal or destruction of these mines.  They are a major obstacle to permitting the safe return of the refugees and allowing them to begin cultivating their land.  We and the United Nations are pushing the Soviets to stop laying mines, remove the mines they can, and provide information on minefield locations so that any remaining mines can be removed quickly.

I mentioned at the onset my profound belief that the United Nations must lead the international community in meeting the challenge of the Afghan refugees. I am convinced it will succeed and, in doing so, help advance interests of major importance to the United States. There are legitimate grounds for criticizing some of the failings of the United Nations. I have done so when I believed such criticism was warranted, as have many Members of Congress.

But, even as we seek to criticize constructively, we must not forget the indispensable work the United Nations does--work essential to global peace, stability, and development; work that benefits directly our national and international interests.

More specifically, the U.N. system is uniquely placed to lead the multinational effort to aid the Afghan refugees. It has the capacity to coordinate and pool resources. Contributions made in isolation by small nations with limited aid programs, for example, would be much less effective and productive than when channeled through the U.N. system. The specialized agencies also have had decades of experience managing the various issues associated with major refugee programs (e.g., distributing food aid and providing health care). Finally, the United National can undertake refugee programs in countries such as Iran where individual nations cannot. For all these reasons, the U.N. effort on behalf of the Afghan refugees is important and should be supported.

## Conclusion

In conclusion, the international community faces a major challenge. We will not relax our vigilance until the last Soviet troops are gone, until all the refugees who want to return are able to do so, and until the proud Afghan people have established, through self-determination, a representative government that serves their needs and sustains their traditions.

Let me assure you that the Administration will work closely with other donors, the U.N. coordinator and U.N. agencies, and the Congress in the critically important endeavor. We will do our share to transform this challenge into an achievement.

# REAFFIRMING OUR SUPPORT FOR AFGHAN CAUSE

The Afghan resistance is within sight of the goals for which it has struggled with such courage and determination over the last nine years -- an Afghanistan freed of the Soviets' brutal occupation and a government reflecting the will of the Afghan people. The recent visit of an Afghan resistance delegation led by current Alliance Spokesman Professor Burhanuddin Rabbani provided an opportunity to reconfirm basic U.S. policy principles.

This administration and the Congress have provided strong, sustained support for the Afghan freedom fighters. President Ronald Reagan, Vice President George Bush and Secretary of State George Shultz reaffirmed U.S. support in the recent series of meetings with the resistance. The consultations also confirmed that the resistance has not been and will not be intimidated by recent Soviet military escalation and threats, nor deterred from achieving complete independence for their country.

Simultaneously with their military advances, the Mujaheddin are actively pursuing a peaceful political settlement. While in the United States, Mr. Rabbani elaborated on the resistance's proposal for a national assembly (shura) to start the process leading to a broad-based, representative government established through self-determination.

The proposal contrasts with various power-sharing concepts advanced by the Soviets and the Soviet-backed regime (PDPA) in Kabul; their objective is to assure a formal role for the PDPA in any future Afghan government, a position the Mujaheddin hold to be unacceptable.

---

Appeared in The Washington Times, November 28, 1988.

The U.S. position is clear and consistent -- while we have no blueprint of our own, we will support a political arrangement that ensures the establishment of a broad-based government that fulfills the aspirations of the Afghan people for self-determination.

In our view, the proposal advanced by Mr. Rabbani on October 31 offers a promising opportunity. The point to keep in mind is that the future development of Afghanistan is for the Afghan people themselves to decide. We have urged the Soviets to talk directly with the resistance.

During the recent discussions, the U.S. and Afghan interlocutors agreed that after the war is over major refugee repatriation and reconstruction requirement must be met. Mr. Rabbani expressed gratitude for past U.S. humanitarian assistance -- more than $750 million since 1980, far more than provided by other donors. During fiscal 1989, U.S. bilateral and multilateral humanitarian assistance to Afghanistan will total around $150 million.

Since the resettlement and reconstruction needs far exceed the resources of any one donor and the needs will be long-term, the United States supports the United Nations' taking the lead in mobilizing humanitarian assistance for the Afghan people; we agreed to support Mr. Rabbani's plea for emergency provision of food aid, medical needs and mine-clearing assistance.

The United States, other major donors, and the resistance agree that U.N. assistance must not be provided through the illegitimate regime in Kabul, or in any way that the Kabul regime could manipulate to its political advantage. The United Nations understands the strength of our position on this issue.

The Soviet Union must accept the reality that freedom is coming soon for Afghanistan. This will not be changed by an intensification of Soviet military action, which will be no more successful than earlier efforts to break the will of the Afghan people or the steadfastness of their supporters in Pakistan, the United States and throughout the world. We have made this clear to Moscow.

To paraphrase Mr. Shultz' comments in the joint press meeting with Mr. Rabbani on November 9, the Soviets should never have invaded Afghanistan; they should not be there now; and the only way to resolve the problem is for them to leave -- the sooner, the better.

In signing the Geneva Accords, the Soviets assumed a formal international obligation to do just that no later than February 15, 1989. They reconfirmed this obligation with the consensus resolution on Afghanistan adopted by the U.N. General Assembly on November 3.

The international community expects them to meet that obligation, not least because the domestic and foreign-policy costs they will incur if they fail to do so would be enormous.

# THE UNITED NATIONS AS PEACEKEEPER

## I. INTRODUCTION

In September 1988, during President Reagan's final address to the United Nations, he turned to Javier Perez de Cuellar and said, "Mr. Secretary General, through your persistence, patience and unyielding will, [you] have shown, in working toward peace in Afghanistan and the Persian Gulf, how valuable the United Nations can be." Within days, U.N. peacekeeping forces were awarded the Nobel Peace Prize. This certainly is a dramatic change. After almost a decade in which U.N. peacekeeping efforts seemed to have withered on the vine, U.N. peacekeeping today is playing a large role in many critical areas. It deserves a serious review.

While the United Nations was founded "to save succeeding generations from the scourge of war" (Charter Preamble) and "to maintain international peace and security" (Article I), peacekeeping as such is not mentioned in the Charter and the term itself did not come into use until a decade later. The founders of the U.N. had their eyes set on grander things. They envisioned the U.N. as organizing a system of collective security, in a world largely disarmed in which the Security Council would enforce the peace. The legal basis for the Security Council's action was contained in Chapters VI and VII of the Charter; and the veto assured Permanent Members that no action could be taken contrary to their fundamental interests.

That was the ideal in 1944. The realities of the Cold War from 1945 on demonstrated the impracticality of such grand thinking and rendered

---

Appeared in <u>World Outlook</u> (Dartmouth College), Winter 1989, No. 8.

inoperable the Charter provisions concerned. For collective security, the United States turned to like-minded nations which joined it in establishing the North Atlantic Treaty Organization (which, interestingly, reaffirms the signatories' adherence to the Charter and justifies NATO's central obligation as an expression of collective defense under Article 51 of the U.N. Charter).

What subsequently happened in the U.N., however, was both constructive and creative. Chapter VII fell into disuse (until it was revived in Resolution 598 1/), but the United States, working with like-minded countries and with members of the Secretariat such as former Under Secretary General Brian Urquhart, created Chapter "6 1/2" which allowed the U.N. through peacekeeping operations to do more than simply encourage the peaceful settlement of disputes but to stop short of enforcement action. U.N. peacekeeping developed as an extra-constitutional device which responded to real requirements in conflict situations. It provided contending parties with a way out of confrontation and, significantly, for many years was viewed as a way of allowing the U.S. and the USSR to avoid military involvement in Third World conflict situations and thus reduce the risk of superpower confrontation.

During its more than 40 years of existence, U.N. peacekeeping operations have enjoyed mixed success. According to Secretary General Perez de Cuellar, since the founding of the United Nations more than 20 million people have died in well over 140 armed conflicts. What does that mean for U.N. peacekeeping and its role in today's world?

The reality is that the U.N. is not, and cannot be, in a position to end all conflicts, whether they involve Viet Nam, the Beagle Channel or Eritrea. It is able, in certain circumstances, to contain conflict, to ameliorate its impact, and to provide an impetus for peaceful settlement and a means to bring the parties together on the terms conducive to resolving their differences. While this role is not all encompassing, when performed well it can be critical. The U.N.'s peacemaking and peacekeeping roles are distinct parts of the same process. In Afghanistan and Iran-Iraq, the U.N. is playing both. In Namibia and Angola, the U.N. will concentrate on the latter function.

Since its inception, the United Nations has had thirteen significant peacekeeping operations (excluding the international force in Korea, an enforcement action which was not under direct U.N. control). Some of these efforts have been deemed successful, while others have failed to achieve reasonable expectations.

Nonetheless, today we face profound opportunities, and many challenges, for the United Nations in the peacekeeping area. As one U.N. observer quipped. "Peace seems to be breaking out all over." In

Afghanistan, Iran-Iraq, Namibia, Cyprus, the Western Sahara, and Kampuchea (Cambodia), the U.N. is moving center stage in helping to resolve significant regional conflicts which have cost many lives and, in some cases, become tinderboxes with the potential to explode into major power confrontations.

While it is important for the United States to recognize and support the significant positive role played by the U.N. in the peace process, it is equally important not to be caught up in the euphoria of this apparent new momentum nor to lose sight of the practical limitations of the U.N.'s capacity in this area. A new and heightened sense of realism is needed so that we may learn from the peacekeeping endeavors of both the past and present, and improve and strengthen the United Nations as a peacekeeping tool.

The effectiveness of U.N. peacekeeping patently depends on the willingness of the belligerents to accept a U.N. peacekeeping role. The availability of a U.N. presence can hasten a cessation of hostilities by providing an honest broker between the parties, an objective means to verify ceasefire agreements, moral pressure on the parties not to renew fighting, and a justification to accept what would otherwise be a politically embarrassing defeat. In short, while the U.N. cannot impose peace in a conflict situation, it can play an important facilitating role.

## II.  CHARACTERISTICS OF U.N. PEACEKEEPING FORCES

Article 43 of the U.N. Charter called for member countries to make available to the Security Council, on its call, forces and facilities as may be deemed necessary for the maintenance of international peace and security. The machinery proposed in Article 43 created unrealistic expectations. Even if it had been possible to reach agreement on the composition and administration of the U.N. forces under Article 43, it is quite problematic whether it would have been able to be used. One can be almost certain that one permanent member or another would have felt utilization of Article 43 would have been to the disadvantage of his interests and therefore used the veto.

Indeed, this was the fundamental weakness of the Military Staff Committee, which was created by the Charter to assist the Security Council and was to consist of the "Chiefs of Staff of the permanent members of the Security Council or their representatives." Despite apparent renewed Soviet interest in resurrecting the moribund MSC, there is no reason to believe it would be any more effective today than it was in 1945. The practical consequences of relying on the MSC would be to weaken the pragmatic institution of U.N. peacekeeping as it has evolved in the past four decades.

The concept of peacekeeping as it has evolved in the U.N. is an outgrowth of the "preventive diplomacy" ideas of the United Nations' second Secretary General, Dag Hammarskjold. Hammarskjold considered it part of the task of the U.N. Secretariat to help stabilize areas of conflict so that parties might be brought together. He felt this was particularly necessary in those parts of the world from which the European colonial powers were withdrawing, lest the United States or the Soviet Union be drawn into a simmering dispute. In the 1950s and 1960s, when East-West confrontation cast a shadow over the process of decolonization, the institutions of the United Nations took an active role on several fronts, including peacekeeping.

Peacekeeping, as it evolved within the United Nations, represents an innovation. It is not, however, the enforcement envisioned under Chapter VII of the Charter. Peacekeeping operations can only be set with the agreement of the parties in conflict. The United Nations' aim in these operations is not to enforce peace but to contain explosive situations and give peace a chance. The forces are present with the consent of the host governments and are not supposed to interfere in domestic politics. On the whole, they are lightly armed for self-defense purposes only.

Peacekeeping forces are made up of troops mainly from small or non-aligned states, only exceptionally accepting contributions from a permanent member of the Security Council.2/ Peacekeeping operations are created essentially as holding actions, designed to halt or control the conflict while concerted efforts are made to bring the warring parties to the negotiating table. They also can serve as a transition mechanism which provides the time and helps create the climate necessary to bring about a peaceful settlement.

Peacekeeping operations have traditionally been employed in regional conflicts. Typically they fulfill two types of roles: (a) peace observation, which involves the limited monitoring and reporting of a conflict situation; and/or (b) traditional peacekeeping, meaning the interposition of an impartial and objective third party to help create and maintain a ceasefire and form a buffer zone between opposing forces.

United Nations peacekeeping efforts operate under specific mandates set by the U.N. Security Council, where the United States has a veto. Often, they seek not to enforce a particular settlement but to prevent the spread of an already existing conflict under an established term of reference. They exist to supervise or observe a ceasefire, a disengagement or the status quo, though their presence may eventually contribute to peaceful solution of the dispute. And, in some cases, they are long-lasting operations whose very presence serves to inhibit fighting and reduce tensions in areas of conflict, such as in Cyprus or southern Lebanon.

Another requirement of a successful peacekeeping operation is a broad political consensus among the interested parties for its mandate. It requires the continuing support of the countries or parties principally concerned in the conflict, as well as the continual active support of the Security Council, particularly the five Permanent Members who can alter or terminate its mandate during periodic renewals. In addition, the states contributing troops have to be satisfied that the effort is worthwhile for their participation to continue.

From the outset, U.N. peacekeeping operations have been by nature sui generis, based on specific needs and tailor-made for the situation at hand. In opposing the idea of a permanent U.N. force, Dag Hammarskjold believed that: "We need really to cut the suit to the body. . . . We cannot afford, or usually have, a wardrobe sufficiently rich and varied to be able to pick out just the right suit as the situation arises. It is much better to have the cloth and go into action as a good tailor, quickly when the need arises."

Since the first U.N. peacekeeping effort in Palestine in 1948, peacekeeping operations have become an important technique in international conflict management. The call for multinational peacekeeping forces to help control regional conflicts has become virtually automatic, notwithstanding the mixed record of success over the last 40 years. There are presently seven operations under way involving some 12,500 troops. These peacekeeping efforts range from 38 observers along part of the India-Pakistan border to a buffer force of 5,700 troops in southern Lebanon. Other major conflicts--Angola/Namibia, Cambodia, and Western Sahara-are candidates for peacekeeping forces, perhaps within the coming months.

Most U.N. peacekeeping operations have fulfilled a useful purpose in one way or another. The UNEF II and UNIFIL operations are just two "case studies" which point to the need to study past endeavors in order to understand the current capabilities and limitations of U.N. peacekeeping.3/

UNITED NATIONS EMERGENCY FORCE, 1973-1979 (UNEF II).

The Arab-Israeli October 1973 War presented a risk of escalation to superpower involvement and thus impelled a recourse to the U.N. despite the deep divisions among the powers over the war. Through acrimonious debate, the Security Council produced three resolutions in rapid succession calling for a ceasefire, the last establishing a new U.N. Emergency Force under the operational control of the Secretary General, who was in turn subject to the authority of the Security Council. The resolution also approved a set of general guidelines for the day-to-day management of the Force. With slight modifications, these guidelines have formed the basis for managing all subsequent U.N. peacekeeping efforts.

While in existence, UNEF II went through three phases:  as an interposing force and observation element between the Egyptian and Israeli armies; then as an instrument to control the process of separation and disengagement; and finally as a force that manned the zone of disengagement (from base camps located on the Egyptian side).

UNEF II functioned effectively and was an important factor in creating the circumstances which made possible the subsequent Egyptian-Israeli peace agreement.  While it had been anticipated that another U.N. force would be created to replace UNEF II in supervision of the terms of that agreement, Arab and Soviet opposition made that impossible.  A non-U.N. multilateral force, supported by the United States and others, was created for that purpose, and UNEF II came to an end in 1979 when its mandate was not renewed by the Security Council.

UNEF II is frequently cited as a model for future peacekeeping forces.  It dealt with a dangerous situation in which the great powers had an interest but were not directly involved; it had the support of the parties at conflict and the membership of the Security Council as well as the troop contributors; and it had a clear and realistic mandate.  It was established, moreover, in a way which clearly defined the ultimate authority of the Security Council for its establishment but gave broad latitude to the Secretary General for its operational direction and administration.

## UNITED NATIONS INTERIM FORCE IN LEBANON (UNIFIL)

Following the invasion of southern Lebanon in 1978, the Security Council called for the withdrawal of Israeli forces and set up UNIFIL to confirm that withdrawal, assist the Lebanese Government to ensure the return of its effective authority in the area, and restore international peace and security.  After the Israeli invasion of 1982, the Council called for UNIFIL to remain in the area with the same mandate.

The United States has strongly supported the contribution of UNIFIL as providing an element of stability in volatile southern Lebanon.  Israeli views over the years have been mixed, however, and the U.S. Congress has funded UNIFIL at about half the level of our assessment because of concerns that it not affect, nor substitute for Israel's security zone and military operations.

While the United States and other countries see UNIFIL as playing an important role and worth keeping, it is often cited as a case of the U.N. being called upon to perform an impossible task.  Concerns regarding UNIFIL have centered on two factors.  First, UNIFIL was faced with an unrealistic mandate in that it was asked to provide a buffer between contending forces--as had been the goal in the UNEF effort--and to help restore the sovereignty of the central government--as had been the goal in the ONUC (Operation des Nations Unies au Congo) effort--but without receiving the requisite authority or strength to do so. And, second, the situation, as it evolved, lacked the full support of all the parties and factions involved and, therefore, the essential element for succeeding in its mission.

Despite these concerns, however, there is no doubt that the withdrawal of UNIFIL would have serious consequences for the stability of the region. Further, peacekeeping endeavors such as UNIFIL illustrate the continued commitment of a significant number of stable, medium-size countries which have maintained their contributions and kept their troops intact, despite the hundreds of fatalities that have occurred. These countries have followed through with their commitment to peacekeeping not because of any particular national interest, but rather as an expression of idealism, to do what is required to be in a sense a good citizen of the world community. This commitment has provided the Secretary General with a relatively large pool upon which he can draw for these operations and, also, has provided a means by which countries can bring about engagement for the resolution of regional conflicts.

Although it is difficult to characterize them neatly as either successes or failures, one can state that U.N. peacekeeping has run into trouble when it has tried to overreach its mandate-that is, by attempting to enforce or impose particular political solutions. This was the case with the Congo operation in 1960-64. UNEF II, on the other hand, is an example of a peacekeeping operation which basically outlived its need when the parties themselves reached agreement outside of the U.N. framework. With UNEF II, the peaceful settlement process was what led to the Camp David agreement between Egypt and Israel. Again, the U.N. can facilitate but not impose solutions.

The U.N.'s record in peacekeeping and conflict resolution also demonstrates a significant adjustment by the Security Council over its history. On certain occasions the Security Council has been called upon to give an opinion, even where it cannot by its own strength enforce that judgment. It can lay down the general guidelines for the settlement, as over the Middle East in 1967. If both parties are willing it can even resolve an issue, as over Bahrain. In other cases it can indicate the procedures that may in turn lead to a settlement, as over Berlin in 1948. It can call for a ceasefire; in the past the Security Council has called for ceasefires in the Middle East four times, and four times they have been accepted. And today there is a new ceasefire in the Iran-Iraq war consequent to Security Council Resolution 598. At the least, the Security Council can censure and condemn. If these judgments are unanimous, they can influence action.

Although Security Council pronouncements can carry considerable weight, they normally cannot be enforced. Under Chapter VII, however, a decision on measures to be taken to maintain or restore international peace and security has the force of international law, and under the Charter, which is a treaty, all states are required to accept and carry out this decision. Nonetheless, Chapter VII has almost never been used; and if a government believes that its vital interests are at stake, the Security Council's influence may only be weak. For example, the Soviet Union blatantly ignored Security Council condemnation in its actions over Hungary and Czechoslovakia. But in most cases governments are influenced, however slowly, by international pressure to modify their policies to avoid public condemnation.

Just as the injunctions expressed by the Security Council have limitations, so do the situations where the United Nations can assert itself in a peacekeeping effort. U.N. peacekeeping operations are those involving military personnel, but without fully effective enforcement powers. They are established by the United Nations to help maintain and restore peace in areas of conflict. But again, the U.N. cannot do this unless the parties themselves wish to seek a solution and accept, at least, the general mandate of the operation.

### III. U.N. PEACEKEEPING TODAY

The United States' policy in recent years of firm, active engagement at the United Nations has begun to achieve significant results in many areas of U.N. activity. Although the U.N. General Assembly remains a highly politicized arena which frequently adopts positions inimical to U.S. interests, there have been over the past two years major positive shifts in support of U.S. interests. One of the most important developments has been the new U.N. peacekeeping operations in Afghanistan, the Persian Gulf and, potentially, southern Africa which reflect a reinvigoration of the Security Council and of the role of the Secretary General in the resolution of regional disputes.

Each of these three situations - Afghanistan, Iran-Iraq and Angola/Namibia - highlights the resurgence of the U.N. as a peacekeeping tool. But each also illustrates the continuing need to have a realistic understanding of the limits on what the U.N. can be expected to accomplish. In addition to the U.N.'s efforts and initiatives, the policies of the Reagan Administration and U.S. pressures have played a significant role in bringing about the circumstances whereby the major players have agreed to come to the negotiation table in these conflicts.

### AFGHANISTAN

The Afghanistan situation provides an excellent example of how various complex factors--the political cooperation of the superpowers, the role of international organizations in limiting the use of force, and the general exhaustion of the belligerents--can all work together in helping to achieve an end to regional conflicts.

By itself, the United Nations was incapable of compelling the Soviet Union to end its brutal occupation after it invaded Afghanistan in December 1979.    Unfortunately, it took eight years of conflict and violence, involving the loss of approximately one million lives, before the Soviets made the decision to pull their troops out of Afghanistan.    The Geneva Accords, which were signed on April 14, 1988, provided the framework for implementing the basic decision on troop withdrawal which Moscow had already made.    They also provided a significant face-saving device for the Soviets by allowing them to escape from the growing economic and military costs of what had become a political and military quagmire for them.

The strength, faith and endurance of the Afghan freedom fighters played a major role leading to the signing of the Accords.  And the strength and durability of U.S. direct support was, clearly, a decisive factor in the equation.  At the same time, the United Nations itself contributed in two important ways to the successful outcome at Geneva.

First, the U.N. provided the forum through which the attention of the world community continually was focused on Afghanistan.  As the years of Soviet occupation dragged on, it would have been all too easy to have forgotten the plight of the Afghan people if this forum did not exist. Following the Soviet invasion, each year the U.N. General Assembly passed identical resolutions on Afghanistan, calling for the withdrawal of foreign forces, the establishment of a broad-based government through self-determination, the safe and honorable return of the refugees and a non-aligned Afghanistan.  These resolutions were passed by overwhelming majorities and served as a major rallying point, particularly for the Islamic nations to demonstrate their opposition to the Soviet Union.  By assuring that the Afghanistan issue would remain before the world community, the U.N. resolutions were very important in raising the diplomatic costs to the Soviets of their aggression.  They clearly established that the Soviet action would not be legitimized over time and that the Soviet-installed puppet regime in Kabul would be seen as illegitimate. That regime continues to be viewed in that light by most of the world's governments.

Secondly, using the authority of his office, the Secretary General appointed a special negotiator, Diego Cordovez, who was charged to explore with the parties involved ideas and ways of resolving the crisis. Thus, the proximity talks began and the U.N. fulfilled a crucial role as the central "broker" between the contending parties.    Although these negotiations, too, would drag on for some years, several key ideas developed during the talks were incorporated into the final Geneva Accords of April 1988.

The Accords also established a new peacekeeping operation: the United Nations Good Offices Mission in Afghanistan and Pakistan (UNGOMAP). A modern version of the earliest U.N. peacekeeping operations, UNGOMAP's primary purpose is underlined by the name given it by Diego Cordovez--a good offices mission. In essence, UNGOMAP was created to monitor the implementation of the Geneva Accords. Its primary function is to monitor the Soviet withdrawal and to investigate reports of violations of the Accords by participating parties.

UNGOMAP's operation is conducted by approximately 50 observers and additional support staff, with offices in both Afghanistan and Pakistan. Since its inception, it has actively pursued its mandate. It confirmed that the Soviets met the August 15, 1988 date for withdrawal of half of its more than 100,000 troops from Afghanistan and has investigated numerous border violations.

The UNGOMAP operation is not in any sense a "classic" U.N. peacekeeping force, such as the Cyprus operation or that which is being established along the Iran-Iraq border. In the case of the latter, a peacekeeping force has been interposed between two armies with the fundamental mandate of maintaining a ceasefire between two parties and preventing a new round of hostilities from breaking out while peace negotiations proceed. In contrast, UNGOMAP's principal function is to monitor the withdrawal of one army. It also investigates charges of violations of the Accords between the various parties. Finally, UNGOMAP has no mandate with regard to internal conflict between the Resistance forces and those of the illegitimate regime in Kabul.

There are many political, economic and social aftershocks of the Afghanistan conflict that will entail a continuing role for the United Nations in the months ahead. The safe and honorable return of six and one half million refugees and displaced persons within Afghanistan will be, for example, an essential element in the establishment of a broad-based, responsive Afghan government through self-determination and to regional stability and security. Given the size of the task, the expertise required, and the funding needed, only the United Nations can lead this effort.


IRAN-IRAQ

The bloody eight-year war between Iran and Iraq is another example of a regional conflict in which the U.N. has long sought to facilitate a settlement, yet only achieved a breakthrough once the parties themselves finally concluded that it was in their respective interests to negotiate. By mid-summer 1988, both sides had fought themselves to exhaustion. With both sides now interested in a peaceful settlement, the U.N. has recently been able to put into effect a ceasefire and initiate direct talks between the parties.

From the outbreak of the Gulf war in 1980, the U.N. has devoted considerable efforts to resolving the conflict.  The Security Council has considered the issue regularly, adopting a series of resolutions calling for an end to hostilities.  U.N. Secretary General Perez de Cuellar and his predecessor, Kurt Waldheim, both launched numerous initiatives in attempts to mediate a settlement.  As the Secretary General's Special Representative in the early 1980s, former Swedish Prime Minister Olaf Palme shuttled between Baghdad and Tehran, trying to hammer out agreement on compromise proposals.  Yet, all these efforts proved unsuccessful, principally because one of the belligerents, Iran, was not interested in a settlement on the terms being offered.

In the early stages of the war, Tehran rejected ceasefire proposals because Iraqi troops were still on Iranian soil.  Later, when Iran gained the advantage on the battlefield, repelled the Iraqis and captured Iraqi territory, Iran refused U.N. peace overtures because it was bent on achieving victory: namely, the overthrow of Saddan Hussein and the Beathist regime in Baghdad.  Thus the fighting continued, with Iran pursuing its war aims and Iraq fighting an increasingly desperate defensive war.

During the first several years of the Gulf war, many in the international community remained relatively unconcerned, content to let these two nations fight it out.  Some even argued it was beneficial to keep Iran and Iraq preoccupied with the war, thereby limiting their ability to cause mischief elsewhere in the region.  By 1986, however, this perception began to change as the international community became alarmed over the threat to neutral shipping in the Persian Gulf and the danger that the conflict might spread to neighboring countries.

Two important developments resulted: First, the Western countries, following U.S. leadership, decided to increase their naval strength in the region to counter the threat; and, second, in July 1987 the Security Council, in an unprecedented move, unanimously adopted Resolution 598, which demanded an end to the fighting and provided a comprehensive framework for a negotiated settlement.

Western fleets in the Gulf proved to be a reasonably effective deterrent against Iranian troublemaking, limiting the number of attacks against neutral vessels and providing a visible sign of political support for our Arab friends in the region.  Implementing Resolution 598 proved more difficult.

Although Iraq promptly accepted the resolution, Iran equivocated, professing to accept parts of 598 while trying to redefine the resolution to its own advantage.  The United States, with allies Britain and France, led efforts in the Security Council to impose an arms embargo against Iran for failure to comply with this mandatory resolution. However, other members of the Council--notably the Soviets--balked, generally out of concern over damaging their relations with Iran. As a result, Resolution 598 remained unimplemented for almost a year, and the war dragged on.

In July 1988, Iran suddenly and unexpectedly announced its formal acceptance of Resolution 598 and willingness to negotiate peace on its terms. Overnight, the peace process was energized. Why the turnaround? Many factors contributed to Tehran's strategic decision.

First and foremost, Iran had suffered a series of major defeats on the battlefield, including loss of Iraq's strategic al-Faw peninsula, which Iran had captured in 1986 at great human cost. These military setbacks contributed to political unrest already brewing inside Iran, fueled by economic distress in Iran's war-ravaged economy. The U.S. and allied naval presence demonstrated the West's resolve to protect its interests in the Gulf and successfully countered Iranian attempts to intimidate its Arab neighbors. Additionally, the international reaction to the accidental downing of Iran Air flight 665 in July 1988 gave proof of Iran's increasing international isolation.4/

Believing that continuation of the war was undermining the mullahs' regime and threatening the Islamic Revolution itself, Tehran reluctantly concluded that it was in its best interests to seek peace, even on the heretofore distasteful terms of Resolution 598. Revitalizing his good offices mission, Secretary General Perez de Cuellar moved quickly to capitalize on this breakthrough. On August 20, 1988, the Security Council approved his arrangements for an early ceasefire and the initiation of direct talks in Geneva between Iran and Iraq on implementing the various provisions of Resolution 598.

Given the complex issues at stake and the high degree of enmity and suspicion between the parties, the negotiations are expected to be lengthy and contentious. To handle the talks on a day-to-day basis, the Secretary General appointed Jan Eliasson, Sweden's Ambassador to the U.N., as his special representative. Eliasson's selection was crucial in that he had already earned the trust and respect of both sides, having assisted Olaf Palme during earlier mediation efforts.

While Ambassador Eliasson and U.N. negotiators attempt (with firm backing from the Security Council) to work out arrangements to implement Resolution 598, a fragile ceasefire is holding on the front. Here, again, the U.N. stepped in with creation of a peacekeeping operation to monitor the ceasefire: the United Nations Iran-Iraq Military Observer Group (UNIIMOG).

Consisting of 350 observers from 24 countries deployed along both sides of the Iran-Iraq border, plus major military support elements, UNIIMOG has done a remarkable job to date in keeping the peace in an extremely volatile environment. The United States has been one of UNIIMOG's strongest supporters, providing extensive logistical support to supplement our financial assistance.

As the troubled peace talks continue, UNIIMOG will continue to play a key role in preserving the truce. The presence of these observers signifies that the international community has a vested interest in preventing a resumption of hostilities and in restoring peace and stability to the Gulf. Ultimately, however, peace can only be assured by agreement between the parties themselves, having recognized that it is not in their interests to pursue their political objectives by military means.

## ANGOLA/NAMIBIA

The current, sudden major progress toward settling the conflict over Namibia involving South Africa, Angola, and the Southwest African Peoples Organization (SWAPO)--and the related serious threat of Cuban military forces in Angola and the need for internal reconciliation in that country--is actually the culmination of more than ten years of diplomatic efforts. It also is a function of changing regional and international political dynamics which have caused the participants to reassess their behavior and move in the direction of accepting the U.N. as a vehicle to implement an acceptable settlement once current negotiations are concluded successfully.

One of the longest ongoing peacekeeping attempts, the current combined U.S. and U.N. effort to settle the Angolan/Namibian problem dates from 1978 and the passage of Security Council Resolution 435 establishing the United Nations Namibia Transition Assistance Group (UNTAG). Once the group is installed in Namibia, UNTAG's mandate will be to assist the Secretary General's Special Representative for Namibia to carry out the mandate conferred upon him by the Security Council in Resolution 431 (1978), namely, to ensure the early independence of Namibia through free elections under the supervision and control of the United Nations.

The South African Government agreed in principle to the creation of an independent Namibian state as early as 1978 and accepted the idea of an UNTAG military presence in March 1979. However, it was not until the advent of the Reagan Administration, with a southern Africa policy based on the complementary goals of a regional political settlement and an end to apartheid in South Africa, that the political calculus in southern Africa began to change sufficiently to make an actual settlement possible.

By mid-1982, when a Namibia/Angola settlement initially appeared within reach, preparations for UNTAG were far advanced. The Western five-nation contact group (Canada, West Germany, France, the United

Kingdom and the United States), which had been attempting to mediate the issue, envisioned UNTAG as comprising a military component of up to 7,500 troops, and a civilian unit of 1,500.  Progress appeared sufficient enough that troop contributors were identified and agreed by all sides.

The implementation of Resolution 435 was expected to take one year during which time UNTAG would remain in existence.  The concrete steps in the implementation process were then, and remain: cessation of all hostilities; free and fair elections for a Namibian constituent assembly; drafting and adoption of a constitution by the constituent assembly; and attainment of independence via the coming into force of the constitution.

The specific tasks assigned to UNTAG would include the following: monitoring the cessation of hostilities as well as the restriction of opposing forces to their bases and the phased withdrawal of South African military units; surveillance of borders and prevention of infiltration; monitoring the demobilization of the Namibian territorial and ethnic forces; and supervision of free elections (primarily the responsibility of the UNTAG civilian component).

UNTAG never moved beyond the planning stage in 1982, foundering on South Africa's fears that the implementation of Resolution 435 would result in a SWAPO-led government in Namibia.  After that time, the Contact Group mechanism slowly atrophied while the United States continued sporadic discussions on its own.

Serious negotiations emerged again only within the last year, when the principal parties, South Africa and Angola, appeared to have recognized that the costs of continuing the conflict far outweighed the benefits.  The Angolans were not only battling the South Africans but also were engaged in an internal battle with UNITA (the National Union for the Total Independence of Angola which has received U.S. assistance in its 13-year war with Angola's Cuban-backed government).  The South Africans, once considered an unbeatable military force, recognized a formidable foe in the Soviet proxy Cuban forces assisting the Angolans, and the cost in lives and treasury was becoming more than the South African public would tolerate.

This recognition of the changed cost-benefit analysis by Angola and South Africa resulted, with the assistance of U.S. mediation, in an agreement on Principles for a Peaceful Settlement in Southwestern Africa on July 20, 1988.  This agreement calls for, inter alia, the implementation of Resolution 435, the total withdrawal of Cuban forces from Angola,the respect for the sovereignty and borders of all states, agreement by the states not to permit their territory to be used for aggression or violence against other states, and the reaffirmation of the right of the peoples of the southwestern region of Africa to self-determination, independence and equality of rights.  The main issues remaining in the negotiations are agreement on a short, explicit timetable for Cuban troop withdrawal, and the need for further explicit understandings among the Angola factions.

The recognition by Angola and South Africa of the futility of their conflict, and their willingness to do something about it, might have been more diificult to achieve if the U.N. were not ready and able to provide a mechanism for ensuring that the fundamental security interests of the two countries could be safeguarded if they ceased fighting, and for mobilizing the significant resources needed to accomplish these ends. For the South Africans this means they no longer need a military presence in Namibia. For the Angolans this means they no longer need to use Cuban troops to achieve the objectives of the Marxist regime which now governs in Luanda.

As in 1982, the U.N. again is finalizing plans to deploy UNTAG. The plans are for UNTAG to monitor an immediate ceasefire, the restriction of armed forces to pre-designated areas, the establishment of a 100 kilometer-wide demilitarized zone along the Angolan-Namibian border and the phased withdrawal of South African troops. The civilian component is to establish field offices to facilitate elections and to assist the return of approximately 76,000 refugees.

The U.N. is currently re-examining UNTAG's proposed size and composition given the general improvement in the political and negotiating environment. As noted above, however, not all the hurdles to a settlement have been overcome. It may still take hard bargaining until the parties feel confident that their basic security interests have been protected. However, now that they recognize the political calculus in southern Africa has altered, and that a viable U.N. exists in which there is a strong consensus in favor of peacekeeping, underpinned by a climate of cooperation between the U.S. and USSR, a solution to this problem appears at last to be feasible.

### IV.  TOWARD THE FUTURE...

With respect to the so-called "peace epidemic" that has been lauded in recent months with an emphasis on the U.N.'s peacekeeping endeavors, two additional conflicts--Western Sahara and Cambodia--now pose significant challenges and opportunities for U.N. peacekeeping activity. The complex nature of these conflicts further underscores the need for realism in assessing both the limitations and capabilities of the U.N. in furthering peace in critical areas of the world.

### WESTERN SAHARA

The long-running conflict in the former Spanish Sahara had dragged to a virtual stalemate on the ground early this year. following completion of the Moroccan defensive sand wall (the "berm") which effectively blocked the POLISARIO guerrillas from the useful portion of the territory.

Meanwhile, internal and regional developments led to a warming between Morocco and Algeria (the POLISARIO's patron) and their eventual reestablishment of relations on May 16, 1988. (The United States, friendly with both countries, remained apart from the conflict and encouraged both sides to resolve their differences through negotiations.) In this context, the proximity talks which Secretary General Perez de Cuellar had been conducting began to bear fruit, and at the end of August, the parties announced their agreement in principle to a series of proposals leading to a ceasefire and a referendum on self- determination.

The Security Council met in September and authorized the Secretary General to appoint a Special Representative, who will negotiate the final details and supervise a resultant peacekeeping operation to manage the ceasefire and referendum. The size and parameters of that operation are still to be determined, but it will have to manage the territory during the transition, much as UNTAG will do in Namibia.


### CAMBODIA

A number of players in the Cambodian conflict, including Prince Sihanouk (the leading candidate to head a coalition government), have suggested peace plans which include an international peacekeeping force. The role envisioned for this force has ranged from a limited operation, primarily to monitor Vietnamese withdrawal, to an extensive force which would supervise a ceasefire and even disarm Khmer Rouge factions.

The parties may not opt for a U.N.-organized peacekeeping force because of Vietnamese and Khmer Rouge opposition. However, there are several other mechanisms available to sponsor an international peacekeeping presence. Any full-fledged peacekeeping operation in Cambodia admittedly will be an ambitious undertaking with the need to resolve one of the key dilemmas in a Cambodian settlement: the reining in of the military power of a potentially hostile Khmer Rouge. There are roughly 100,000 armed Cambodians among the four factions, including 40,000 Khmer Rouge. Thus, it conceivably could take a ten thousand-man force to accomplish this task, although a much smaller force is likely should the U.N. be asked to take on the job.


### V. ...AND BEYOND

Additional peacekeeping operations over the next few years could have several consequences--not all of them positive--for the West. In particular, the recent increased Soviet interest in peacekeeping carries the danger of further Soviet manipulation of the United Nations. Additional peacekeeping operations also would result in increasing financial demands on the United States.

Since the founding of the United Nations, the Soviets have clashed with the United States over U.N. peacekeeping operations in three major areas: control of operations, troop composition and selection, and financing. The paramount issue for the Soviets has been the division of responsibilities between the Security Council and the Secretary General-- that is, the degree of control the Security Council should exercise over a peacekeeping operation once launched. The Soviet goal is to retain the ability to veto all aspects of peacekeeping by giving the Security Council operational control over peacekeeping operations. To this end, the Soviets want to reinvigorate the Military Staff Committee, which the Security Council also would control.

On October 4, 1988, Soviet Deputy Foreign Affairs Minister Vladimir Petrovsky held a press conference at the United Nations regarding a series of Soviet proposals for "strengthening" the U.N. I met with Mr. Petrovsky the following day to discuss these proposals, which would include reactivating the Military Staff Committee as well as broadening the U.N.'s peacekeeping role. Under the Soviet recommendations, the Security Council would act "to stave off emerging conflicts by setting up observer posts in explosive areas;" these operations would be established "to protect states from outside interference;" and "U.N. personnel could be sent at the request of only one party to be stationed on its territory."

These proposals are linked to a larger package the Soviets have been circulating recently as part of their draft resolution on a "Comprehensive System of International Peace and Security" (CSIS). The CSIS, which was first introduced at the 41st U.N. General Assembly in 1986, would replace the present system of international security with a so-called "comprehensive system" that purports to encompass all aspects of international relations in one package. The United States opposes the overall concept because it could, in our view, lead to eventual redefinition of the Charter; the establishment of a new, costly and redundant structure within the U.N. system; and the further politicization of the U.N. system. Furthermore, now that the U.N. is reforming its administration and budgeting, curbing its politicization and name-calling, and reinvigorating its peacekeeping role, we should not be seeking new, sweeping "comprehensive" changes. There already is a "comprehensive system" for International security. It is the U.N. Charter. And to date it appears that the Soviet proposals are more propaganda than substantive.

Current peacekeeping operations are working well due to the fact that each is individually tailored to meet operational demands in the area in which it is operating. The superpowers traditionally do not provide troops; yet the Soviets' current plan would envision allowing the five

Permanent Members of the Security Council to contribute troops to peacekeeping activities. It is the U.S. view that this would further politicize these operations and, therefore, undermine their effectiveness.

In addition, the U.N. Charter confers on the Security Council the primary responsibility for the maintenance of international peace and security. The Security Council already has the authority to investigate any dispute or situation that might lead to international friction or give rise to a dispute. Thus, the Soviet proposal to establish "observer posts in explosive areas" is simply unnecessary. While the United States would be prepared to look at any proposal within this context on its merits, it believes that a more effective use of resources would be to concentrate on getttng at the root causes of conflicts rather than establishing a static presence which would only monitor their symptoms.

While there has been an evolution over the last several years with respect to Soviet declaratory policy toward the U.N.'s role as an institution for resolving conflict, Soviet actions have not always matched their words. For example, the Soviets supported Resolution 598 but stymied its implementation. They agreed to the Geneva Accords on Afghanistan, but violated their spirit by high altitude bombing and attacks on Pakistan. They have taken some useful steps in support of some U.N. peacekeeping, but they continue to advocate the resurrection of the Military Staff Committee. In sum, there has been an interesting development in Soviet policy which suggests the need for exploring wider U.S./USSR bilateral discussions on the resolution of regional disputes, as well as the need to indicate to the Soviets that we are willing to see how serious they really are.

In conclusion, at this time of increased U.N. involvement in peacekeeping initiatives, it is essential that we study the reasons events have joined to create this opportunity and that we learn the lessons of history and of these current conflicts, so that we may better understand precisely what the U.N. is able to contribute in resolving these conflicts. Any unrealistic expectation that the U.N. can overreach its mandate or try to assert or impose solutions will only serve to undermine its effectiveness. It will strain its resources. And it will necessarily bring into question its critical impartiality.

Whether by bridging a gulf of remaining differences or merely providing a graceful exit, or the political justification that the respective goverrments can use with their own situations at home, the United Nations has a role. It does not impose peace. However, it can act as a midwife, a facilitator, a promoter of peace. This is a limited role--but an enormously important one.

1/     Security Council Resolution 598 of July 1987, which established a basis for ending the Iran-Iraq war, was a mandatory resolution. Under the Charter and under international law, all states are required to abide by its provisions. Although Resolution 598 demanded an immediate ceasefire, it took a year before Iran reached agreement to abide by its terms. Several months later, the two parties are still negotiating through the Secretary General over how to interpret and implement the mandatory requirement of withdrawal "without delay." Clearly, U.N. practice is not as cut and dried as the Charter drafters decreed--nor can it be.

2/     Currently, U.S. and Soviet military personnel participate directly in only one U.N. peacekeeping operation--the U.N. Truce Supervision Organization, headquartered in Jerusalem--although the US does indeed assist such operations in various capacities, such as the US airlift of U.N. forces in Cyprus, Lebannon, Iran-Iraq and elsewhere.

3/     A more extensive discussion of U.N. peacekeeping operations up to 1988 will be appearing in the near future as part of a special publication of this paper by the Foreign Service Institute's Center for Studies of Foreign Affairs.

4/     Despite efforts by Iran to obtain a clear condemnation of U.S. actions, the Security Council on July 20, 1988, unanimously adopted Resolution 616 which expressed the Council's distress at the downing of the Iranian airliner and welcomed the investigation of the International Civil Aviation Organization (ICAO). The resolution also expressed condolences to the families of the victims, urged compliance with international rules on safety of civil aviation, and stressed the urgency of ending the Gulf war through implementation of Resolution 598.

AFGHANISTAN: TURNING THE CORNER


When the Reagan administration came into office in 1981, the Soviet Union's brutal aggression against Afghanistan seemed unstoppable. Having overrun that small, nonaligned, independent country, Moscow appeared poised to challenge fundamental U.S. interests in the oil-rich Persian Gulf region and in South Asia. The United Nations seemed helpless to contribute to finding peace in this troubled area. Indeed, rather than vigorously pursuing its Charter-prescribed role as peacemaker, the U.N.'s primary attention centered on larger budgets, more personnel, vague political and economic programs, and name-calling resolutions all too often directed at the United States.

Eight years later, a remarkable transformation has occurred -- prompted in large part by the firm, strong, and consistent policies of the United States, led by President Reagan and Secretary of State George Shultz and receiving strong bipartisan congressional support. The Soviets are withdrawing their troops from Afghanistan, holding out the prospects of the Afghans again having the right and opportunity to determine their own government and future. U.S. interests in the Persian Gulf are more secure today than they have been in a decade, and the foundation has been laid for greater stability and security in South Asia.

Many people and countries contributed to this remarkable transformation. Far and away the most important were the brave Afghan freedom fighters who refused to be cowed by the military might and technological superiority of the Soviet superpower. Their determination to keep fighting until the invading forces were forced to withdraw stands as testimony and inspiration to those who aspire to and those who support

Appeared in The World & I, March, 1989.

national independence and self-determination.  Pakistan, which housed millions of refugees and aided the resistance despite threats, bombing attacks, and terrorism, deserves praise and respect.  The United States and other nations provided indispensable support to the resistance.

The United Nations also has played a critical role -- and, in so doing has, in many respects, lived up to the expectations of its founders.  It served as the facilitator for a settlement -- tirelessly promoting mediation and providing the forum to which the parties could turn when the objective conditions on the ground made clear that peace was preferable to continued conflict and bloodshed.  With the unwavering backing of Secretary-General Javier Perez de Cuellar, Diego Cordovez labored indefatigably and imaginatively, finally mediating a comprehensive plan that represented the first step toward peace -- the Geneva Accords of April 1988.  While monitoring the implementation of the Geneva Accords, the U.N. now, under Humanitarian Assistance Coordinator Prince Sadruddin Aga Khan, is taking the lead in formulating the international effort to assist more than five million Afghan refugees and approximately one to two million displaced persons to return to their homes and begin rebuilding their war-devastated country.

No one expected the Soviets to be forced out of Afghanistan quickly.  Unfortunately, much time, great effort, the loss of countless human lives, and the material destruction of much of the country occurred before Moscow understood the necessity of pulling back its invading forces.  In the meantime, it was important that Afghanistan remain at the center of attention of the international public and the community of nations; the tragedy of the invasion could become even greater if world opinion lost sight of the Afghan disaster and the valiant efforts of the Afghan freedom fighters.

Over the years, U.S. officials have provided regular background briefings in the international press about military, political, and economic developments in the war.  Congress has passed numerous resolutions condemning Soviet aggression and calling for Afghan self-determination. Annually, on the anniversary of the Soviet invasion, the Department of State has issued a comprehensive report (prepared by its Bureau of Intelligence and Research), summarizing what had occurred in Afghanistan and assessing its meaning; this information was widely disseminated abroad.  The Department of State also sponsored several public forums on the Afghan situation.

The United States has strongly supported the Pakistani-sponsored U.N. General Assembly resolutions on Afghanistan.  In New York, we preferred to play a supportive role--to demonstrate that the invasion of Afghanistan was not an East-West issue, but instead a matter of sovereignty versus aggression, with which all nations could identify. Repeated U.N. resolutions have called for the preservation of Afghanistan's sovereignty, territorial integrity, nonalignment, and political independence; the right of the Afghan people to self-determination; the withdrawal of foreign (that is, Soviet) troops; and the return of the refugees in safety and honor. The resolutions have helped center world attention on Afghanistan; year after year, the international community has overwhelmingly reiterated its opposition to the Soviet invasion. By reiterating in eight successive U.N. resolutions that the Afghan people had the right to determine their own form of government, the international community clearly has affirmed its belief that the Kabul regime is illegitimate (notwithstanding the fact that the regime represents Afghanistan in the United Nations).

As determined as our efforts were to facilitate the mujahideen struggle and publicize Soviet atrocities, the United States had unwaveringly supported the mediation efforts undertaken by the special representative of the secretary-general, as well as mediation attempts by other organizations, such as the Organization of Islamic Conference. After the first few years of the war, however, only the United Nations persisted in its efforts to negotiate an end to the conflict.

In supporting mediation, the United States made clear that its first objective was the withdrawal of Soviet forces from Afghanistan. The United States rejected any arrangement that would have legitimized the Soviet presence, provided for a gradual withdrawal of Soviet forces (such as the original four-year timetable suggested by the Soviets), or legitimized the Soviet-backed regime in Kabul. In short, the United States opposed any settlement through mediation that would have preserved the status quo or recognized the imposition of Soviet control over Afghanistan, whether through its armed forces or puppet regime.

In his article "Inside the Afghan Talks" (Foreign Policy, Summer 1988), Selig S. Harrison claims that in 1983 an opportunity was lost to negotiate as settlement, primarily because the United States was unwilling to encourage Pakistan to test then Soviet Premier Yuri Andropov's reported intention to withdraw. Harrison finds the U.S. action "regrettable" because Andropov reportedly was willing to withdraw Soviet forces--though not prepared to state the timing or circumstances under which he envisioned withdrawing them. That evasiveness and vagueness, however, was precisely the problem. The principal issue of negotiation for the United States and Pakistan was to achieve a strict Soviet withdrawal timetable that would be implemented in a relatively short period. What is regrettable is not U.S. firmness in pursuing its policy goals, but the Soviets' inability to make the decision in 1983 that they finally made five years later--after hundreds of thousands more casualties and further massive destruction of the countryside.

## The Achievement of Geneva

Finally, the Soviets accepted the inevitable. Even though their troop strength had grown to 115,000, they finally drew the correct lesson from the battlefield: The resistance, fired by faith and nationalism, could not be defeated. They also incurred major political costs, as the United States and other nations kept the fate of the Afghan people and the cruelty of the Soviet aggression before the world community.

On April 14, 1988, Moscow agreed to sign the Geneva Accords. The accords are a major historic achievement. Soviet forces are withdrawing from Afghanistan, following an internationally recognized timetable. Without this commitment, their withdrawal could--and events of November 1988 (when it was announced that the withdrawal was being suspended) suggest would--have been delayed. In signing the accords, the Soviets have acknowledged that they were unable to break the political will of the Afghan resistance or the military stalemate that had developed. Implementation of the accords will help create the conditions whereby the people of Afghanistan, exercising their right to self-determination, will be able to establish a broad-based nonaligned government. It also will facilitate the return to their homes of the more than five million refugees living outside Afghanistan and the one to two million displaced persons inside the country.

The accords do provide something of a face-saving mechanism by which the Soviets could extricate themselves from Afghanistan. It also is true that they do not signify a military defeat for the Soviet Union in the classic sense of the word; that is, the physical destruction of most or all of the Soviet army in Afghanistan. However, with its global perspective, the purpose of U.S. policy was not to help inflict a total military defeat on the Soviets nor to fight the Soviets to the last Afghan in an effort to do so. The primary U.S. objective was to compel the withdrawal of Soviet troops. As Zalmay Khalizad pointed out last summer in the National Interest, the withdrawal itself is "a strategic defeat for the Soviets with profound and wide-ranging implications."

There have been those who have claimed that the accords are a "sellout" of the resistance and of U.S. policy. This position has been best articulated by Rosanne Klass in an article in the Summer 1988 edition of Foreign Affairs. Klass argues that the accords (1) do not deal with "the Soviet presence" in Afghanistan except "tangentially"; (2) will pave the way for the consolidation of communist control over the country because "by 1986 Moscow had had time to strengthen its puppet regime in Kabul" -- the implication being that despite the withdrawal of "uniformed Soviet forces," Moscow will still be left in effective control of Afghanistan; and (3) are a reversal of U.S. policy as repeatedly stated "since the Soviet invasion."

Taking the last point first, the U.S. government has remained consistent in its policy toward Afghanistan. The policy objectives that were set in the period following the Soviet invasion -- withdrawal of Soviet troops and the reestablishment of a nonaligned Afghanistan, the establishment of a broad-level government through the exercise of self-determination, and the return of the refugees in safety and honor--remain the same. And it is those guidelines that argue for the support of the accords.

There are no illusions that the accords can or will solve all of the problems associated with the long, brutal, and tragic Afghan war. There remains the formidable problem of providing for the resettlement of the refugees and reconstruction of the country. Moreover, the shape of future Afghan political arrangements remains unclear. We do not know precisely what form Afghan self-determination will take; that is an issue for the Afghans to decide. But no genuine act or process of self-determination can succeed, nor will most of the refugees return, until all Soviet troops are withdrawn. The critical value of the Geneva Accords is that they establish a firm timetable for withdrawal to which the international community holds the Soviets accountable.

Turning to the other points, Klass is simply wrong in her assertion that the Soviet obligation to withdraw is "tangential" to the accords. The accords consist of the two bilateral agreements between Pakistan and Afghanistan, the "Declaration on International Guarantees" signed by the United States and the Soviet Union and the "Instrument on the Interrelationship for the Settlement of the Situation Relating to Afghanistan" signed by the United States and the Soviet Union. Although the time frame of the withdrawal (that is, one-half of the troops by August 15, 1988, and the rest by February 15, 1989) was agreed upon by the Soviets and the Kabul regime, that time frame is explicitly incorporated into the Interrelationship Instrument. It is an integral part of that instrument and, therefore, part and parcel of the overall accord package.

Klass' charge that the accords will pave the way for the consolidation of communist control of Afghanistan is apparently based on her interpretation of what led the Soviet Union to agree to the accords in the first place. In addressing that question, Klass misrepresents that military situation that formed the backdrop for the Geneva agreement. She concedes that "the increasing effectiveness of the resistance forces may have prodded the Soviets to conclude they would face growing problems in the future." Nonetheless, she appears to attribute Soviet agreement to withdraw to what she apparently perceives as the strength of the Soviet client regime in Kabul and to the Soviets' confidence that they could maintain "effective control" without a residual troop presence. This seems to imply that the Soviets had achieved at least a temporary victory in Afghanistan.

No reputable observer of Afghan affairs, inside or outside the U.S. government, shares this assessment. The Soviet-backed Kabul regime has been riddled with factionalism and its army marked by high rates of desertion and a lack of fighting spirit. Even before Soviet troop withdrawals commenced, the resistance controlled most of the countryside. The Kabul regime could hold major cities, but only with the help of Soviet military support.

As Soviet forces have pulled back from eastern, southern and western Afghanistan, the strength of the resistance has become even more apparent. The Kabul regime has lost significant amounts of additional territory--including a number of important provincial capitals, towns, and garrisons--to the mujahideen. As a result, the resistance now completely controls the Panjshir and Konar valleys, strategic areas bitterly contested for the last eight years. Major cities such as Jalalabad, Ghazni, Gardez, and Kandahar are cut off from the surrounding countryside and can be supplied only with great difficulty. As the Soviet troop withdrawal proceeds, the military initiative will continue to pass to the resistance.

Klass' insinuation that the Soviet Union will achieve the kind of "effective control" by stealth that it could not attain with more than 100,000 troops is simply fantasy. To buttress her case, she has resorted to alleged reports from defectors claiming the existence of a "secret" Afghan army numbering between 18,000 and 20,000. This claim is highly suspect. But even if the regime has hidden reserves of this relatively small size, the author fails to demonstrate rigorously how regime forces will hold out in the face of what she herself describes as "the almost universal hatred of the people."

In the final analysis, the Klass article shows the remarkable capacity of some detractors of the Reagan administration to mistake an important foreign policy achievement for defeat.

### The U.N. Contribution

The Geneva Accords did not emerge by magic. They were the culmination of a long process of political and military pressure and on-again, off-again mediation activities. The United Nations was an important, persistent actor in this process. In a broader context, the accords can be seen as part of a new pattern of opportunity for U.N. peacemaking and mediation around the globe. The United Nations is moving to center stage in helping to resolve significant regional conflicts that have cost many lives and, in some cases, become tinderboxes with the potential to explode into major power confrontations.

As a result, some observers have claimed that "peace is breaking out all over" and that the U.N.'s peacekeeping horizons are limitless. That is not the case; there are practical limits to the U.N.'s peacekeeping capabilities. The effectiveness of U.N. peacekeeping patently depends on the willingness of the belligerents to accept a U.N. peacekeeping role. The availability of a U.N. presence can hasten a cessation of hostilities by providing an honest broker between the parties, an objective means to verify cease-fire arrangements, moral pressure on the parties not to renew fighting, and a justification to accept what would otherwise be a politically embarrassing defeat. In short, while the U.N. cannot impose peace in a conflict situation, it can play an important facilitating role.

In the case of Afghanistan, the United Nations did not compel the involved parties to sign the accords; it did not impose the Geneva solution. Mitigating pressures and circumstances outside the U.N.'s purview led to the decision--particularly on the part of the Soviets--to participate in that process. The important role that the U.N. played was to serve as catalyst for ideas about how issues could be resolved and to provide a forum to which the parties could turn once the decisions were made to participate.

Also, as indicated earlier, the U.N. provided the international community with a forum in which to express its collective condemnation of the Soviet invasion and to criticize the illegitimate Kabul regime. Through this process, the Soviet Union was unable to relegate its actions to the margins of the international community's consciousness.

Once the accords were signed, the U.N. provided a face-saving monitoring mechanism--UNGOMAP (the United National Good Offices Mission to Afghanistan and Pakistan)--to oversee the withdrawal of the Soviet forces. The importance of UNGOMAP lies in the fact that it provides an impartial body, acceptable to all parties, which can monitor the withdrawal.

The U.N. will continue to have an important role in Afghanistan in the years to come. It continues to be active in the search for an internal political solution for Afghanistan. Also, it will lead the international effort to assist the resettlement of Afghanistan's refugees and the reconstruction of the country.

The United States strongly supports the U.N.'s humanitarian assistance effort. It recognizes that, over the long term, the U.N. agencies, including the multilateral development banks, must supply the major share of external assistance for the reconstruction and development of Afghanistan. We support U.N. Coordinator Prince Sadruddin Aga Khan and his achievements to date. We also welcome the progress that already has been undertaken by the U.N. High Commissioner on Refugees, the World Food Program, and other agencies to prepare for the return of the refugees and displaced persons, and to plan for the future development of the country.

The United States believes, however, that certain basic principles must underlie the U.N. effort to ensure success of its program. First, U.N. assistance must go directly to the Afghan people and remain strictly humanitarian in nature. It must not be provided in a way that can be manipulated by others to gain political advantage. Specifically, U.N. assistance must not flow through the current illegitimate Kabul government. We believe U.N. officials understand the strength of our concern and that of other major donor governments.

Second, in looking for pragmatic solutions, humanitarian aid programs should be strictly prioritized. The needs are large and diverse, but only a rigorously phased approach can work.

Third, the U.N. agencies must direct increased, concentrated attention on how to effectively implement the relief programs they are planning. This must be done in conjunction with Afghans--not by outsiders alone, regardless of their good intentions. Our own successful bilateral cross-border program has demonstrated that programs succeed in Afghanistan only when Afghans are deeply involved in all aspects of decision making. The First Consolidated Report described with clarity and precision the problems for which relief is needed. The ways and means to implement the relief are an even greater challenge that must be tackled vigorously.

## Into the Future

The withdrawal of Soviet occupation troops from Afghanistan represents one of the Reagan administration's top foreign policy achievements. Soviet aggression has been blunted, the Brezhnev Doctrine undermined, and the threat to Western interests in South Asia and the Persian Gulf reduced.

But the game is not yet over in Afghanistan. We have not yet achieved all of our policy objectives: the complete withdrawal of Soviet military forces followed by the establishment of a broad-based Afghan government through self-determination and the return and resettlement of the refugees.

The achievement and consolidation of these objectives will advance the important U.S. objective of promoting regional stability. A broad-based, legitimate Afghan government will be better able to heal the wounds and repair the damage done by the war and resist future Soviet efforts to manipulate internal Afghan politics and Afghan foreign policy in ways that would be inimical to good relations with Afghanistan's neighbors, such as Pakistan. It also will contribute to internal Pakistani stability and development by assuring that the refugees return to and stay in Afghanistan, thereby removing an enormous economic and social burden. In a wider context, stability in South Asia contributes to our overall effort to stabilize the situation in the Gulf following the winding down of the Iran-Iraq War.

To maximize the chances of achieving our objectives for Afghanistan, we must maintain an engaged policy by sustaining high-level, visible, political attention toward Afghanistan and by maintaining U.S. bilateral and multilateral aid contributions to Afghanistan. We will need to work closely with all interested parties to strengthen Afghan political and administrative capabilities as well as to bring about the return of the refugees.

### Lesson Learned

The success of the Afghan policy provides several lessons for future foreign policy management, including:

The critical need to **develop bipartisan congressional support**. The administration, through early consultation with Congress, must fashion comprehensive policies that clearly support U.S. interests and that can be clearly articulated and garner congressional support. Follow-up and continuous consultations with key Capitol Hill leaders should become routine. The Afghan policy has enjoyed strong support in the legislative and executive branches. Even though Afghanistan might be considered a relatively "easy" issue on which to achieve such a consensus, without careful management between the administration and Congress, such consensus could have quickly eroded.

The importance of **policy consistency**. Policy consistency starts with a clear definition of policy goals and the tactics needed to reach them. These tactics may have to change over time, but the goals generally should remain constant. Otherwise, national will weakens, particularly since it often takes considerable time to achieve basic national goals. In Afghanistan, it took nine years, but our course was steady because our goal was clear, understandable, and supported by the international community.

The significance of **energizing the international community**. The Soviets were unable to legitimize their activities in the international arena. They were consistently on the defensive. International public opinion and the community of nations kept the Afghan issue from becoming solely a superpower squabble in which other nations should step to the sidelines. Afghanistan was an Islamic issue; it was a nonaligned issue; it was an issue for the entire community of nations, as well as a problem between the United States and the Soviet Union.

The **willingness to take risks**. The resistance fought the Soviets to a standstill because it had the weapons capable of compelling that development. For that to happen, however, the United States had to be willing to take some calculated risks and to provide the resistance with weapons of sufficient sophistication and firepower to meet the tactical objective of imposing a stalemate on the Soviets. In other words, the United States had to be willing to act if its policy goals were to be achieved.

Afghanistan has suffered an enormous tragedy and injustice at the hands of the Soviets and the Afghan Communist Party. Hundreds of thousands of people have lost their lives or been permanently maimed, and much of the country had been destroyed. It will take a generation or more for Afghanistan to recover what has been lost. But the resiliency, fortitude, and strength of character that the Afghan people have displayed in the past demonstrate that they are capable of successfully meeting the challenges of the future.

Under Reagan's guidance, the United States instituted a series of policies designed to help the Afghan people regain control of their lives and country. Much has been done toward achieving that objective. More, however, needs to be done. In the coming months and years, the United States must be there to help the Afghan people in the tasks that lie ahead by providing political and economic support. As Reagan stated in his Afghan Proclamation in 1988, the United States "will join other nations and international organizations to help the Afghans rebuild their country and their institutions." Having come this far, we could do no less.

PART SIX

THE U.N. AND ARMS CONTROL

# PAKISTAN HAS CALLED OUR BLUFF ON THE NUCLEAR ISSUE

Stopping the spread of nuclear weapons is a delicate business and a deadly important one.

Of all the dangers from nuclear weapons that today imperil mankind, none is greater than the spread of the bomb into the hands of terrorists or an unstable regime. The more countries that acquire the bomb, the more neighbors will feel compelled to develop the bomb for their own protection. The more countries that hold the nuclear bomb, the less safe we all are.

Twenty-five years ago, President John F. Kennedy saw the possibility of a world in the 1970s with 15 to 25 nuclear-weapon states, a situation he regarded as "the greatest possible danger." Instead, the 1970s closed with five declared weapons states (China, France, United Kingdom, USSR and U.S.), one state that has launched a peaceful explosion (India) and one or two that were believed to be just below the explosion threshold (Israel and South Africa).

While we can take some comfort that President Kennedy's worst fears about nuclear proliferation have not been realized, there is reason for immediate concern about the increasing complexity of stopping the spread of the bomb. And, there is growing cause for alarm that Pakistan may be continuing to pursue its nuclear weapons program single-mindedly.

The best way to maintain the status quo of just five declared nuclear-weapon nations is to control nuclear technologies and materials. But over the past decades, more and more nations have developed sophisticated nuclear scientists, knowledgeable and experienced.

Appeared in The Chicago Tribune, August 5, 1987.

Simultaneously, more nations have become suppliers of both technologies and materials.

During the Reagan adminstration, the nuclear non-proliferation regime has been strengthened. Today there are stronger cooperation efforts to inhibit the transfer of sensitive nuclear material, equipment and technology. Also, there has been progress at restricting access to delivery systems. Earlier this year the United States and six allies signed an agreement to put export controls on missiles and missile technologies. The International Atomic Energy Agency has strengthened its technical assistance program and made critical advances in its safeguard system to detect whether a nation is diverting nuclear materials from peaceful purposes to possible weapons programs. More nations have signed the nuclear non-proliferation treaty. The U.S. has sought to conclude additional bilateral agreements such as the important U.S.-China agreement signed in 1984. And the U.S. has become a more predictable and competitive participant in international nuclear cooperation.

Today, Pakistan presents a singularly important challenge to these advances in the non-proliferation regime.

Between 1981 and 1987 the U.S. gave $3.6 billion to Pakistan. The U.S. has used its aid and other aspects of its relationship with Pakistan to influence Pakistan.

The U.S. has supported the country's transition from military rule to constitutional government. The U.S. concerns over human rights contributed to the end of Pakistan's eight-year old martial law in 1985. Similarly, the U.S. has worked with Pakistan to reduce the illicit production of opium and to improve drug enforcement. However, it does not appear that the U.S. has had like success at halting Pakistan's efforts to rapidly develop a nuclear bomb.

Pakistan has operated and expanded its clandestine enrichment facility at Kahuta. It has operated a clandestine plutonium and reprocessing facility at the Pakistan Institute for Science and Technology. Pakistan has expanded its nuclear weapons design team at Wah and stepped up imports of nuclear warhead components. A few years ago, Pakistanis were caught in Houston illegally trying to export devices used in triggering nuclear explosives. Pakistan's Kanupp reactor had had failures in its safeguard system, making plutonium diversion possible. President Zia ul-Haq has said that Pakistan can build the bomb whenever it wishes.

Now the U.S. must accept the fact that a Pakistani native, Arshad Z. Pervez, was arrested in Philadelphia July 10 on charges of seeking to illegally export 25 tons of special steel alloy to Pakistan. The steel can be used in a facility to make enriched uranium.

In response to U.S. concerns, Pakistan has denied that efforts to smuggle illegal materials used in making nuclear weapons had the support or approval of the government. And Pakistan has issued an arrest warrant for retired general Inam ul-Haq, who allegedly directed Pervez in his search for the sensitive nuclear-related materials. State Department officials have welcomed these developments. But is it enough? Isn't it likely that even if Pervez was not an official agent of the Pakistani government, he was acting with their knowledge?

It appears that Pakistan has called our bluff on the nuclear issue. Other countries are watching.

Quiet, cooperative diplomacy, as a general rule, is the best diplomacy. But given the importance to all the world of nuclear non-proliferation and given the alarming record of Pakistan in the area, quiet diplomacy simply is not enough right now.

The United States has many important global security interests. Among them is providing support for Pakistan in its vital role in opposing Soviet occupation of Afghanistan. Pakistan is carrying an enormous burden in caring for three million Afghan refugees and standing up to Soviet pressure and intimidation. But even these important interests must be subordinate to a flagrant and provocative challenge to U.S. security interests in the non-proliferation regime.

The administration, in consultation with Congress, should suspend military aid to Pakistan until there is a resolution of the serious issues raised by charges that Pakistan has tried to illegally acquire material for nuclear weapons. The deadly important business of stopping the spread of the bomb dictates no less dramatic a step.

# THE UNITED NATIONS AND DISARMAMENT

Let me begin by congratulating you [Permanent Representative Paul Engo from the Republic of Cameroon] on the assumption of the chairmanship of this Working Group with a subject--namely U.N. disarmament machinery--which is of particular interest to my delegation in the context of the ongoing U.N. reform efforts. I would note that this agenda item has been the subject of discussion in a working group which you yourself have chaired at the U.N. Disarmament Commission (UNDC) in recent years. I am confident that your able stewardship of that group will serve you well as you guide the deliberations of the present working group.

I wish to preface my remarks with the observation that the work of this special session should be viewed in the broader context of overall international relations. The primary objective of the United Nations, as stated in its Charter, is to maintain international security and peace. In pursuing our work here, as in other U.N. bodies, we must keep this objective firmly in mind; and in considering proposals related to disarmament, we must weigh them against this objective. We also must work to ensure that all of our efforts support another fundamental principle of the United Nations--namely, freedom.

Security, freedom, and peace must be our watchwords. That is why the United States cannot subscribe to the notion that arms control and disarmament agreements should be pursued merely for the sake of agreement. Rather, in our view, arms control and disarmament agreements must make sense only to the degree that they make a realistic contribution to a more secure, free, and peaceful world. Arms are the symptom, not the cause, of distrust and tension. Agreements to limit and reduce the level of

Statement before Working Group II of the Third U.N. Special Session on Disarmament, New York, New York, June 7, 1988.

armaments are useful when they can help to reduce distrust and tension, which lie at the root of all conflicts, but such agreements cannot do the job alone. Real arms control, applying to all nations, will be feasible only when the causes of distrust and tension are addressed and resolved.

## Accomplishments

For its part, the United States has been engaged in a broad range of activities--bilateral and multilateral--aimed at promoting enhanced security, freedom, and peace for all nations. We are proud of our record and take satisfaction in the solid accomplishments we have achieved thus far, for these should serve as an example for the rest of the world.

In the bilateral field, the INF [Intermediate-Range Nuclear Forces] Treaty stands as the first agreement in history to provide for actual reduction of nuclear weapons by eliminating an entire class of such weapons, and contains unprecedented, stringent verification provisions which can serve as the model for future agreements. We are continuing negotiations with the Soviet Union toward an agreement on strategic nuclear weapons which could lead to far more substantial reductions, and we are pursuing exchanges on nuclear testing through a step-by-step approach to resolve verification concerns to make possible the ratification of existing treaties.

But our efforts have not been confined to the bilateral sphere. The United States has been an active participant in a wide range of multilateral arms control and disarmament negotiations. We played a leading role, for example, at the Stockholm Conference on Confidence- and Security-Building Measures and Disarmament in Europe, which reached agreement in September 1986 on specific measures to reduce the risk of war in Europe as a result of miscalculation or misunderstanding. Similarly, the United States has been energetic in the talks in Vienna, which we hope will lead to a negotiation between the member states of NATO and the Warsaw Pact on conventional arms control in Europe from the Atlantic to the Urals.

Finally, I hardly need to remind the delegates of the leading role we have exercised at the Geneva Conference on Disarmament (CD) in the negotiations for a comprehensive, effectively verifiable and truly global ban on chemical weapons. These negotiations are proceeding on the basis of a U.S. draft treaty text which was introduced by Vice President Bush to the CD in 1984. In the intervening years, the negotiations have increasingly focused on the tough issues, particularly effective verification. Much work remains to be done to overcome the substantial obstacles which remain. We will need to deal realistically with these issues and ensure that any agreement that is reached accords with our primary objective of security, freedom, and peace.

This solid record, which speaks for itself, stands in rather sharp contrast with the situation which prevails elsewhere in the world. Most of the initiatives I have just cited fall within the East-West and/or European context. Yet, it is appropriate to note that, in the decades since the end of World War II, the conflicts which have ravaged the world and sapped its human and material resources have taken place in regions outside this arena--in Africa, Asia, and Latin America.

There gave been scores of such conflicts, which have exacted a staggering toll of casualties. Probably the most destructive and protracted regional conflict of recent times is the ongoing war between Iran and Iraq. It has been estimated that, in the nearly 8 years since this war erupted, several hundred thousand people have been killed. The war between Iran and Iraq also highlights several of the most disturbing recent trends in regional conflicts: the increasing sophistication and deadliness of modern conventional weapons and the resort to chemical weapons.

Thus, it is fair to ask: What are other countries, of other regions, doing concretely to contribute to a more secure, free, and peaceful world? What steps have regional groups and individual states outside of Europe taken to reduce tensions and remove the sources of conflict? Other regions of the globe have been subjected to the destabilization and human losses caused by local conflict, but what have the states of those regions done to reduce tensions and the likelihood of conflict?

The answer is: in many regions, far too little. The United States is doing its part in cooperation with its allies and friends, but other countries need to do theirs. All nations should acknowledge and assume their share of responsibility for maintaining peace and security within their respective regions through such activities as confidence-building measures and reductions in their arsenals of conventional weapons. This is a challenge which deserves the full attention of all participants at this special session.

The maintenance of international peace and security is the primary purpose of the United Nations, according to the Charter. The organization can play, and does play, a constructive role in this vital endeavor in a variety of ways. For example, the Security Council's efforts over the decades in peacekeeping operations and the resolution of regional conflicts have made contributions to promoting peace and security in many parts of the world.

Outside its main organs, there are components of the U.N. system which also contribute to a more secure world. Based on my own experience, I would particularly cite the work of the International Atomic Energy Agency (IAEA) in safeguarding the international nonproliferation regime under the Non-Proliferation Treaty as an important example of the multilateral cooperation in this regard. During my years as U.S. Representative to the IAEA, I was pleased and proud to promote the safe and peaceful uses of nuclear energy and to ensure that nuclear materials are used for strictly peaceful purposes.

## Questionable U.N. Activities

At the same time, however, there are instances of U.N. activities--especially in the field of arms control and disarmament--which make only a marginal or even negative contribution to a more secure, free, and peaceful world. Over the years, the United Nations has accumulated an elaborate--some would say excessive--structure of activities and mechanisms ostensibly designed to promote and encourage the arms control and disarmament process. Yet, by its very nature, this structure has become unwieldy and, at times, detrimental to improving the climate for negotiations.

For example, every fall the First Committee of the General Assembly routinely considers and adopts literally scores of resolutions on subjects ranging from the so-called urgent need for a comprehensive nuclear test-ban treaty to the importance of multilateral negotiations at the CD to prevent an arms race in outer space. Not only is there a surplus in the number of such resolutions but there is also a surfeit of unrealistic, hyperbolic formulations in their texts.

The United States endorses and supports the various proposals which have been made to rationalize the work of the First Committee by such devices as confining its consideration of individual agenda items to alternate years. We will continue to promote such proposals, but, more to the point, we would hope that member states would exercise greater restraint in the language of the resolutions which they introduce. Rhetorical, polemical texts on the so-called urgent need for a comprehensive test ban, for example, are hardly conducive to the climate affecting the serious negotiations now underway between the United States and the Soviet Union on nuclear testing issues.

The plethora of resolutions considered annually by the First Committee leads me to my final point, which directly relates to the deliberations of this working group: at a time of continuing financial crisis over the organization, the U.N. machinery in the field of disarmament needs to be rationalized, streamlined, and made more cost effective. My delegation applauds the welcome first steps toward this end, such as the proposals which have been made in the UNDC working group over which you have presided, Mr. Chairman, and the adoption last year of Resolution 42/42N entitled "Rationalization of the work of the First Committee." We hope and expect that, consistent with the request of that resolution, the committee will implement the recommendations contained therein at the 43rd General Assembly.

## Room for Further Improvement

But more needs to be done. For example, one cost-saving measure would be for the First Committee and the Disarmament Commission to adopt the practice of summary records rather than verbatim records. Consideration should also be given to adjourning those U.N. subsidiary bodies which have failed to achieve substantive progress. I note that such a step has already been taken in the case of the Ad Hoc Committee on the World Disarmament Conference. During the course of this working group's deliberatons, my delegation will offer other ideas.

Consistent with our views on the need to streamline the disarmament machinery, the United States does not perceive any need to create new, duplicative U.N. mechanisms in this field. We are aware of proposals from some member states for the establishment of new organs, such a U.N. verification mechanism and an international outer space inspectorate. I wish to reiterate that my delegation will continue to oppose such proposals on both financial and, more importantly, substantive grounds.

We also are aware of proposals by some states that certain components of the U.N. system which have heretofore not played a role in disarmament should be accorded such a role. The United States believed that we already have sufficient U.N. bodies to consider the broad agenda of arms control and disarmament, as manifested in this special session, for example. To accord a role in disarmament matters to other bodies would diffuse the overall focus of discussion. This would be a prescription for failure.

The U.S. delegation approaches the work of this working group, and of the special session overall, in a positive and constructive spirit. We trust that all other delegations will adopt a similar approach. For, if our work here is to contribute to a more constructive atmosphere for the conduct of arms control and disarmament negotiations, we must be realistic and avoid divisive proposals and overly ambitious concepts which clearly are not susceptible to consensus. We must recognize that while the General Assembly provides the central forum for deliberations, at which all member states are able to express their particular concerns about arms control and disarmament, the conduct of negotiations lies outside our purview but can be, and is, influenced by what we accomplish here. Whether the outcome of this special session contributes to the international environment in which further agreements can be reached and implemented will largely depend upon a realistic and reasonable approach by all of us assembled here.

PART SEVEN

THE U.N. AND THE MIDDLE EAST

# SERPENTS IN THE U.N.

On November 10, 1975, a date already infamous in history as it marked the 37th anniversary of Kristallnacht, the United Nations General Assembly (UNGA) adopted Resolution 3379. This resolution, ostensibly intended to renew the U.N. Decade to Combat Racism, has become instead an embodiment of one of the most pernicious and racist propositions of modern times. Resolution 3379 ends with the determination that "Zionism is a form of racism and racial discrimination." The membership of the General Assembly agreed to that determination by a 2 to 1 margin.

The total incompatability with the U.N. Charter of the concerted campaign against Israel is a matter of concern for the United States as a founding member of the U.N.. We must recognize that the U.N. was founded on the very same principles which have guided our own national experience; belief in the rule of law, in peaceful settlement of disputes, and in the freedom and dignity of the individual. All of these principles are called into question by the U.N.'s affirmation of the equation of Zionism with racism.

The persistence of the Zionism = racism equation, then, is not solely a matter of concern to Israel or the Jewish community. Zionism has long been recognized as the Jewish "national liberation movement," and as such is no more racist than similar movements associated with black South Africans, or Namibians, both of which have been endorsed in numerous UNGA resolutions. Thus, the condemnation of Zionism in the face of open and fervent support for other National Liberation Movements (NLMs) demonstrates blatant hypocrisy by the U.N. General Assembly.

---

Appeared in _Midstream_, January, 1989, Volume XXXV, No. 1.

Moreover, inasmuch as Zionism = racism is clearly an attempt to delegitimize Israel, it is a grave derogation from the premises upon which the U.N. was founded. The First Article of the U.N. Charter provides for the sovereignty of each member state. Inherent in the reciprocal recognition of sovereignty by each and every U.N. member is the reciprocal recognition of the right to exist of each and every member state. The Zionism = racism proposition attempts to deprive Israel, a state created by the U.N., of ethical legitimacy. It is a part of a wholesale effort to defame Israel, deprive it of legitimacy and ultimately expel it from the U.N. Islamic countries, allied with the Soviet bloc, have pushed through the UNGA some 415 resolutions since 1972 singling out Israel for criticism.

For these reasons, the continuing refusal of a majority of the U.N. to reject the Zionism = racism formula is a grave peril to the U.N. itself. It calls into question the fundamental values of U.N. membership as contained in the Charter, it marks the majority of the U.N.'s membership as inconstant and hypocritical, and destroys the U.N.'s credibility in making a contribution to the peaceful solution of the problems which confront the Middle East. The failure of the UNGA to repudiate "Zionism is racism" is a cancer that saps the U.N.'s fundamental strength and should be a matter of concern to all who believe in the importance of the U.N. Charter.

At a time when the U.N. is receiving credit as a facility for helping arrange peaceful solutions to regional conflicts, the U.N.'s membership must examine its adherence to the Zionism = racism proposition a new and consider how this pernicious formula detracts from the U.N.'s credibility. In order to be restored to the tenets of its Charter, the U.N. clearly must repudiate Resolution 3379. Otherwise, the hypocrisy of the voting majority will destroy the value of the organization.

## Political Utility of Resolution 3379

To governments and individuals that value and take seriously the U.N. and its Charter, the revocation of Resolution 3379 must be a high priority. In seeking to do so, however, we must recognize that to its principal sponsors, the resolution is of great political utility. We must be realistic and recognize the UNGA for what it is, a forum where the majority is composed of governments that do not believe in democracy at home and do not respect fundamental Western values. The fact that the U.N. majority support NLMs which do not have their origins in the West and slander Zionism which is one of the oldest NLMs and is rooted in Western civilization, is just one example of the rejection of Western values by most U.N. member states.

Some argue that if the U.S. simply ignores the resolution that it will eventually be forgotten. This argument does not take into account the numerous resolutions which reiterate Resolution 3379 each year. In addition, the Zionism = racism formula was interjected into an agenda item concerning the effort to combat and eradicate racism. The interjection of the Zionism = racism equation perverts the debate on this important subject and prevents the U.S. from making a contribution to U.N. deliberations and to the U.N.'s efforts to eradicate racism, which are centered in the UNGA Third committee. For these reasons the U.S. can never ignore Resolution 3379.

To cease our opposition to the Zionism = racism formula also would call into question our moral steadfastness in seeking a just solution to the Middle East conflict. It would undermine our credibility with all parties in that region, Israel itself, as well as its enemies.

In seeking to overturn the resolution, we must realistically appraise the political forces which make it an attractive formula to a majority of U.N. member states. Like a good move in Chess, the Zionism = racism proposition accomplishes many things for its proponents. By linking Zionism to racism, anti-Israeli forces in the U.N. were able to harness the energy of the well-organized and broadly-based anti-Apartheid movement. Zionism = racism cemented relations between the Arab and African blocs in the U.N.. (The African group is the single largest voting bloc in the U.N. and is one of the most disciplined.) In return for supporting African interests in condemning South Africa, Arabs won African support for anti-Israeli resolutions since Israel was now, according to the perverse U.N. optic, a bastion of "racism" on the same par as the government of South Africa.

The General Assembly cannot be rated highly as a political power. Its relevance in world affairs instead is derived from its authority in reflecting the opinion of mankind. Many, if not most, U.N. members value highly their participation in the U.N. because it enhances the prestige of their government at home, The entire foreign policy of some countries is largely centered on the U.N.. And in the UNGA, words have power. It is for these reasons that the Zionism = racism formulation was a masterstroke of propaganda. "Racism" has long been one of the greatest sins of which government or individuals can be accused. In the U.N. lexicon it is closely associated with the greatest of all crimes -- Genocide -- and other crimes against humanity.

Zionism has long been the term applied to the legitimate aspirations of the Jewish people for a homeland. It also has been a term utilized by the most vehement anti-Semitic forces. The Tsarists fabricated the infamous **Protocols of the Elders of Zion** and conducted a defamatory campaign to whip up public opprobrium against Russian Jews. Under the Nazis, the **Protocols** were constantly used to justify the genocidal measures employed against the Jewish population of every country that fell under the Nazi shadow. The "Zionism is racism" formula thus linked a concept that is completely legitimate, but under attack, with an absolute evil.

The injection of anti-Israel polemics into the racism issue at the U.N. also served anti-Israel interests by carrying the efforts to isolate Israel to another level. Previously, these efforts had resided in the U.N.'s political organs -- the UNGA plenary, the Special Political Committee and the Security Council. With the adoption of Resolution 3379 the campaign against Israel moved into new territory, from the political level to the moral-ethical human rights level. The resolution thus marked a continuation of the effort to isolate Israel by other means. It opened another U.N. forum to anti-Israel polemics.

## Consequences Outside the U.N.

The move to brand Zionism a form of racism had repercussions outside the U.N. of utility to its proponents. Chief among these was driving a wedge between black and Jewish communities in the United States and elsewhere. A bevy of anti-Semitic hate groups in this country and others have trumpeted the U.N. resolution as "proof" that the international community supports their extremist positions. Anti-apartheid groups citing the proposition contained in Resolution 3379, have voiced concern that Israel and its supporters here are seeking to secretly undermine their efforts to end the reprehensible apartheid system in South Africa. This is an especially vicious slur against Israel and Jews in America who, of course, take civil rights issues very seriously. Jews have figured prominently in the vanguard of the American civil rights movement.

Resolution 3379 assists the forces of radicalism in the U.N. and particularly in the Middle East by exacerbating suspicion and hostility on both sides of the issue, ultimately making peace more difficult to achieve in that troubled region. It attempts to discredit those sympathetic to Israel and makes it impossible for Israel to have any confidence whatsoever in the U.N. as a facilitator in attaining a peaceful resolution to the conflict in the Middle East.

Again, the "Zionism is racism" issue strikes a blow at the heart of the U.N. Charter as it represents an attempt to deprive a member state of its very legitimacy, and hence, implicitly of its right to exist. The continuation and constant reiteration of the "Zionism is racism" proposition in the U.N. is like a malignancy that may be dormant, but which can be ignored only at the gravest peril to the patient. It undermines the U.N.'s credibility by calling into question the willingness of the U.N. majority to abide by the fundamental tenets of the U.N. Charter.

While far from a frivolous endeavor, the "Zionism is racism" formula can never achieve what its proponents most desire -- the expulsion of Israel from the U.N. by branding it as an international pariah. The challenge to Israel's credentials which was initiated prior to the 1982 UNGA, and turned back at that time when the U.S. made it clear that it would withdraw from the U.N. if Israel's credentials were denied, has become little more than a ritual which is now turned aside procedurely with overwhelming support in the UNGA.

It also has become clear the "Zionism is racism" is completely irrelevant to any eventual outcome in the Middle East. The governments which support the "Zionism is racism" proposition do so cheaply and without much commitment. It is an example of the penchant in the UNGA for the adoption of sweeping and excessive declarations that have no validity in the real world. The majority which supports Resolution 3379 creates a false impression of the actual correlation of political forces in the Middle East, and only exacerbates tensions making a solution more difficult by contributing to the intransigence of the Arab states and others hostile to Israel.

These factors in turn contribute to the widespread perception that the UNGA is politically impotent and morally bankrupt. They dramatically highlight the flawed diplomacy practiced by too many U.N. member states: too often seized with issues of narrow interest and excluding issues which concern the interest of the whole body.

It will be no easy task to break the large coalition of African, Arab, and Soviet bloc states that support the Zionism equals racism proposition. It remains a pillar of the effort to propel Israel into pariah-state status. It serves the powerful but narrow interests of its principal components. However, if explored in relationship to the principles and spirit of the U.N. Charter, the proposition is clearly at odds with the purpose of the U.N.. Accordingly, there should be a window of opportunity now opening because of the renaissance of faith that the U.N. is an important institution in world politics. Supporters of the U.N. Charter must now assert themselves to make the organization true to itself once again. In this regard repudiating Resolution 3379 ought to be a high priority.

### Successful Challenges by the U.S.

During the past seven and a half years the U.S. has become increasingly experienced in the conduct of multilateral diplomacy. It has worked hard to eliminate the blatant anti-Americanism contained in certain U.N. resolutions, as well as the rhetoric bandied about in the halls of U.N. meetings. Thanks to the concerted and conscientious efforts of U.S. Ambassadors to the U.N., Moynihan, Kirkpatrick and Walters, the "kick-me" sign now has been taken off the back of the U.S. Representative to the United Nations. We have successfully challenged the pervasive double standard by confronting serious human rights abuses. Earlier this year the U.S. won a significant victory in persuading the U.N. to investigate the human rights situation in Cuba.

The U.S. must now concentrate on building upon these successes by tackling one of the most egregious examples of bias within the U.N. In seeking to bring about a repudiation of the "Zionism is racism" formula, we will have to adopt a subtle and tenacious strategy that will utilize the full panoply of U.S. diplomatic assets. African countries which have little direct interest in the Middle East political equation should be targeted.

Twelve years ago, when the Arab oil producers' politico-economic clout was in the ascendancy, many of these African nations were brought into the anti-Israeli ford by promises of increased economic aid from wealthy Arab states. By and large these promises have not been kept, and the U.S. should be able to use the incipient disillusionment to its advantage in divorcing the Africans from the Arab bloc at the U.N.

One of the secrets to U.S. previous successes, particularly on Cuban human rights, in the U.N. has been the bi-partisan involvement of the Congress. In the case of the odious "Zionism is racism" formula, the strong opinion of Congress is on the record. A joint resolution of the Congress, adopted late in 1987, directs the U.S. Representative to the U.N. to support efforts to overturn Resolution 3379. The interest and backing of Congress always strengthens the hand of Administration foreign policy initiative because the role of Congress in setting foreign aid levels is well understood in the developing world. It also helps to establish the broad-based support for an initiative in the minds of some who would otherwise doubt the seriousness or steadfastness of resolve on the part of the Administration.

Successful multilateral diplomacy also requires the clear support and visible involvement of the President and other high-level Administration officials. President-elect Bush has to make a commitment to overturning the "Zionism is racism" proposition. He should be prepared to personally weigh in with the heads of state of countries which we will attempt to enlist to support our effort. Presidential interest and involvement also is essential in mobilizing the full commitment of the U.S. foreign policy bureaucracy.

There has been a clear change in the U.N. in the past few years. Thanks to the firm leadership of the United States, the most extreme tendencies of some U.N. members to engage in harsh rhetoric and politicization, which had the effect of undermining the principle of universality and the spirit, if not the letter of the U.N. Charter, have abated. Thanks to the prospects for solution of regional conflicts in Afghanistan and the Persian Gulf, there is renewed faith in the U.N.'s mechanisms for peacekeeping. The improved atmosphere at the U.N. now makes it propitious to move to erase what remains a dark stain on the reputation of the U.N., the "Zionism is racism" equation. In doing so, the United States and other countries which trul;y believe in what the Charter stands for, must be clear and steadfast in opposing the pernicious implications of this equation. The majority which support "Zionism is racism" must be convinced that their adherence to the proposition damages the U.N. organization and cannot be tolerated.

# THE U.N. AT LEAST SHOULD DO NO HARM

No issue has bedeviled the United Nations more than the Middle East conflict. Tragically, the U.N. has exacerbated the problem more than helped resolve it. This month, with the prospects of real progress emerging in that troubled region, the U.N. again may harm the Middle East peace process rather than nurture it.

The Palestine Liberation Organization and radical Arab states have turned the U.N. into a forum for waging war against Israel by other means. In 1975, the U.N. membership passed Resolution 3379, a pernicious proposal asserting that "Zionism is a form of racism." This gave greater political and intellectual credibility to attacks on Zionism. It also endowed that attack with the moral value and legitimizing force accorded U.N. resolutions.

The enemies of Israel used the U.N. majority to pass a resolution whereby their distorted propaganda could become the conventional wisdom of large segments of the international community. Thus began a constant assault within the U.N. to delegitimize Israel.

To date there have been more than 150 anti-Israel resolutions passed in the Security Council, General Assembly and the Commission on Human Rights. Israel has been the most frequent target of U.N. resolutions condemning or deploring its actions by a ratio of more than 10 to 1.

By the early 1980s, over 50 percent of the time spent in Security Council meetings was taken up with vilifying Israel and over 25 percent of the time in General Assembly sessions was devoted to vituperations against

Appeared in The Chicago Tribune, May 16, 1989.

the Jewish state.   Every year since 1982 in the General Assembly and within the U.N.'s specialized agencies, the PLO and radical Arab states have sought to deny Israel active membership.

And not a single General Assembly resolution on the Arab-Israeli conflict calls for negotiations between the parties.

The U.N. has not been an arena for conflict resolution in the Middle East.   Quite the contrary, it has been used for political posturing, name-calling and polarizing the parties.   As a result, during the last 18 months the U.N. has helped advance resolutions of regional conflicts in Afghanistan, Iran-Iraq and southern Africa, but it has been unable to make a positive contribution in the Middle East.

Today there is movement in the Middle East.   In December, Chairman Yasser Arafat said the PLO's long history of terrorism would stop.   In a dramatic reversal of the group's policy and practice, he acknowledged Israel's right to exist. This was a significant event. Yet the PLO continues to support in moral and material ways the violent intifada, or uprising, in Israel.

Israel is adjusting to the new situation.   Prime Minister Yitzhak Shamir and his aides have been meeting with a variety of West Bank and Gaza Strip Palestinians for months.   There is growing debate among Israeli leaders about what can and should be done.   They heard Arafat's words; now they ask for some time to see if the PLO's actions match the December pledge.

Just recently there was a further development that may prove significant.   Arafat said the PLO Charter, which calls for the destruction of Israel, is null and void.   This is a profound rhetorical shift.   He said he favors a Middle East peace settlement based on the existence of Israel and a Palestinian Arab state.

Whether these developments will translate into concrete confidence-building measures toward peace is unknown.   But the possibility for progress does exist.   However, events in Geneva this month may damage the process.

There is a move to grant the PLO full membership in the U.N.'s World Health Organization as the representative of the proclaimed Palestinian state.   This move is contrary to international law that requires a "state" to exercise effective governmental control over the territory it claims as its own.

If the U.N. membership recognizes the PLO as a state with full membership in the World Health Organization, it would bestow legitimacy on the self-proclaimed Palestinian entity, making it even more difficult to advance Middle East peace.    Both Israel and the United States oppose creation of a separate Palestinian state.   The U.N. would be used to further polarize the parties, not reconcile them.

The Arab-Israeli problem can be resolved only through negotiations between the parties and confidence-building, not through unilateral acts such as the declaration of Palestinian statehood.    The question of Palestinian statehood has to be addressed in direct negotiations.    Giving U.N. legitimacy to that unilateral act just compounds the problem.

U.N. members must reject this move to recognize the PLO as a state.   If the world body cannot advance peace in the Middle East, at least it should avoid compounding the difficulties.

**MAKING THE PEACE: A 15-Session Violence Prevention Curriculum for Young People** *by* Paul Kivel & Allan Creighton, with Oakland Men's Project

This is a widely used violence prevention curriculum for youth-group leaders and educators. The exercises, roleplays, and discussion guidelines help students to explore the roots of violence in the community and their lives; deal with dating violence, fights, suicide, guns, and sexual harassment; and develop practical techniques for stopping violence.

*192 pages ... 15 photos ... 35 handouts ... Paperback $24.95*

**MAKING ALLIES, MAKING FRIENDS: A Curriculum for Making the Peace in Middle School** *by* Hugh Vasquez, M. Nell Myhand, Allan Creighton, and the Todos Institute

More than 30 innovative classroom sessions address diversity and violence issues that middle-schoolers face. Some of the themes are: What respect is; Who am I / Who are my people?; and How can I be safe? This carefully crafted work will be a valuable resource for middle-school personnel and teachers of violence prevention, youth development, conflict resolution, social studies, art, and theater.

*192 pages ... 15 photos ... 48 handouts ... Paperback $29.95*

**DAYS OF RESPECT: Organizing a School-Wide Violence Prevention Program** *by* Ralph Cantor, with Paul Kivel, Allan Creighton, and the Oakland Men's Project

This is a step-by-step guide for staging a collaborative, schoolwide event to celebrate and teach respect and tolerance. It brings young people, teachers, parents, and the community together; emphasizes hands-on practice in building nonviolent relationships; and includes planning outlines, checklists, timetables, and exercises on gender and race.

*64 pages ... 6 photos ... 21 handouts ... Paperback $14.95*

**HELPING TEENS STOP VIOLENCE: A Practical Guide for Counselors, Educators, and Parents** *by* Allan Creighton with Paul Kivel

Teenagers may be subjected to violence at home, at school, and in society. This book helps adults help teenagers to help themselves out of the cycle of abuse and to find ways to deal with and reduce the violence around them. The authors weave issues of gender, race, age, and sexual orientation into frank discussions of violence and its roots.

*168 pages ... 16 photos ... Paperback $16.95 ... Spiral bound $21.95*

**To order see last page or call (800) 266-5592**

## LOVING YOUR PARTNER WITHOUT LOSING YOUR SELF
*by* Martha Beveridge, MSSW

This book explains how to maintain your sense of self in a relationship. Beveridge, an experienced therapist, shows why romantic relationships often deteriorate from intense love into day-to-day struggles that tear couples apart, and gives practical and unique strategies for transforming these struggles into deeper intimacy. These include:

- getting past the ABCs (Attacking, Blaming, Criticizing)
- recognizing the symptoms of poor boundaries (clinging, jealousy, acting single, running away)
- dealing with the smokescreen issues (time, money, sex)

*256 pages ... Paperback $14.95*

## CREATING EXTRAORDINARY JOY: A Guide to Authenticity, Connection and Self-Transformation
*by* Chris Alexander, with a foreword by Deborah Waitley

Extraordinary joy is a state of deep satisfaction and continuous delight that comes when we really like who we are, how we live, and what we do. The key to this is synergy: making connections that energize and inspire us beyond the ordinary.

Using timeless teachings, images from nature, powerful exercises, and real-life examples, Chris Alexander describes the seven steps that can put synergy in your life and create the most important sort of happiness: an immoderately, exuberantly joyful life.

*272 pages ... Paperback $15.95*

## I CAN MAKE MY WORLD A SAFER PLACE
Words by Paul Kivel, illustrations by Nancy Gorrell

With simple text, eye-catching drawings, and reader activities such as mazes and crosswords, *I Can Make My World a Safer Place* engages young readers in thinking about and acting to promote peace at home, in the neighborhood, and in the world. Topics covered include: Teasing and bullies – Fights, gangs, and weapons – Personal safety from physical, emotional, and sexual abuse – Public safety in the community – Toys and violence in the media.

Each section encourages young people not only to stay safe, but also to get involved in increasing community safety.

*96 pages ... 90 illus. ... Paperback $11.95*

**All prices subject to change**